RELIGION, GE
E\

Religion, Gender and Sexuality in Everyday Life

Edited by

PETER NYNÄS
Åbo Akademi University, Finland

ANDREW KAM-TUCK YIP
University of Nottingham, UK

Routledge
Taylor & Francis Group

LONDON AND NEW YORK

First published 2012 by Ashgate Publishing

Published 2016 by Routledge
2 Park Square, Milton Park, Abingdon, Oxfordshire OX14 4RN
711 Third Avenue, New York, NY 10017, USA

First issued in paperback 2016

Routledge is an imprint of the Taylor & Francis Group, an informa business

British Library Cataloguing in Publication Data
Religion, gender and sexuality in everyday life.
   1. Sex--Religious aspects. 2. Sexual minorities--
   Religious life. 3. Muslim gays--Social conditions.
   4. Religious minorities--Attitudes.
   I. Nynas, Peter. II. Yip, Andrew K. T., 1963-
   200.8'66-dc23

Library of Congress Cataloging-in-Publication Data
Nynas, Peter.
   Religion, gender, and sexuality in everyday life / by Peter Nynas and Andrew Kam-Tuck Yip.
      p. cm.
   Includes bibliographical references and index.
   ISBN 978-1-4094-4583-8 (hbk.) 1. Religion and culture--Case studies.
   2. Sex role--Case studies. 3. Sex--Case studies. I. Yip, Andrew Kam-Tuck. II. Title.
   BL65.C8N96 2013
   200.81--dc23

                                                                          2012022235

ISBN 13: 978-1-138-25124-3 (pbk)
ISBN 13: 978-1-4094-4583-8 (hbk)

Contents

List of Tables

Notes on Contributors

Peter Nynäs is Professor of Comparative Religion and Director for the Centre of Excellence in Research which manages the research programme *Post-secular Culture and a Changing Religious Landscape in Finland* (PCCR, http://web.abo.fi/fak/hf/relvet/pccr) and project leader for *Viewpoints to the World: Prototypes of Worldview and their Relation to Motivational Values in Different Social Movements*, funded by the Academy of Finland. His main areas of research have been psychology of religion, emotional geography and intercultural encounters. The edited books *Transforming Otherness* (2011) and *Post-secular Society* (2012), were both published by Transaction. Within PCCR he is now undertaking a case-study on LGTB activism in the religious field in Finland focusing on the intersection of themes such as agency, subjectivity, space and imagined bodies.

Andrew Kam-Tuck Yip is Professor of Sociology at the University of Nottingham, UK. His research interests include contemporary religious/spiritual identities, sexual identities, youth culture, ageing, and human rights. His writings have appeared in journals such as *British Journal of Sociology*, *Sociology of Religion*, *Theology & Sexuality*, *Sexualities*, *Sociological Research Online* and *Contemporary Islam*. He is also the author of *Gay Male Christian Couples: Life Stories* (1997); and co-author/co-editor of *Lesbian and Gay Lives over 50* (2003), *Queer Spiritual Spaces: Sexuality and Sacred Places* (2010), *Religion, Youth and Sexuality: A Multi-faith Exploration* (2011), and *The Ashgate Research Companion to Contemporary Religion and Sexuality* (2012).

Vanja Hamzić is Lecturer at City University London and Visiting Lecturer at King's College London. He has researched and worked with gender-variant and/or sexually diverse Muslim collectives in Europe, the Middle East, South Africa and Southeast Asia. In his native Bosnia and Herzegovina, he has founded *Logos*, an inter-faith non-patriarchal organisation, and worked as the Editor-in-Chief of *Abraham*, a magazine for culture of inter-religious dialogue. His main legal anthropological research involves the process of human subjectivity formation along the geographic, political, cultural and religious fault lines, with a focus on normativity, ritual, gender and sexuality. His recent publications include Control and Sexuality: The Revival of Zina Laws in Muslim Contexts (*Women Living Under Muslim Laws*, December 2010), co-authored with Dr Ziba Mir-Hosseini; and 'The Case of "Queer Muslims": Sexual Orientation and Gender Identity in International Human Rights Law and Muslim Legal and Social Ethos', *Human Rights Law Review* 11(2): 237–74 (2011).

Kenneth Houston was an associate and research intern with the International Conflict Research Institute (INCORE) at the University of Ulster, Northern Ireland. He has now joined the Faculty of Webster University at its Thailand Campus, where he lectures in International Relations. He has published on the subject of religion in politics and society in several journals such as *Religion, State and Society*, *Journal of Critical Globalisation Studies* and *Religion Compass*.

Rusi Jaspal is Research Fellow and Social Psychologist at the University of Nottingham, UK. He holds degrees from the University of Cambridge, the University of Surrey and Royal Holloway, University of London. His research has addressed issues concerning the construction and management of sexual, ethnic and religious identities particularly among ethnic and religious minority groups in Britain. Currently, he is conducting a study on the lived experiences of non-heterosexual Iranian migrants in Britain and Canada. He has published his work in peer-reviewed journals such as *British Journal of Social Psychology*, *Mental Health, Religion and Culture* and *Journal of Homosexuality*. Rusi Jaspal is co-editor (with Glynis Breakwell) of *Identity Process Theory: Identity, Social Action and Social Change* (Cambridge University Press, 2012).

Sarah-Jane Page completed her doctorate at the University of Nottingham in 2009 and she has held research posts at both the University of Nottingham and Durham University. She is currently a lecturer in the School of Languages and Social Sciences at Aston University. Her research interests focus on the study of religion, gender, sexuality, embodiment, feminism, youth, parenthood, and clergy families. She was the Research Fellow on the *Religion, Youth and Sexuality: A Multi-faith Exploration* project (www.nottingham.ac.uk/nottingham/rys).

Wim Peumans is an anthropology Ph.D. candidate at the *Interculturalism, Migration and Minorities Research Centre*, University of Leuven, Belgium. As a Fellow of the Research Foundation Flanders he studies transgressive sexualities and Muslim subjectivities in Belgium. His master's thesis on sexual migration to Belgium won the biannual *Marguerite Lefèvre Award for Genderstudies* (2010, Academische Stichting Leuven) and was published as a book: *Seks en stigma over grenzen heen – homoseksuele en lesbische migranten in Vlaanderen en Brussel* (Acco Publishing, 2011). He has several forthcoming articles in international peer-reviewed journals: one on 'sexual migration' and another on 'sexuality, disability, body aesthetics and performance art'.

Bernadetta Siara is currently writing up her doctoral thesis at City University, London, United Kingdom. The thesis focuses on gender and sexuality in the migration context with recent Poles to the UK as a case study. She has been a visiting lecturer at City University London, where she has been involved in teaching sociology and research modules. She has also spent a number of years working as a researcher at the University of Westminster and Middlesex University, both in London. She published on the issues around negotiating gender and ethnic identity in cyberspace (Siara 2009) and on the constructions around body, gender and sexuality in the migration context (Siara 2011, 2012).

Christiane Stallaert is an Anthropologist and Hispanist; Professor of Anthropology at the Catholic University of Leuven, Belgium (Interculturalism, Migration and Minorities Research Centre, Department of Anthropology) and Professor of Iberian Studies, Translation and Intercultural Communication at the University College of Antwerp, Belgium. Her main fields of research are inter-ethnic and inter-religious relations, ethnicity and nationalism, conversion, migration and translation. She was a visiting professor at the Ecole des Hautes Etudes en Sciences Sociales (Paris), University of Santa Catarina (Brazil), University of Konstanz (Germany), as well as several Spanish universities (Madrid, Tarragona, Universidad Internacional Menéndez y Pelayo, La Coruña). She is the author of, among other works, *Ni una gota de sangre impura. La España inquisitorial y la Alemania nazi cara a cara* (2006; Naar eigen beeld en gelijkenis, 2010), *Perpetuum Mobile. Entre la balcanización y la aldea global* (2004), and *Etnogénesis y etnicidad en España. Una aproximación histórico-antropológica al casticismo* (1998; Etnisch nationalisme in Spanje. De historisch-antropologische grens tussen christenen en Moren, 1996).

Melissa M. Wilcox is Associate Professor and Chair of Religion and Director of Gender Studies at Whitman College, USA. She is author or co-editor of several books and numerous articles on gender, sexuality, and religion, including *Coming Out in Christianity: Religion, Identity, and Community*; *Queer Women and Religious Individualism*; and (with David W. Machacek) *Sexuality and the World's Religions*. She is also author of the forthcoming volume, *Religion in Today's World: Global Issues, Sociological Perspectives*, and is currently at work on a book on the Sisters of Perpetual Indulgence.

Sara Zalcberg is a doctoral student at the Department of Sociology and Anthropology at the Hebrew University of Jerusalem, Israel. Her fields of specialty include gender, sexuality and religion; deviance and crises in closed communities; and the ultra-Orthodox Jewish society. Another field is the rehabilitation of offenders in religious settings. She published a book chapter based on the thesis: Zalcberg, S. (2004), 'The process of adopting a religious Jewish lifestyle among criminals', in: A. Levi, A. Shedmi and Y. Kimm (eds), *Seekers of Justice: Crime and Law Enforcement Research in Israel* [in Hebrew], 487–510, Tel-Aviv: Cherikover Publications.

Sima Zalcberg holds a Ph.D. in sociology and anthropology and taught in The Program in Contemporary Jewry, Faculty of Jewish Studies, Bar-Ilan University, Israel. She is involved in studying the ultra-Orthodox society, focusing mainly on issues of religion and gender. Her major research projects involve the study of the control of sexuality and the norms of modest dress for women among the most extreme ultra-Orthodox groups. One of her latest articles – 'Shouldering the burden of the redemption: How the "fashion" of wearing capes developed in ultra-Orthodox society' – was published in *Nashim: A Journal of Jewish Women's Studies & Gender* 22: 32–55 (2011).

Acknowledgements

Many of the chapters in this volume have their origins in work presented at the international conference *The Politics of Living Religion/Spirituality and Gender/Sexuality in Everyday Context*. Organised by the editors of this volume, the conference was held in London on 24 and 25 May 2011. We gratefully acknowledge the generous funding from the Centre of Excellence in Research which manages the research programme *Post-secular Culture and a Changing Religious Landscape in Finland*, for having enabled the productive and meaningful dialogue.

Chapter 1

Re-framing the Intersection between Religion, Gender and Sexuality in Everyday Life

Andrew Kam-Tuck Yip and Peter Nynäs

This volume brings together eight contributions by an international team of scholars, exploring the intersection between religion, gender and sexuality in contemporary societies. While the examination of this intersection does not constitute a new topic, we argue for the need to re-frame this intersection in order to capture its diverse facets and outcomes. This is an important endeavour in light of recent debates concerning the location and persistence of religion in contemporary society on the one hand, and the hitherto narrow focus on religion as an intrinsically constraining and restrictive force in relation to gender and sexuality. We would argue that, in order to fully understand this intersection, we need to not only re-evaluate the relationship between religion and gender and sexuality, but also the character and role of religion itself in contemporary society.

The empirical focus of the contributions in this volume covers an extensive geographical area, including the UK, USA, Pakistan, Indonesia, Belgium and Israel. They collectively illustrate the multi-faceted and intricate nature of the intersection between religion, gender and sexuality – and the multiple outcomes this entails – on local, national and global levels. In terms of religious traditions, the contributions engage with Christianity, Islam, Hinduism, Sikhism and Judaism. Before introducing each of the contributions, we would like to discuss three unifying themes that contextualise this volume conceptually.

The Relocation and Persistence of Religion in Contemporary Society

The recent debate on religion has to a large extent stressed that processes on a macro level have implications for how we comprehend religion. At the heart of this debate concerning the location of religion lies the issue of secularisation. The erosion and decline of religion was long considered to be an inevitable feature of modernity (e.g. Bruce 2002, 2011). However, the validity of this claim or ideology has become increasingly questioned and more nuanced understandings of religion have emerged which take into serious consideration historical, geopolitical and socio-cultural specificities. Within this framework, religion is viewed as a complex and multidimensional phenomenon that takes different forms depending on the varying trajectories of modernisation and social differentiation across different historical, national, social and cultural contexts (e.g. Davie 2007, Turner 2011). Indeed, the recognition of multiple modernities has sensitised scholars to multiple manifestations of the complex relationship between modernity and religion.

The main challenge to the secularisation thesis comes from the observation that it often occurs concurrently with different forms of counter-developments (e.g. Berger 1999, Davie 2007, Turner 2011). At the background of the resurgence of religion we find many different processes such as the proliferation and persistence of religions within immigrant communities, the rise of charismatic movements, the establishment of new religious movements and the growth of non-institutional spiritualities. These counter-developments challenge earlier expectations about a linear progression of secularism and modernisation.

However, in order to comprehend better the postsecular condition and the resurgence of religion we need to make a distinction between, on the one hand, a shift in religiosity; and on the other, a shift in awareness or consciousness of religion and religion-related issues. Habermas puts emphasis on this shift in consciousness when he claims that 'in terms of *sociological indicators* ... the religious behaviour and convictions ... have by no means changed to such an extent as to justify labelling these societies "postsecular"' (Habermas 2008: 17, his emphasis).[1] We can however, according to Habermas, address the growing public consciousness that has in particular been brought about by different processes that have undermined the secularist belief in the disappearance of religion, the connection of religion with global conflicts, the rise of religious voices in connection with value-laden civil and political issues and controversies, and increasing immigration. Therefore, we need to address the postsecular in terms of a relocation of religion and not in terms of a process opposite to or in contrast to secularisation. Further, this requires from us investigations of the reconfigurations and implications that are involved in the relocation of religion.

These trends have marked many modern societies and it has become more and more obvious that religion as such does not lose relevance and influence in society, politics, culture, or in the everyday lives of individuals. Therefore, in the debates about these contradictory trends of, on the one hand, continuing religious decline, and on the other, enduring religious vitality, scholars have pointed to the relevance of a range of alternative interpretive frameworks, such as de-secularisation, re-socialisation, de-Christianisation, and the emergence of a postsecular society (Casanova 1994).

In addition to these forms of the changes addressed above, we also have to take into account how the new cultural and religious complexity as such involves a quite different change in the religious landscape. Even though scholars who

---

1   For a further discussion of Habermas' account of the concept of postsecularity see e.g. Dillon (2010), Harrington (2007), McLennan (2010), and Moberg et al. (2012).

address the resurgence of religion have shed light on different aspects, the focus has been on qualitative change. In this respect, Frisk (2009: iii) has provided a general overview of this change and how it is linked to globalisation:

> As to the changes, each author describes them a little differently, but there are a few characteristics that several of them bring up ... Eclecticism and syncretism; emphasis on personal experience at the expense of ideology or dogma; uninstitutionalism or religiosity in the private mode; radical egalitarianism or recognizing each person as his/her own spiritual authority; self-spirituality or a shift from God to human being; and emphasis on this-worldliness rather than emphasizing life after death ... Globalization is of course only one of the processes triggering this shift, but I think that as a major cause it has been quite neglected in the discussion so far.

Indeed, one very striking feature of the contemporary religious landscape is the emphasis on working with oneself, more specifically with one's mind, body and spirit, as well as emotions, goals, values and relations. This has been referred to as 'the subjective or expressive turn of culture' (Heelas and Woodhead 2005), 'the de-differentiation of the person' (Davie 2007) or 'self-realization' (Hervieu-Legér 2000). The wide range of what we regard as popular culture has come to play an ever more important role in the distribution of religious and spiritual beliefs, ideas, practices and identities and may become influential for religious life of both individuals and groups (e.g. Lynch 2007, Partridge 2004, 2005).

Many post-institutional forms of religiosity are characterised by the privatisation of religion, a dimension that has further been reinforced also by secularism. Despite these strong influencers in the religious landscape in the West, we can also point at its counterpart, namely deprivatisation. Part of the resurgence of religion today is about how religion makes a comeback in the public sphere within modern democratic polities (Koenig and Guchteneire 2007). Much of the growing public awareness that Habermas (2008) refers to – as mentioned above – has emerged from 'the dilemmas posed by religious otherness', and focused on reframing 'the ongoing tensions between religious cultures and civic political life' (Dillon 2010: 141–2). Therefore, the resurgence of religion is in many ways a societal issue and challenge, rather than simply a private matter.

It should not be neglected that an important background to this 'new' presence of religion in the public sphere and the rise of public awareness of religion-related issues is formed by new media technologies, as Lynch et al. argue, '[C]ontemporary media and culture encourage the "deregulation" of religious ideas and symbols, allowing them to circulate through society in ways that are increasingly beyond the control of religious institutions' (2012: 1). Indeed, new media technologies could enable religious discourses to play a strong role in the public sphere and the nexus of religion and media need to be thoroughly explored (Moberg and Granholm 2012). Furthermore, the changing media landscape has also affected power relations between religious groups and other institutions, and has made possible new and innovative forms of both collective and individual religious agency. Indeed, in many western societies we have witnessed how various forms of media provide new and significant platforms for debates and negotiations about sexuality and gender and how these platforms make space for a plurality of both religious and secular voices and claims.

Central to many received perspectives on secularisation was also the assumption that there is an inherent 'incompatibility between some features of "modernity" and religious belief' (Taylor 2007: 543). Turner has made a relevant observation when he claims that modern nation-states have become increasingly compelled to organise and regulate religion through a plethora of policies. He refers to this as the 'management of religions' (2011: 175–84), but this is also a matter of sovereignty. Connolly has addressed the paradox of sovereignty in late modernity, and how this paradox is reinforced by intertwined local and transnational processes and instances that compose 'a plurality of forces circulating through and under the positional sovereignty of the official arbitrating body' (2005: 145). In other words, the contemporary 'postsecular' condition also implies that we are required to account for a society that is characterised by a cluster of discursive public processes rooted not only in established institutions, but also in highly significant broader social movements and cultural trends that strive to transform their particular positions into legitimate societal values and practices.

However, taken together many of the above mentioned shifts in the religious landscape in Western societies involve a relocation of boundaries and blurring of previously more clearly marked and differentiated 'secular' and 'religious' spheres. Smith argues this point well:

> [O]utside the sphere of secular public discourse... there are circles of discourse
> that are metaphysically and theologically much thicker ... So the challenge, it
> seems, is... to figure out whether and how and on what terms to admit such
> thicker belief into public discourse. (2010: 215)

Smith's question is topical in many Western cultural and societal contexts and surfaces in several contributions in this volume. It addresses problematic issues such as plurality versus shared norms and values, and the preconditions for the organisation of a publicly justified language. On the one hand, when engaging in public civic and political debate religious individuals and groups need to translate 'their religious norms into a secular idiom' (Dillon 2010: 146). Therefore, when we take a closer look at debates around a contested issue that involves both 'religious' and 'secular' parties, the difference between a 'religious' idea or argument as opposed to a 'secular' one is not necessarily clear (Dillon 2010). We can therefore question how reasonable it is to presuppose that the dichotomy between secular and religious is meaningful at the level of individual self-identification. Contemporary social actors are increasingly prone to blur the boundaries between different sectors of knowledge and in juxtaposing scientific, religious, esoteric and therapeutic discourses and practices (Furseth 2006). In this respect, Turner (2011) contends that the world of the sacred appears to be shrinking and the separation of the sacred and the profane evaporating in contemporary societies. Hence, to continue regarding religion versus secularity implies a simplistic and problematic distortion of what is a very complex phenomenon.

From an exploration of the relocation of religion it is clear that encounters, debates and conflicts between voices affiliated with religious or non-religious positions become a much more complex issue than merely one concerning the bridging of differences with regard to formal theologies or worldviews. These complexities need to be addressed from several vantage points. The relevance of power relations within religious and secular institutions and in their interplay should not be ignored. It might be assumed that the contemporary condition raises many challenges for contemporary social actors. Focusing on the emotional aspect, Riis and Woodhead discuss the tensions and contradictions in contemporary society, arguing that 'different domains of a polycentric society pursue their values self-referentially' and that '[m]any individuals find their lives dispersed between competing symbolic and social systems, while seeking a unified and consistent biography' (2010: 204). This tension entails a paradox of the demand for freedom and autonomy, and the call for commitment and surrender.

As we indicated in the beginning of this chapter, a crucial point for future research is therefore how we approach religion; what we highlight, include and exclude. In other words, we need to face the question of the location of religion, and from what we have stressed above this is not a simple task since it seems to indicate significant reconfigurations of, for instance, the private and the public, and the sacred and the secular. Indeed, problematising received understandings of the very category of 'religion' has become a topical question in research on religion. It seems to us that it is worthwhile in this context to point out Taira's (2010) and Turner's (2011) term 'liquid religion' (with reference to Bauman's (2000) concept of 'liquid modernity'). In this connection, Lassander (2012) argues that we have to abandon outdated categories and models, and approach religion as a hybrid, namely the reconfigurations of religion without reducing it to social or psychological components without each acknowledging the other. He refers to the model of 'vernacular religion' and how an individual's religion is a process dependent on what she/he does with the religion, how she/he talks about it; what social actors are involved and how they are engaged. This kind of holistic process might prove fruitful, leading to a form of critical openness.

This way to address religion may prove fruitful when exploring the intersection of contemporary religion from a perspective of the everyday, in particular when we acknowledge how this is embedded in a complexity of social, political and cultural processes, both local and transnational in nature, and how received categories such as 'religious' and 'secular', and 'public' and 'private', dissolve and manifest themselves in novel and decisive ways.

The Contestation of Gender and Sexuality in Contemporary Society

Gender and sexuality are two key markers of an individual's identity, particularly in our highly sexualised and mediatised culture. In social research, gender and sexuality have often been studied separately – with the former focusing primarily on women, and the latter, lesbians and gay men. In the everyday context, however, gender and sexuality are mutually implicated and inextricably linked. In other words, we live our gender and sexual identities in relation to each other; and others relate to us based on their perceptions of our gender in connection to our sexuality, and vice versa. For instance, masculinity is not only about norms, subjective feelings and bodily performances associated with being a man; it is also about desiring a woman as a sexual object – and vice versa. Thus, to be a man, it is not sufficient to just feel and act like a man, but such feeling and 'acting out' only makes sense if it includes desiring women (Dennis 2003). Masculinity, therefore, is traditionally constructed in a heteronormative fashion. Homo-intimacy and homo-eroticism are consequently discouraged, and indeed forbidden, precisely because they disrupt the gender and sexual script which dictates that a man must desire women in order to be a 'proper' man (e.g. McCormack and Anderson 2010, Richardson 2010).

Similarly, in conservative spaces and cultures, cross-gender behaviour often leads to stigmatisation not only because of the transgression of gender dichotomy *per se*, but also because of the assumption that such gender transgression simultaneously disrupts the dualistic sexual regime (i.e. the association between masculinity in women with lesbianism, and effeminacy in men with male homosexuality).

The above examples demonstrate that gender and sexuality are not only about personal identity, embodied subjectivities and bodily performances; they are also about social organisations, structures and relationships. Chambers articulates well the close relationship between gender and sexuality in his definition of heteronormativity as 'the assemblage of regulatory practices, which produces intelligible genders within a heterosexual matrix that insists upon the coherence of sex/gender/desire' (2007: 667).

Indeed, gender and sexuality pertain not only to the personal and private, but also the social and public. With reference to sexuality, for instance, Weeks argues that:

> Sexuality as a theme, a set of pleasurable and sometimes painful practices, a theoretical space, and a site of political passion, ethical debate and social mobilization, is a focus of ever-growing ideas, debate, conflict and creativity …
> Sexuality may be about bodies, but it is also about society. (2011: xi, xii)

Indeed, sexuality – and gender, for that matter – is not only about an individual's feelings, desires and emotions, it is also about the social structures within which such feelings, desires and emotions are located, understood and lived out.

The living out of such subjectivities in a power-infused interactional web – with its inequitable distribution of, and access to, capital of various kinds – makes salient the political dimension of gender and sexuality.

Recent decades have seen the problematisation and politicisation of gender and sexuality, thanks primarily to the strenuous efforts of gender and sexual 'Others'. Social movements since the 1960s, such as feminism, as well as lesbian and gay politics, have exposed and disrupted the tyranny of traditional gender and sexual orders that hegemonise dualistic ways of being, seeing and relating. These movements' liberatory and emancipatory energies – often anti-authoritarian, anti-institution and self-prioritising – have also opened up new legal and social possibilities of envisioning and living gendered and sexual life (e.g. Rahman and Jackson 2010, Trappolin et al. 2012, Weeks 2007). In fact, their justice-seeking agenda has led to the incorporation of 'intimate/sexual citizenship' and 'gender citizenship' into academic theorising as well as into policy and political formulations of citizenship in relation to equality, democracy and human rights (e.g. Lister et al. 2007, Oleksy 2009, Plummer 2003, Richardson and Monro 2012). There have been many positive outcomes of this development. The hegemonic status and legitimacy of traditional cultural scripts of gender and sexuality have been profoundly challenged by competing scripts favouring diversity and difference (e.g. Jackson and Scott 2010). New research has also shown that homophobia is declining amongst certain segments of the young heterosexual male population (e.g. McCormark and Anderson 2010, McCormack 2012).

In spite of such progressive developments in law and various arenas of social life, it would be erroneous to assume that equality is firmly in place in the national and international gender and sexual landscape. National, regional and global analyses continue to attest to undeniable progress, but in tandem with setbacks and recalcitrant resistance to change. The landscape is, at best, uneven; whether it is about the men-privileging 'double standard' that continues to inform gendered bodily performances, or the heterosexual-favouring access to reproductive and fertilisation technologies and legal protection of partnerships and families (e.g. European Union Agency for Fundamental Rights 2010, McRobbie 2008, Trappolin et al. 2012, Walby 2011).

Furthermore, there could be rapture between the commitment to gender justice (i.e. specifically, equality between women and men) and sexual justice (i.e. specifically, equality between heterosexual and LGBT people). The assumption that these two types of justice are concomitant and complementary has not been borne out consistently in empirical research. Some individuals – including activists – who support gender equality in the name of social progress continue to oppose endeavours to recognise certain manifestations of homosexuality such as the legalisation of same-sex partnerships, and same-sex families particularly when children are involved. Often undergirding their rationale with conservative religious and cultural discourses, such individuals construct the sexual justice agenda as corrosive of morality and social fabric (e.g. Yip 2008, 2012, Yip et al. 2011).

In sum, then, while progressive developments in the past decades have undoubtedly empowered and enabled social actors to exercise individual and collective agency, thereby constructing a gender and sexual landscape more tolerant of diversity and difference, the destination has not yet been reached, and the journey continues. The contestation of gender and sexuality continues to be an everyday lived reality.

Everyday Life and Intersectionality:
Putting Religion, Gender and Sexuality Together – and Stirring

Research often focuses on the socio-politically significant – thus public – issues. Consequently, the everyday is associated with the 'mundane' – and often the private – less deserving of research attention. We would contend that everyday life is a microcosm of social life on a macro level. Everyday life is characterised by messiness, fluidity and 'taken-for-grantedness'. It is constituted by – and is constitutive of – identities, subjectivities, experiences, emotions, bodies and desires that are lived out on individual and collective levels of spaces and politics. This emphasis further involves an ambition to raise issues concerning the dynamics related to the ways in which individuals – as social actors – appropriate, negotiate, reinterpret, transgress, invert and challenge various normative practices and spaces (e.g. Miller 2008, Pink 2012). Indeed, Scott asserts that everyday life has three dimensions:

> [It] is that which we presume to be mundane, familiar and unremarkable ... that which is routine, repetitive and rhythmic ... our everyday lives appear to us as private and personal, the product of our individual choices. (2009: 2)

However, we must stress that a shift towards the everyday context does not exclude awareness of the social and political aspects. The everyday is located within a power structure. Thus, it is a highly relevant task to explore such dimensions from a perspective of the everyday context, because the everyday is negotiated and managed through conformity and resistance – in other words, lived – under various structural constraints (e.g. May 2011).

One of the key features of the everyday context is intersectionality, the meeting and interplay between social categories and identities. None of us lives everyday life on the basis of a singular and unitary identity. Rather, we are an assemblage of multiple identities, and we may foreground a specific identity in a given context, contingent upon a host of factors such as expediency and the desire to be included. While identity politics often mobilises one shared identity label or marker in order to maximise political mileage, even the most committed of activists does not live her/his life exclusively on the basis of that singular identity. Her/his everyday life is embedded within a power-infused interactional web which requires her/him to function as an individual with multiple identities, or at least context-specific identifications (Richardson and Monro 2012; Taylor et al. 2012). With specific reference to ethnicity, race and nationalism, Banton offers important insights about multiple belongings and intersectionality:

> [E]very human is assigned to, and identifies with, many social categories; each identification entails costs and benefits. The interrelation between categories presents a generalization of what is currently known as intersectionality. The relative importance of categories changes as individuals trade off advantages associated with one form of social alignment for that of another. (2011: 199)

In the same vein, Lahire also argues for the plurality of the individual social actor: 'Behaviours and practices can only be understood as the intersection of embodied dispositions ... each singular individual can be the bearer of a plurality of dispositions and straddle a plurality of social contexts' (2011: xi-xii). For religious social actors, the intersection between their religious, gender and sexual identities could be an explosive encounter. From the secularist point of view, religion represents traditionalism, authoritarianism and institutionalism, whose relationship with gender and sexuality is characterised by tension and conflict. Therefore, religion is considered an intrinsically constraining and restrictive force, policing gendered and sexual subjectivities and practices. This particular construction of the nature of this intersection is reflective of the ideological underpinnings of secularism itself. As Jakobsen and Pellegrini argue, 'Secularism is central to the [European] Enlightenment narrative in which reason progressively frees itself from the bonds of religion and in so doing liberates humanity' (2008: 2). The secularist assumption is that its emancipatory and liberatory powers would permeate all aspects of social life. In other words, the assumed decline of religion and the corresponding ascendency of scientific reason and rationality would empower individual agency and social life, including how gender and sexuality are understood and lived. This perpetuates a one-dimensional construction of religion as restricting and oppressive of gender and sexuality, particularly gender and sexual 'Others' inhabiting marginal spaces outside of the patriarchal and heteronormative kernel of power. In other words, the secular paradigm presumes not only the unscientific, but also the patriarchal and heteronormative nature of religion.

This perspective has been repeatedly proven to be limiting and biased, thus fails to capture the multi-faceted and nuanced nature of how religion, gender and sexuality are lived in everyday life. It over-emphasises the structural power of religion and downplays the agency of religious actors for creativity, resistance and transformation on the personal and social levels. It also fails to give due recognition to religiously-inspired and religiously-informed gender and sexual subjectivities that could be liberating and meaningful on multiple levels (e.g. Hunt 2009, Hunt and Yip 2012). It is therefore not too difficult to understand the often misplaced and palpable anti-religious sentiments in feminist and queer politics and communities. In such discourses and spaces, religion constitutes an 'Other' that needs to be kept at the margin, if not eliminated altogether. Unfortunately, such discourses often turn a blind eye to the progressive gendering and queering efforts which aim to make theology, religious spaces, beliefs, and practices more inclusive and respectful of diversity (e.g. Browne et al. 2010, Wadud 2006). There is no denying that the intersection between religion, gender and sexuality – as manifested in controversies pertaining to homosexuality, veiling and access to religious leadership – constitutes a site of contestation. Nonetheless, it is also a site of creation and transformation. The contentious nature of each of them – and their interrelationship – is precisely the reason why they also unleash the potential for change that transform individual lives and socio-political arrangements. Contestation, then, delimits as well as opens up new possibilities of living and relating (e.g. Yip Forthcoming, Yip with Khalid 2010).

If we accept that identities are intersecting rather than singular and unitary, particularly within the 'messiness' of the everyday context, then this opens up new possibilities of sociological imagining. This relates to the postsecular paradigm in significant ways, and indeed to the re-framing of religion, gender and sexuality. King expresses well the fluidity of the postsecular paradigm:

> Postsecularism can be defined as a renewed openness to questions of the spirit, but one that retains the habits of critical thought which partially defines secularism. 'Questions of the spirit' is just one way to put it; one may prefer 'a renewed engagement with religion' or 'questions of faith'… To open up those questions, to engage with an open mind in these debates, yet to retain the specifically secular critical stance towards unsupported metaphysical assertions – this juxtaposition can broadly be called postsecular. (2009: 11–12)

King presents here a particular view of the postsecular with important normative trajectories. It implies a postsecular paradigm that is non-dualistic and eschews from a militant and extremist ideology of the incompatibility of religious sensibility and scientific thinking. Such a paradigm would emphasise the co-existence of secularism and religion, and the multi-directional possibilities of their relationship. In the same vein, Connolly argues that societies marked by diversity require a 'deep pluralism', meaning that a renegotiation of 'the ethos of sovereignty in the contemporary context requires an audacious pluralization of the sacred and a corollary relaxation of what it takes to defile the sense of the sacred embraced by you, me, or others' (2005: 147). We think this renewed and revised relationship will contribute to the re-framing of the intersection between religion, gender and sexuality. We hope that this volume's exploration of how religion, gender and sexuality are lived in the everyday context will offer conceptual and empirical insights about the limitations of the secular paradigm; therefore the exciting possibilities that the postsecular paradigm could offer.

The Chapters

The eight chapters in this volume engage with the three themes we discussed above in cross-cutting and distinctive ways. Collectively, they demonstrate that the intersection between religion, gender and sexuality has a salient political dimension, and this is manifested on the personal, institutional and cultural levels within national, regional and international contexts. In Chapter 2, Hamzić turns our attention to the case of gender-variant and sexually non-heterosexual Muslims in Pakistan and Indonesia, specifically their strategies of survival and resistance within the context of two intersecting hegemonic identitarian/ ideological discourses. These discourses refer to the nationalistic Muslim theopolitical reductionism and (neo)liberal homonormative identity politics originating from the Global North. Both discourses have a common feature in that they are exclusionary to the kaleidoscope of gender and sexual subjectivities. His study reveals the strength and creativity of the social actors and communities concerned to not only resist such hegemonic discourses, but also cultivate self-understandings and communitarian belongings that transcend national, cultural and religious specificities. Such possibilities are an outcome of 'the emanation of a distinct *alterspace* which these communities have learnt to occupy, that cuts across the hegemonic identity tropes whilst retaining an operative and conceptual *différance*'.

In Chapter 3, Wilcox uses the example of the Sisters of Perpetual Indulgence to explore the ways in which spirituality, parody and politics are intertwined. She argues that, in the exploration of the Sisters' spiritual orientations, political activism and service particularly to the LGBT community, the 'postsecular', namely, the breakdown of the secular-religious dichotomy can be evidenced. Wilcox asserts that this does not denote the dialogue between the religious and the secular; rather, it involves 'a melding of the two until, at least at the margins, each becomes indistinguishable from the other'. She concludes her analysis of the Sisters' 'parodic politics' – which combines seriousness and parody, in their effort to confront the homophobia of the Church through subversive performance – that they, as 'religious nones', and as nuns, 'are betwixt and between, working in the postsecular gray area that is both secular and sacred, neither secular nor sacred'.

Focusing on the lived experiences of Sikh, Hindu and Muslim young women and men in the UK, Page and Yip, in Chapter 4, present insights into the everyday management and negotiation of these young adults, which also implicate their family, kinship network, religious and cultural communities, as well as mainstream society. Their examination of the specific issues of marriage and virginity demonstrates that these young adults draw from multiple religious and secular discourses to negotiate such significant issues. Furthermore, the process of negotiation and its outcomes are highly gendered: young men, compared to young women, generally demonstrate a greater degree of agency in resisting and reconfiguring dualistic religious and cultural scripts on gender and sexuality. Thus, the 'double standard' continues to assert much greater pressure on young women to discipline their embodied gender and sexual subjectivities and performances.

In Chapter 5, Jaspal, adopting the identity process theory – a socio-psychological theory explicating identity construction, threat and coping – throws light on the lived experiences of British Muslim gay men of Pakistani descent. Focusing on how these men manage religious and cultural homophobia, Jaspal presents narratives pertaining to three themes: identity dissonance and feelings of shame and guilt; managing ingroup norms, God's norms and the experience of fear; and managing interpersonal relations and anger. He argues that the participants consistently manifest negative emotions of shame, guilt, fear and anger when reflecting upon being Muslim and gay. Therefore, many of them engage in intrapsychic strategies for coping, such as denial and compartmentalisation, as well as self-withdrawal from religious and cultural communities. He concludes that this scenario significantly threatens identity coherence, self-esteem, and social relationships; and that, in such a context, 'being Muslim and gay can induce "hyper-threats" to identity'.

In Chapter 6, Siara turns the spotlight on Poles living in the UK. Capitalising on the experiences of the participants' migration from a religiously and politically conservative space in terms of gender and sexuality matters, to one that is more progressive, Siara examines the participants' attitudes towards abortion and homosexuality specifically. Her findings show that men – particularly those who are religious – appear to be more likely to oppose abortion and homosexuality. Women, on the other hand, demonstrate more tolerance on such matters, and religiosity does not seem to play a significant role in this respect. Siara argues that Britain's more progressive gender and sexual culture and actual contacts with lesbians and gay men also cultivate in her participants more tolerant attitudes towards abortion and homosexuality. Siara challenges the pervasive assumption about the high level of religiosity amongst the Polish community and the corresponding religiously-informed conservative attitudes towards gender and sexuality issues. She argues that the picture, particularly within the migration context, is far more complex.

In Chapter 7, Peumans and Stallaert use a case study to illustrate 'the queering of conversion'. Focusing on the life journey of a white Marxist Belgian gay man, Wout, who converts to Islam *vis-à-vis* increasing Islamophobia in Belgian society, Peumans and Stallaert demonstrate that conversion is a kind of experimental cultural passage in search of the right path for the individual's biographical narrative, through a process of trial and error. They argue that an individual's reorientation to a new belief system is based on a pre-existing identity and embodied worldview. They conclude that, '[I]n a project of queering conversion, sexuality takes up a central place … Queering conversion also stresses the political meanings around sexuality. Sexuality is in this sense very much a public and political matter'. Indeed, as their participant Wout demonstrates, coming out as Muslim and gay is a matter of honour, and this conscious political act entails benefits but also costs.

Focusing on the ultra-Orthodox Jewish community in Israel, Zalcberg and Zalcberg, in Chapter 8, present an analysis of this community's socialising agents in the constructions of the body and sexuality. Their chapter explores three empirical themes: the mechanisms that perpetuate the prohibition of any discussion of the body and sexuality; the channels through which the participants obtain information about sex regardless of this prohibition; and the ramifications of the silence and silencing within this community. Their findings show that this community – through its various socialisation agents – systematically constructs silence around sexuality matters, and silences the potential for query. This entrenched silence and systematic silencing generate ignorance about sexuality, thus many participants report a sense of guilt and confusion about adolescent physiological changes, and beyond. Compared to women, some men nonetheless gain sexual knowledge from peers and by exploring 'forbidden literature' – secular texts that discuss the body or sexuality. Zalcberg and Zalcberg also argue that the ramifications of community silence and silencing are immense, leading to the notion of 'sin' and further silencing through mutual policing and surveillance amongst young people themselves.

Last but not least, Houston, in Chapter 9, demonstrates that the political dimension of the intersection between religion, gender and sexuality is not confined to the personal and community levels, but also the global. Houston analyses the prominent and problematic role of corporate religion in international policy debates about gender and sexuality issues, such as reproductive healthcare and equality for lesbians and gay men. Employing Foucault's concept of 'governmentality', Houston argues that, far from being relegated to the private sphere, religion – specifically in the form of religious authority structures – continues to play a significant role in policy debate and formulation, manifested in its continued influence on policies and development efforts on gender and sexual minorities by the European Union and the United Nation. Houston concludes with the caution that political activism of conservative monotheistic religions constitutes a recalcitrant impediment to the formal equality of gender and sexual subjectivities.

References

Banton, M. 2011. A Theory of Social Categories. *Sociology* 45(2): 187–201.

Bauman, Z. 2000. *Liquid Modernity*. Cambridge: Polity Press.

Berger, P.L. 1999. *The Desecularization of the World: Resurgent Religion and World Politics*. Washington DC: The Ethics and Public Policy Center.

Browne, K., Munt, S.R. and Yip, A.K.T. 2010. *Queer Spiritual Spaces: Sexuality and Sacred Places*. Farnham: Ashgate.

Bruce, S. 2002. *God is Dead*. Oxford: Blackwell.

Bruce, S. 2011. *Secularization: In Defence of an Unfashionable Theory*. Oxford: Oxford University Press.

Casanova, J. 1994. *Public Religions in the Modern World*. London: University of Chicago Press.

Chambers, S. 2007. 'An Incalculable Effect': Subversions of Heteronormativity. *Political Studies* 55(3): 656–79.

Connolly, W.E. 2005. *Pluralism*. London: Duke University Press.

Davie, G. 2007. *The Sociology of Religion*. London: Sage.

Dennis, J.P. 2003. Heteronormativity, in *Men and Masculinities: A Social, Cultural, and Historical Encyclopaedia*, edited by M. Kimmel and A. Aronson. Santa Barbara, CA: ABC CLIO.

Dillon, M. 2010. Can Postsecular Society Tolerate Religious Differences? *Sociology of Religion* 71: 139–56.

European Union Agency for Fundamental Rights. 2010. *Homophobia, Transphobia and Discrimination on Grounds of Sexual Orientation and Gender Identity*. Luxembourg: Publications Office of the European Union.

Frisk, L. 2009. Globalization: A Key Factor in Contemporary Religious Change. *Journal of Alternative Spiritualities and New Age Studies* 5. Available at http://www.asanas.org.uk/files/005Frisk.pdf [accessed 1 March 2012].

Furseth, I. 2006. *From Quest for Truth to Being Oneself. Religious Change in Life Stories*. Frankfurt am Main: Peter Lang.

Habermas, J. 2008. Notes on Postsecular Society. *New Perspectives Quarterly* Fall: 17–29.

Harrington, A. 2007. Habermas and the 'Postsecular' Society. *European Journal of Social Theory* 10: 543–60.

Heelas, P. and Woodhead, L. 2005. *The Spiritual Revolution: Why Religion is Giving Way to Spirituality*. Oxford: Blackwell Publishing.

Hervieu-Legér, D. 2000. *Religion as a Chain of Memory*. Cambridge: Polity Press.

Hunt, S. 2009. *Contemporary Christianity and LGBT Sexualities*. Aldershot: Ashgate.

Hunt, S. and Yip, A.K.T. 2012. *The Ashgate Research Companion to Contemporary Religion and Sexuality*. Farnham: Ashgate.

Jackson, S. and Scott, S. 2010. Rehabilitating Interactionism for a Feminist Sociology of Sexuality. *Sociology* 44(5): 811–26.

Jakobsen, J.R. and Pellegrini, A. 2008. *Secularisms*. Durham: Duke University Press.

King, M. 2009. *Postsecularism: The Hidden Challenge to Extremism*. London: James Clarke & Co Ltd.

Koenig, M. and de Guchteneire, P.F.A. 2007. *Democracy and Human Rights in Multicultural Societies*. Aldershot: Ashgate.

Lahire, B. 2011. *The Plural Actor*. Cambridge: Polity Press.

Lassander, M. 2012. Grappling with Liquid Modernity: Investigating Postsecular Religion, in *Postsecular Society*, edited by P. Nynäs, M. Lassander and T. Utriainen. New Brunswick and London: Transaction Publishers.

Lister, R., William, F. and Anttonen, A. 2007. *Gendering Citizenship in Western Europe*. Bristol: The Policy Press.

Lynch, G. 2007. *The New Spirituality. An Introduction to Progressive Belief in the Twenty-first Century.* New York: I.B. Tauris.

Lynch, G., Mitchell, J. and Strhan, A. 2012. Introduction, in *Religion, Media and Culture: A Reader*, edited by G. Lynch, J. Mitchell and A. Strhan. London and New York: Routledge.

McCormack, M. 2012. *The Declining Significance of Homophobia: How Teenage Boys are Redefining Masculinity and Heterosexuality.* Oxford: Oxford University Press.

McCormack, M. and Anderson, E. 2010. 'It's just not acceptable any more': The Erosion of Homophobia and the Softening of Masculinity at an English Sixth Form. *Sociology* 44(5): 843–59.

McLennan, G. 2010. Spaces of Postsecularism, in *Exploring the Postsecular: The Religious, the Political and the Urban*, edited by A.L. Molendijk, J. Beaumont and C. Jedan. Leiden: Brill.

McRobbie, A. 2008. *The Aftermath of Feminism: Gender, Culture and Social Change.* London: Sage.

May, V. 2011. *Sociology of Personal Life.* Basingstoke: Palgrave MacMillan.

Miller, D. 2008. *The Comfort of Things.* Cambridge: Polity Press.

Moberg, M. and Granholm, K. 2012. The Concept of the Postsecular and the Contemporary Nexus of Religion, Media, Popular Culture, and Consumer Culture, in *Postsecular Society*, edited by P. Nynäs, M. Lassander and T. Utriainen. New Brunswick and London: Transaction Publishers.

Moberg, M., Granholm, K. and Nynäs, P. 2012. Trajectories of Postsecular Complexity: An Introduction, in *Postsecular Society*, edited by P. Nynäs, M. Lassander and T. Utriainen. New Brunswick and London: Transaction Publishers.

Oleksy, E.H. 2009. *Intimate Citizenships: Gender, Sexualities, Politics.* London: Routledge.

Partridge, C. 2004. *The Re-enchantment of the West (vol. 1): Alternative Spiritualities, Sacralization, Popular Culture and Occulture.* London: Continuum.

Partridge, C. 2005. *The Re-enchantment of the West (vol. 2): Alternative Spiritualities, Sacralization, Popular Culture and Occulture.* London: Continuum.

Pink, S. 2012. *Situating Everyday Life: Practices and Places.* London: Sage.

Plummer, K. 2003. *Intimate Citizenship: Private Decisions and Public Dialogues.* Seattle: University of Washington Press.

Rahman, M. and Jackson, S. 2010. *Gender and Sexuality: Sociological Approaches.* Cambridge: Polity Press.

Richardson, D. 2010. Youth Masculinities: Compelling Male Heterosexuality. *British Journal of Sociology* 61(4): 737–56.

Richardson, D. and Monro, S. 2012. *Sexuality, Equality and Diversity.* Basingstoke: Palgrave Macmillan.

Riis, O. and Woodhead, L. 2010. *A Sociology of Religious Emotion.* Oxford: Oxford University Press.

Scott, S. 2009. *Making Sense of Everyday Life*. Cambridge: Polity Press.

Smith, S.D. 2010. *The Disenchantment of Secular Discourse.* Cambridge, MA: Harvard University Press.

Taira, T. 2010. Religion as a Discursive Technique: The Politics of Classifying Wicca. *Journal of Contemporary Religion* 25(3): 379–94.

Taylor, C. 2007. *A Secular Age*. Cambridge, MA: Harvard University Press.

Taylor, Y., Hines, S. and Caset, M.E. 2011. *Theorizing Intersectionality and Sexuality*. Basingstoke: Palgrave Macmillan.

Trappolin, L., Gasparini, A. and Wintemute, R. 2012. *Confronting Homophobia in Europe: Social and Legal Perspectives*. Oxford: Hart.

Turner, B.S. 2011. *Religion and Modern Society: Citizenship, Secularisation and the State.* Cambridge: Cambridge University Press.

Vincett, G., Sharma, S. and Aune, K. 2008. Women, Religion and Secularization: One Size Does Not Fit All, in *Women and Religion in the West. Challenging Secularization*, edited by K. Aune, S. Sharma and G. Vincett. Aldershot: Ashgate.

Wadud, A. 2006. *Inside the Gender Jihad: Women's Reform in Islam*. Oxford: Oneworld.

Walby, S. *The Future of Feminism*. Cambridge: Polity Press.

Weeks, J. 2007. *The World We Have Won: The Remaking of Erotic and Intimate Life*. London: Routledge.

Weeks, J. 2011. *The Languages of Sexuality*. London: Routledge.

Yip, A.K.T. 2008. The Quest for Intimate/Sexual Citizenship: Lived Experiences of Lesbian and Bisexual Muslim Women. *Contemporary Islam* 2(2): 99–117.

Yip, A.K.T. 2012. Homophobia and Ethnic Minorities in the UK, in *Confronting Homophobia in Europe: Social and Legal Perspectives*, edited by L. Trappolin, A. Gasparini and R. Wintemute. Oxford: Hart.

Yip, A.K.T. Forthcoming. When Religion Meets Sexuality: Two Tales of Intersection, in *Sexual Diversity and Religious Diversity*, edited by P. Dickey Young, H. Shipley and T. Trothen. Vancouver: University of British Columbia Press.

Yip, A.K.T., Keenan, M. and Page, S. 2011. *Religion, Youth and Sexuality: Selected Key Findings from a Multi-faith Exploration*. Nottingham: University of Nottingham.

Yip, A.K.T. with Khalid, A. 2010. Looking for *Allah*: Spiritual Quests of Queer Muslims, in *Queer Spiritual Spaces: Sexuality and Sacred Places*, edited by K. Browne, S.R. Munt and A.K.T. Yip. Farnham: Ashgate.

Chapter 2

The Resistance from an Alterspace: Pakistani and Indonesian Muslims beyond the Dominant Sexual and Gender Norms

Vanja Hamzić

Introduction

This chapter presents a comparative critique of the two hegemonic discourses which challenge the social integrity and agency of individuals and communities in Pakistan and Indonesia who are outside the dominant sexual/gender matrices and politics. The first identified discourse is that of Muslim theopolitical reductionism, which – by regulating sexuality and gender – aims at achieving or retaining political power. The second stream is that of (neo)liberal homonormative identity politics, seeking to monopolise sexual/gender plurality wherever possible, thus asserting its global relevance and a *will to represent* all those who diverge from the perceived heterosexual path. The origins and ideological apparatus of these discourses supersede national particularities and can, indeed, be analysed as supranational phenomena, present across the porous nation-state, cultural and religious divide.

The ensuing analysis is focused on the effects of these discourses on specifically *Muslim* sexually diverse and/or gender-variant individuals and communities in the two Muslim-majority states, whose subjectivities remain intrinsically imbued in their deeply felt religious experience, despite being largely ostracised from the mainstream currents. Their subject positions, thus, necessarily comprise 'a critique from within', because they challenge – from a Muslim perspective – the core moral and social nation-building narratives, which in both societies rely heavily on the limited interpretations of Muslim legal and cultural traditions. They are, however, also 'a critique from outside', because they expose the exclusionary effects of gender/sexual identity politics entrenching the rigid identity scripts to which many of the analysed subjectivities in Pakistan and Indonesia cannot or do not want to subscribe.

It appears that the regulative mechanisms of the two hegemonic discourses are both based on a simultaneous *producing* of the desired forms of sexual/gender behaviour and identities and forceful *reducing* of the behavioural/identitary forms deemed unwanted. This piece attempts to disclose the particularities of these actions, as well as to discern and analyse some resistance strategies devised by the oppressed communities. I argue that the survival and continuous resistance of the researched subjectivities are made possible through the emanation of a distinct *alterspace* which these communities have learnt to occupy, that cuts across the hegemonic identity tropes whilst retaining an operative and conceptual *différance* (c.f. Derrida 1963).

Comparative analyses relating to Pakistan and Indonesia are relatively rare, because the two states are each thought to embody a very different historical, cultural and political ethos from one another. Pakistan is often seen as an increasingly troubled political playground, suffering greatly from the lack of good governance and power-thirsty military, tribal, clerical and political elites whose manoeuvres are often legitimised through an extremist theopolitical discourse (Hamzić and Mir-Hosseini 2010). The prospect of legal and political reforms is slight and hard to predict, not least because of the continuous political instability in the region as a whole (the crises of Afghanistan and Kashmir being amongst its most apparent triggers). Indonesia is, however, perceived as a far more stable and democratic republic, despite numerous internal conflicts alongside the sensitive political, ethnic and religious divide. The country's *reformasi* (reform) movement, which in the late 1990s brought down the authoritarian regime of President Suharto, decentralised the government and enabled a number of important legal and political changes to take hold. Yet it stopped short of resisting the oppressive programmes – coming both from the centre and the peripheries of the country's political system – which aim at regulation of public morality and sexual and gender norms for the sake of political legitimacy and control (Hamzić and Mir-Hosseini 2010).

Despite the above and many other differences, the two states are curiously close in a number of respects directly relevant for the present comparative analysis. Firstly, both of them house astonishingly heterogeneous Muslim communities, the majority of which are Sunni, generally following either *Shafi'i* (in Indonesia) or *Hanafi* (in Pakistan) jurisprudential traditions. These denominational orientations are further complicated by the strong presence of various Sufi orders, leading to what is sometimes called the distinct Indonesian or Pakistani Muslim exegetic path, epitomised in the Javanese mystical way (*tarekat*) and idea of religious law (*sarengat*), as espoused by their spiritual teachers (*kyai* for men and *nyai* for women), and in the Pakistani/Indian Barelvi traditionalist movement. Secondly, as already mentioned, this Muslim intra-religious plurality in Indonesia and Pakistan is complemented by ubiquitous sexual/gender heterogeneity greatly exceeding and defeating both heteronormative and homonormative identitary scripts. The traditional gender-variant groups, most notably the *khwajasara* in Pakistan and *waria* in Indonesia, are amongst more visible examples of such plurality, thus attracting an increasing academic interest (e.g. Boellstorff 2005a, Valentine 2007) and social debate. Thirdly, the two states' political history and legal systems are similar in many ways. Both states have been created in the aftermath of World War II, following the periods of European colonial rule, through the process of political negotiation and nation-building programmes balancing between the largely secular visions of their founders and the cohesive narrative of the common faith, resulting in the new type of Muslim nationalism (Hamzić and Mir-Hosseini 2010). In both instances this resulted in the creation of multi-sourced legal systems, including the antiquated pre-independence colonial laws and the official interpretations of the *shari'a* (God's injunctions contained in the Qur'an and *sunna* – the practice of the Prophet Muhammad), partly based on some classical Islamic jurisprudence (*fiqh*). As it will be shown, this strange mixture of late nineteenth century European morality and the disputable, centuries-old *fiqh* has been particularly salient for the policing of sexuality and gender in Pakistan and Indonesia. Fourthly and finally, both Pakistan and Indonesia boast highly developed civil society movements. Amongst them, the feminist groups have arguably played a key role in framing and sustaining the demands for gender/sexual plurality and justice (Mullally 2006, Rofiah 2010, Shaheed 2010). These and other considerations signal that the environments and experiences of sexually diverse and/or gender-variant Muslims in Pakistan and Indonesia are, indeed, comparable. On this premise, it is plausible that some forms of resistance from an alterspace emerge in other contexts as well, in particular when the communities and individuals struggle against the two identified globalised hegemonic discourses.

Theopolitical Reductionism

I refer to the first analysed hegemonic discourse as Muslim theopolitical reductionism. It is based on the reductionist (literalist, simplistic, tendentious) interpretations of Muslim legal and social tradition, including its sources (Qur'an, *sunna*) and founding principles (for example, *shari'a*), advanced to achieve certain political goals. This discourse is commonly yet problematically branded as 'Islamism'.[1]

One of the key strategies of this stream is to conflate *shari'a* – an ideal of God's injunctions to humankind in need of human interpretation – with the classical jurisprudence (*fiqh*) on the subject. In doing so, the selected interpretations of Muslim scholars from times and contexts much different from the contemporary

---

1   The term 'Islamism' was originally used in eighteenth-century French academia as a synonym for Islam (alongside 'Mohammedanism') and then gradually abandoned in favour of the generic term (Islam). It was rediscovered in the 1980s, again by French academics, but its previous meaning was changed. Today it is generally employed 'to distinguish Islam as modern ideology from Islam as a faith' (Kramer 2003). I find this highly problematic, since it confuses an entire faith system with varying political ideologies. Also, the very absence of such constructs in the articulation of similar phenomena, associable with other religions (e.g. 'Christianism'), suggests a peculiar Orientalist reminiscence in the contemporary scholarship on Muslim political movements (Hamzić and Mir-Hosseini 2010: 190). Hence, the term 'Islamism' or some of its popular synonyms (e.g. 'political Islam') are not used in this chapter.

exigencies of Muslim-majority nation-states of today, are proclaimed sacrosanct, that is to say, beyond critique or much-needed contextualisation. These views are then codified into a variety of legal rules which are unsophisticatedly called 'Islamic law' or, indeed, *shari'a*. Yet the adequacy of the term 'Islamic Law' is dubious, as it refers to instances which can hardly be subsumed under a single denominator, such as, on the one hand, *lex ferenda* (*shari'a*) and, on the other hand, *lex lata* of various Muslim communities, including those based on classical *fiqh*. To maintain the discursive difference between the sources of law, such as *shari'a*, and the law itself effectively means to recognise the role and agency of human interpretation (*ijtihad*) in the lawmaking process. Once this role is revealed, it becomes clear that the contemporary emanations of 'Islamic law' are not the *shari'a, sui generis*, but – at the very least – the mixture of some classical and present-day *fiqh*, and that, as such, they are most certainly mutable, contestable and politically conditioned.

Producing Gender/Sexuality: From Ibuisme to Purdah

Ever since their struggles for independence, which in Indonesia was declared in 1945 and in Pakistan two years later, the political elites of the two countries have embarked on extensive cultural, political and legal reforms aimed at controlling sexuality and gender (Hamzić and Mir-Hosseini 2010). The new vision of the idealised, exemplary Pakistani/Indonesian woman was particularly strongly imposed through a variety of media, including new dress-codes, provisions of family law and cultural and religious policies. These measures combined to create a dutiful gender role which was to serve as the primary identitary and visionary symbol of the new nation, against which the 'complementary' male model was developed (albeit less stringently) and all other gender forms gradually marginalised. Because Muslims comprised the majority population in both states, the production of this nation-building gender (and its accompanying heteronormative sexuality) was particularly geared towards Muslim women and families, even though sometimes furthered by largely secular state elites.

For instance, in Indonesia, during the Suharto era (1965–1998), the state ideologues created and heavily promoted *ibuisme* ('motherism'), which maintained that the ideal Indonesian woman 'is a mother that forgoes all her personal ambitions for the sake of her children and country' (Hamzić and Mir-Hosseini 2010: 52). Against this state gender ideology, the oppositional Indonesian Muslim right-wing political establishments have developed another form of patriarchy, imposing even stricter control of women's sociality, sexuality and gender identity/expression. According to this identitary script, the Muslim women were to be almost exclusively confined to the household and to strictly obey their husbands, the imposed dress-codes and moral rules derived from the reductionist interpretations of Muslim legal and social tradition, including compulsory heterosexuality and monogamy. The two ideological role-models of female gender clashed and combined – and they continue to do so – in a primarily political power struggle.

In Pakistan, a distinct form of liberal bourgeois ideology (Rouse 1988) with largely symbolic Muslim elements was initially developed by the ruling political establishment, in order to galvanise secular (largely upper and middle class) as well as multi-voiced Muslim communities (Hamzić and Mir-Hosseini 2010: 158). It was, however, challenged by a stricter form of (at the time oppositional) Muslim theopolitical reductionism, spearheaded by the *Jamaat-e-Islami* Party, which endeavoured to bring the 'issue' of the female gender (and its distinct nation-building role) to the forefront of its ideological programme. The life-long leader of this faction, Sayyid Abul A'la Maudoodi, published as early as 1939 a book entitled *Purdah*, which has since gone through many reprints and has become an unofficial manifesto of the party's patriarchal vision for the Pakistani Muslim woman (Maudoodi 1967, Pal 1990). Maudoodi's book describes the model Pakistani woman as inferior to men and incapable of performing almost any public work, hence domestic confinement is 'ordained for her by nature' (Maudoodi 1967: 93, 199, Pal 1990: 453). In 1977, when the military *coup d'état* brought into power General Muhammad Zia-ul-Haq, the new ruling elite adopted Maudoodi's *Purdah* as the state gender ideology. A series of far-reaching legal and cultural measures were quickly introduced, which followed (either covertly or overtly) the patriarchal maxim of *chador aur char diwari* ('veil and four walls', meaning that women should be veiled and confined to the household (Mullally 2006: 170)). Zia-ul-Haq's oppressive regime ended abruptly in 1988 following his death in a plane crash, but the legacy of his gender-biased reforms – which he ushered in under the banner of 'Islamisation' of the country's legal system and cultural values – is still deeply felt. The subsequent governments have tried to depart from it to varying degrees, but the continuous activities of the *Jamaat-e-Islami* Party and other right-wing theopolitical forces still manage to keep Maudoodi's and Zia-ul-Haq's vision of *Purdah* influential in the Pakistani politics, law and culture(s).

The production of the oppressive gender models was reinforced with an overarching, strictly heteronormative ideological discourse, which the patriarchal political and religious elites in Indonesia and Pakistan wrongly equated with the historical and present-day Muslim legal and social ethos, contrary to the comprehensive evidence suggesting otherwise (e.g. El-Rouayheb 2005, Habib 2007, Hamzić 2011). Attempts to reduce sexual/gender plurality were particularly undertaken by means of legislative reform.

Reducing Gender/Sexuality: A 'Muslim' Return to Victorian Rigidity?

The elites behind the grand cultural projects in Indonesia and Pakistan, designed to control sexual and gender plurality primarily amongst the Muslim communities, have eventually realised that these efforts will need to be extended into legal provisions, in order to suppress the existent alternative concepts. The concepts which the new laws will have been set to counter and reduce in both countries include various types of same-sex intimacy and relationship; gender identities and expressions well beyond the rigid binary male/female divide; and, overall, far more diverse, culture-specific types of family and kinship, defeating the rigidity of the European 'nuclear family' construct (e.g. Blackburn 2004, Boellstorff 2005a, 2005b). Being deeply rooted in the traditions of the two countries, these multifarious emanations of sexuality and gender could not have been simply culturally discouraged; thus, the punitive and violent force of law has been brought into play.

The model of '*the* family' and sexual/gender relations imposed by the new laws has given a second, more powerful than ever, life to the Victorian (in Pakistan) or Dutch colonial (in Indonesia) mores, which have been preserved by the two states' legal systems (Hamzić and Mir-Hosseini 2010). Studies have already shown how Muslim societies, following the encounters with the European colonialism and imperialism, had simultaneously endeavoured to resist and to embrace certain novel forms of sociality, sexuality and gender (El-Rouayheb 2005, Hamzić 2011, Massad 2007). The remnants of these ambiguous efforts continued to reappear long after the demise of the European empires, wholeheartedly supported by the new liberal capitalist 'free market' dream and the emerging bourgeoisie of the nascent Muslim-majority nation-states.

Paradigmatically, in Pakistan as well as in Indonesia, an astonishingly large number of criminal law provisions, many of which regulate sexual/gender mores, survive unchanged since the colonial times. The subsequent attempts, on the national and/or provincial level, to 'return to the *shari'a*' by legislating (mostly within the domain of criminal and family law) austere control measures, have effectively reinforced (and, in many cases, revived) the European colonial morality, with its stringent patriarchal heteronormativity and gender roles. Instead of offering an alternative to the colonial *Weltanshauung*, the Muslim theopolitical reductionist legal reforms have targeted, by and large, the specific *post-independence* legislation. Thus, some undoubtedly European constructs – such as that of the 'nuclear family' – have been reified as 'truly Muslim' (and Pakistani/Indonesian) and prescribed by law, while the new reforms have challenged the domestic legislation providing – from a Muslim and/or country-specific social perspective – for at least a limited scope of gender justice (e.g., in Pakistan, the 1961 Muslim Family Laws Ordinance or, in Indonesia, the 1945 Constitution).

In Indonesia, a federated presidential republic founded on an ostensibly religion-neutral state ideology, the Muslim theopolitical reductionism primarily reached the domain of law on the provincial, rather than federal level (Hamzić and Mir-Hosseini 2010), following the post-*reformasi* decentralisation of governance (from 1998 onwards). Yet it was complemented by the central government's moral panic[2] and an increasingly insecure position, which gave the Muslim reductionist vision an unprecedented influence. As a consequence, the central legislative

---

2   I use the phrase 'moral panic' to describe the intensity of anxiety expressed in a given group (in the above case, the Indonesian central government) about an issue (above, it is the rise of the Muslim right-wing theopolitical factions) that appears to jeopardise the social order. For a seminal text on moral panic, see Cohen 1973.

organs enacted laws which aimed at a stricter policing of public morality and, thus, of sexuality and gender, most notably the notorious 2008 Pornography Law.

In Pakistan, a parliamentary federal republic in which Islam is considered to be the state religion, the oppressive legislation curtailing sexual and gender plurality was *traditionally* English, i.e. originating in the antiquated nineteenth century colonial criminal laws of the British Empire, which were quite literally 'domesticated' after independence. Thus section 377 of the 1860 Penal Code, still in force in Pakistan, provides for a Victorian formulation and punishment of 'carnal intercourse against the order of nature'.

The situation, however, significantly changed in 1979, when General Zia-ul-Haq imposed, through martial law, the *Hudood* Ordinances, most notably the *Zina* Ordinance, which made the offence of *zina* (adultery) liable to harsh, prescribed (*hadd*) or discretionary (*ta'zir*) punishments (Hamzić and Mir-Hosseini 2010). This led to systematic discrimination and violence against women, on an unprecedented scale. Many of the *zina* cases were, in fact, converted rape charges, which, failing to satisfy the stringent evidentiary requirements (four Muslim male witnesses of good standing), were decided so that the rape victims were accused and sentenced for *zina*. Although being acquitted at the appellate proceedings, numerous women languished in jails for years, awaiting the appellate process to begin (Khan 2003: 77).

The ordinance was finally significantly revised by the 2006 Protection of Women Act. However, on 22 December 2010, the Federal *Shariat* Court declared one provision of this Act relating to *Zina* Ordinance as 'repugnant to Islam' and thus unconstitutional (Shirkat Gah 2010, AHRC 2010). That section (s 11) omitted a provision of the *Zina* Ordinance (s 3) so that it had overriding effect on all other Pakistani laws. Given the special (extra-systemic) position of the Federal *Shariat* Court in the Pakistani legal system, it is hard to predict the effects of this judgment. Presumably, it might at least aggravate the psychological and cultural impact of the *Zina* Ordinance, whose continued and now reaffirmed existence, even without straightforward enforceability, encroaches upon the prospects of change in the state-sanctioned theopolitics.

(Neo)Liberal Homonormativity

There is today quite a well-developed critique of the globalised liberal ideological discourse in sexuality/gender-related contexts. Janet Halley (2006) has shown how the global northern 'governance feminism' has emerged as a power-thirsty, rather than power-defying, ideology which has readily joined the (liberal) state in various hegemonic projects. Duncan Kennedy (2002) has demonstrated how the ubiquitous human rights discourse has become a key constituent in the universalisation projects and the related assimilationist identity politics of various liberal ideological intelligentsias. More specifically, numerous authors (e.g. Altman 2001, Cruz-Malavé and Manalansan IV 2002, Drucker 1996,

Jackson 2009, Long 2009, Puar 2007) have traced the *homonormative* strand of (neo)liberal governance strategies (Duggan 2002), which seeks to forcefully categorise, identify (in *all* historical and, even more importantly, present-day cultures) and then *globally represent* sexual and gender collectives beyond heteronormativity. Finally, an emergent stream of critique (e.g. Abraham 2010, Al-Sayyad 2010) focuses on global northern (liberal) homonormativity affecting various sexually diverse and gender-variant Muslim communities.

The expansionist homonormative ideology, which Paola Bacchetta (2002) dubs the 'from-Stonewall-diffusion-fantasy', promotes, under the guise of skilfully appropriated human rights discourse, a specifically designed liberal identity politics which promises a *guided* gender/sexual 'liberation'. In doing so, although at times admitting diversity beyond and complexity within the ready-made identitarian boxes, this project seeks to *systemically* obliterate the *asymmetries* and *compounds* it stumbles upon in cultures, geographies and histories of its targeted subjectivities. Asymmetries (c.f. Blackwood 2008, Stoler 1997) emerge as the distinct communities this hegemonic discourse encounters, which embody identities and experiences (including those relating to spirituality) beyond or across the proposed identitary matrices, reject or *transform* these models within their own social spatio-temporal domain. Compounds, in turn, are found as the ideologues of homonormativity painfully realise that some of 'their' imagined subjectivities construct their collectives on grounds which transcend their 'mere' sexual/gender difference, towards a multitude of formative factors (again, sometimes, including a specific spirituality). Because these 'irregularities' inexorably disrupt the intended global supremacy of the liberal homonormative project, they are portrayed as inimical to the proposed 'liberty' agenda and earmarked for *assimilation*, by means of donor policies, 'development' strategies, global advocacy and other missionary equipment.

When encountering and 'dealing with' the sexually diverse and gender-variant Indonesian and Pakistani Muslims, the homonormative discourse generally seeks to *define* and *represent* them through an intentionally imprecise (at best) or misconstrued (at worst) taxonomy which denies their multiple asymmetries and compounds as incongruent with the proposed 'fit-all' LGBT label. Unlike the first hegemonic discourse, however, this project cannot directly rely on state power in Pakistan and Indonesia, even though the two countries' officially endorsed and proclaimed heteronormativity helps in formatting 'the other side' (i.e. a juxtaposed homonormative otherworld). Hence, the applied methods differ and take, at times, most subtle shapes and intensities. Their ubiquity and selfsameness (in origins and intentions) are, nonetheless, undeniable, much like the *resistance* (e.g. through rejection, transformation and a specific conceptual and operative *différance*) they come upon in the targeted communities.

Sexual/Gender Plurality in Indonesia and Pakistan

In Pakistan and Indonesia, human genders and sexualities are continuously negotiated, performed, intersected and disrupted with variance, traditions and narratives apparently unintelligible (and, most certainly, unacceptable) to either of the two identified hegemonic discourses.

Firstly, there are 'traditional' subjectivities – such as *khwajasara* (also known as *hijra*) and *zenana* in Pakistan (Naqvi and Mujtaba 1997, Pamment 2010), or *calabai', calalai', bissu* (in South Sulawesi), *warok* and *gemblak* (in Ponorogo, East Java) in Indonesia (Boellstorff 2005a, Hardjomartono 1962, Pelras 1996) – all of which challenge and transgress both heteronormative and homonormative identitary/behavioural criteria.

Secondly, there are more recently emerged subjectivities – such as *gay* and *lesbi* throughout Indonesia, or *tomboi* specifically (although not exclusively) in Padang, West Sumatra (Blackwood 1998, 2005, 2008, Boellstorff 2005a, 2005b, Wieringa et al. 2007) – whose names are *cognates* with the international(ised) terms gay, lesbian and tomboy, yet who *do not share* the same meanings with these terms and their respective subjectivities. Rather, for example, '[b]eing lesbi in Padang is generally understood as an expression of gender rather than a form of sexuality engaged in by two women' (Blackwood 2008: 486). Hence, as Evelyn Blackwood (ibid: 483) warns, '[t]he fixity of identities promoted by such terms as LGBT needs to be reconsidered in light of the tombois, lesbian men, and other masculine females whose lives blur the boundaries of "lesbian" and "transgender"'. In addition, although of relatively recent origin, male-born gender transgressive *waria* claim to be an Indonesia-wide subjectivity that subsumes many previously more visible 'traditional' gender-variant selfhoods, such as that of *calabai'*.

Thirdly, there are those Indonesians and Pakistanis who do feel comfortable with labels such as LGBT and who, presumably, embody them within their current international episteme. Unlike some other critics of sexual/gender imperialism (notably Massad 2007), it seems to me inevitable to recognise these subjectivities *as they are*, that is, as they see themselves. These subjectivities, however, should not be conflated with the previous groups, despite the fact that they sometimes go by virtually the same name (e.g. gay and *gay*).

Fourthly and finally, there are Pakistanis and Indonesians, in particular within certain religious communities, who do not identify with any specific community established, amongst other criteria, on sexual/gender difference, even though their desires, proclivities and/or experience (sometimes) transcend heteronormative and/or homonormative boundaries.

Muslim individuals and communities researched in this chapter belong or travel across all of the above four elementary groups of sexual/gender subjectivities, thereby further dissipating them. This indicates the spatio-temporal relativity of such sexual/gender models, even though it does not imply their eventual dissolution, or *vice versa*. In fact, their transformative (and performative, c.f. Butler 1990) nature seems to be their inherent quality which ensures (c.f. Pamment 2010) that certain identitary tropes persist despite often being at odds with the mainstream sexual/gender scripts.

Homonormative Production/Reduction of Gender/Sexuality

A comparative analysis of the mainline trajectories of liberal homonormative discourse in Indonesia and Pakistan reveals a startling similitude in the approaches used to assimilate the local expressions of sexuality and gender into the preferred universal narratives, augmented by two specific taxonomies – that of LGBT and that of the global (and ubiquitously androcentric) HIV/AIDS prevention discourse. I turn first to the latter narrative, arguing that it does not depart from the liberal hegemonic homonormativity in any significant respect, despite its putative 'cultural sensitivity'.

In Indonesia, since the 1990s, all major projects aimed at prevention of HIV/ AIDS use an epidemiological behavioural category of 'men who have sex with men' (MSM) (translated to Indonesian as '*lelaki suka lelaki*' (LSL) – 'men who like men') to describe male persons who engage in sexual relations with other males. By avoiding local social taxonomies related to such sexual activities, this 'behavioural approach' supposedly manages to avoid the social stigma that many 'MSMs' face. Yet, a number of these programmes include *waria* – a traditional gender-variant identity – in the 'MSM' category, or simply call them 'transgenders' or 'transvestites' (Boellstorff 2005a, Dowsett et al. 2006). The same practice occurs in Pakistan, with *khwajasara* and *zenana* subjectivities (e.g. Imran 2010). Thus, a supposedly 'behavioural category' easily slips into the identitarian concept of 'LGBT', without any attention to local asymmetries, compounds and gender-sex dynamics. The identitary slippage is further evidenced in the emergence of self-contradictory terms within this discourse, such as 'MSM community', 'self-identified MSM', 'MSM peers' and – perhaps most remarkably – 'male partners of MSM' (Boellstorff 2005a: 100).

The situation is further complicated by the fact that the survival of nearly all national or local non-governmental organisations in Pakistan and Indonesia of gender-variant and/or sexually diverse communities often depends on financial aid secured primarily through HIV/AIDS prevention global networks. Organisations unable to obtain such support 'cease to exist after a few years' (Boellstorff 2005a: 143). More often than not, the economic dependency results in deterrence shown towards the liberal donor policies, which not only include specific taxonomies (such as 'MSM' or LGBT) that these organisations are urged to adopt, for instance, in their 'outreach' projects, but also a number of programmatic directions. These stipulations, introduced through the funding application guidelines, project evaluations, international workshops and other similar policy implementation strategies, tend to strongly prioritise liberal sexual/gender values and the related projects of their 'partner' organisations over any other considerations of their supposed constituencies. Hence, catering, for example, for the spiritual needs of the targeted communities, some of which are Muslim-specific, runs very low (or not at all) on the donors' priority list. As a result, the complexity of these communities' sociality and interaction (amongst themselves and with the broader environment) is eschewed in preference for a compartmentalised, unrepresentative view of their supposed sexual/gender specificities. Thus, the adoption and dissemination of donors' taxonomies of gender and sexuality is only the first step in the impoverished programmatic orientations these organisations are led into accepting/devising, which further alienate them from their primary constituencies (e.g. Blackwood 2008). It is with these considerations in mind that I now turn to the liberal LGBT discourse.

The social identitary terms of art linked with a particular sexual/gender experience or proclivity can be traced throughout the historical and cultural plurality of which the contemporary nation-states of Indonesia and Pakistan are composed. The latest aetiological and ethnographic studies (e.g. Boellstorff 2005a, Blackwood 2008, Pamment 2010) which trace and analyse a relatively recent introduction of the key global northern non-heteronormative gender/ sexual concepts – such as 'gay', 'lesbian' or 'transgender' – indicate that various modalities have materialised through which these non-traditional terms of art have been negotiated, transformed, accepted or rejected in the local contexts.

In Indonesia, some researchers linked the emergence of subjectivities known as *gay* and *lesbi primarily* with the national media's growing interest in and coverage of such phenomena, as of the early 1980s, while the concomitant formation of national and local organisations claiming to represent non-heteronormative communities apparently yielded much less dispersed and class-specific impact (e.g. Boellstorff 2005a). Others, however, convey a more complex story of social interactions amounting, indeed, to what Joseph Massad (2007), after Michel Foucault (1978), describes as homonormative 'incitement to discourse'. Evelyn Blackwood, for example, documents (2008: 498) the following conversation between Dedi, a self-defined *tomboi* from Padang, West Sumatra, and a Jakarta-based lesbian activist, in 2004:

Activist:	'What do you consider yourself to be, a man or a woman?'
Dedi:	'I'm like a man'.
A[*ctivist*]:	'That means you're not a lesbian. You're transgender'.

This is but one of a number of examples of how a new global LGBT vernacular, benevolently or not, has been ushered in across the archipelago. By excluding Dedi from the 'purified' definition of *lesbi*, within which the *tombois* of Padang (and elsewhere) have commonly imagined themselves (Wieringa et al. 2007, Blackwood 1998, 2008), the activist from Jakarta attempts to impose a new term of art – 'transgender' – as a 'correct' expression of Dedi's gender/sexual experience. Dedi, however, *resists* this attempt, albeit silently, and returns to Padang in what was still a *space* safe from such discursive interventions, and later confides in the researcher:

Dedi said, 'I didn't say anything then [in response]. I didn't understand "transgender". I'd never heard of it before. But it doesn't matter, I know how I feel'. (Blackwood 1998: 499)

By defending their asymmetries with the global purview, Dedi and others implicitly indicate other shortages in the hegemonic discourse. Some of the existent subjectivities – such as *warok* and *gemblak* actors in Ponorogo, East Java, who traditionally enter a form of same-sex relationship – are primarily *culturally* and *spiritually* rather than *sexually* compelled to such unions (Hardjomartono 1962, Wibowo 1995–1996). Others – most notably *waria* – claim a distinctly *Indonesian* ('archipelagic') self (Boellstorff 2005a). In such narratives of self-definition, religious, national and culture-specific considerations often complement and balance with 'purely' sexual/gender orienting. This may lead to situations and narratives which an outsider's eye can easily label as 'incongruous' or 'self-conflicting', as with the fact that a great number of self-perceived *gay* and *lesbi* Indonesians voluntarily commit to different-sex marriage (ibid). Yet it also signals a complex communitarian and localised experience of selfhood, largely incompatible with and undesirable of the global hegemonic homonormative liberal promise and its intrinsic concept of freedom and interpersonal relations.

Thus, even a 'passive' resistance, as in Dedi's case, warrants recognition and further research. One such 'alternative' – adamant of keeping up with Muslim-specific spiritual (communitarian and individual) self by organising religious study circles – is apparently nascent amongst the *waria* (Courrier International 2008) as well as other non-heteronormative (and non-homonormative) Indonesian subjectivities (Hamzić 2011). Some such developments, including sparse academic works (e.g. Al-Qurthuby et al. 2004), are perhaps not widely popularised, yet they reach their audience through informal social networks and are entirely self-sustainable. They are, hence, operative from an alterspace, which cuts across and vivisects the two hegemonic discourses while remaining – in concept and content – miles away from either of them. Later on in this chapter, I revisit this curious stance in search for some theoretical implications.

In Pakistan, the homonormative discourse does not present itself as openly and ubiquitously as in Indonesia. It is confined, instead, to some privileged sites of HIV/AIDS prevention activism (e.g. Rajabali et al. 2008), upper class socialisation (e.g. Walsh 2006), foreign reports (e.g. IRIN 2005) and neo-Orientalist accounts (e.g. Soofi 2007). For instance, during an interview with a Pakistan-based activist of the Naz Foundation, a grassroots organisation fighting against the HIV/AIDS epidemic (January 2011; on file with author), I was informed that 'very few self-identified *gay* men can only be found in the wealthy upper class circles, particularly in Islamabad', while local identitary nomenclatures related to sexuality and gender prevail in the rest of society. In fact, in the environment so deeply stratified along class/caste, ethnic, religious and political lines of division, whereby the few internal power centres are clearly and steadily demarcated, the prime interest of the global homonormative hegemonic discourse, as an integral element of liberal neo-imperialism, is in pervading those secluded decision-making sites, removed afar from the common society and traditionally receptive of global northern worldviews. 'Preaching to the converted' is largely unnecessary, while unruly masses are not (yet) of interest, except when a proof is needed *elsewhere* (i.e. outside of Pakistan) that the crude LGBT taxonomy applies in this chaotic 'Islamic republic' as well. In such instances, *khwajasara* are regularly defined as 'transvestites, eunuchs and hermaphrodites' (Haider 2009) while stories of discrimination against 'thousands of gay people in Pakistan today' (IRIN 2005) abound. Beyond these cameo appearances in the foreign mediasphere, sexually diverse and gender-variant common Pakistanis are largely left alone, that is, to state and theopolitical elites and their policing of sexuality and gender.

The subversion of hegemonic discourses on sexuality and gender in Pakistan is related primarily to the two grass-roots movements – that of women's rights associations, such as Shirkat Gah (Shaheed 2010), and that of *khwajasara* subjectivities (Pamment 2010). The latter movement – through a variety of actions including public performance, street demonstrations and political organising – is uniquely placed and equipped for resistance, being simultaneously on the margins of societal power and at the centre of public attention:

> The [*khwajasara*] trope – by moving in the third space of gender, class, and politics – has the gift of heroically upsetting the tyranny of boundaries and the secure world of logos, offering a cultural frontier that disturbs the hegemonic designs of the established orders. (Pamment 2010: 48)

A 'third space' (as a form of an alterspace) from which the resistance is contemplated and waged is at times quite literally asserted. The political candidacy of Mohammed Aslam, a *khwajasara* from Abbottabad, in the 1990 elections seemingly came across under the following slogan: 'The men have tried and failed, the women have tried and failed, maybe [*khwajasara*] will do the job better!' (Naqvi and Mujtaba 1997: 266). On the other side of social divide, since 2005, the upper class performer Ali Saleem appears regularly in the mainstream media cross-dressed as the celebrity diva Begum Nawazish Ali, who mocks and satirically interrogates the elite's role in numerous controversial issues, including corruption, class division, dysfunctional judiciary, sexuality and gender-based discrimination and the 'war on terror' (Pamment 2010: 39–40). The inverse logic of the subaltern – powerful *because* of being systemically devoid of power, publicly pronounced and listened to even when criticising the elite *because* they cannot really speak (c.f., *mutatis mutandis*, Spivak 1988) – plays the key role in these subversive performances.

An intrinsic element of the Pakistani *khwajasara* experience and their specific resistance to hegemonic discourses is their faith. Unlike some of their Indian counterparts, the Pakistani *khwajasara* see themselves as descendants of a gender-variant subjectivity of the same name, who were highly respected in the Muslim Delhi Sultanate (1206–1526) and Mughal Empire (1526–1857) (Pamment 2010). Some *khwajasara* further claim that one of the most widely respected early

Sufi female scholars, Rabia al-Adawiyya (717–801) was, in fact, a *khwajasara* herself (ibid). The acceptance of a common spiritual practice (although *nominal* differences are permitted) is a compulsory element of the initiation ritual for all Pakistani *khwajasara*. The pilgrimage to and dancing at shrines of Sufi saints as well as the performance of *badhai* (ritual collection of alms by conferring blessings at birth and wedding ceremonies) are just some of the elements of *khwajasara* hieropraxis that each community member is expected to adopt. Even though this aspect of life is sometimes seen as tainted by prostitution, which has become widespread in the community due to the economic exigencies of their marginalised and restricted social existence, the markedly religious nature of *khwajasara* subjectivity cannot be overstated. As a distinct *spiritual* group, the Pakistani *hijra* challenge the normative limits of mainline Muslim sociality and spirituality when faced with societal plurality (religious, sexual, gender-based, class-based, etc.) and the related Muslim responsibility to ensure social justice (e.g. Qur'an 7:157, 11:29, 49:13, 57:25, 91:8–10).

Reclaiming an Alterspace

In the preceding parts of this chapter, I propose that the resistance of sexually diverse and gender-variant Muslims to the hegemonic discourses comes from an alterspace, a liminal locus based on *différance* as a conceptual and operative strategy. I borrow '*différance*' – one of Jacques Derrida's terms of art (1963) – to describe what simultaneously signifies both 'deferral' and 'difference' (as in the French verb *différer*). 'Deferral' is implied in an endless chain of signifiers employed by the subjectivities in question in order to avoid their assimilation into the desired meaning of either of the two hegemonic discourses. They travel across and temporarily embody the constructed hegemonic identitary models in order to ultimately disrupt, reclaim/transform or reject them, thus performing and proving the malleability of the imposed sexual/gender systems. 'Difference' is strategically employed by these subjectivities to enable and retain a spatial distance from the hegemonic loci, thus allowing for their own alterity to emerge.

This nascent alterspace is *hybrid* (Abraham, 2010) and *liminal*, for it simultaneously embodies *and* disintegrates/resists the hegemonic discourses. Homi Bhabha (2004 [1994]), building on Fredric Jameson's notion of a 'third space' (2002 [1981]), has proposed that

> a *hybrid* third space [emerges] when what is produced by the fusion of parent cultures becomes sufficiently ambivalent that one cannot say where one culture begins and the other ends. (Abraham 2010: 411)

This hypothesis, however, only partly applies to the context that I explore in the present chapter. For the 'fusion' and, indeed, strategic re-appropriation of the two hegemonic discourses is conditioned by *différance*, which in turn provides our subjectivities with a hybrid *and* liminal 'otherworld', whose spatial alterity is their agential and identitary cornerstone.

It would be misleading to inextricably link the emergent alterspace and the subjectivities it hosts with the two hegemonic discourses. Despite the phenomenon of *hybridity*, the aetiological connection between the resisting subjectivities and the hegemonic models they learn to perform (and reform) is but *strategic*. This connection is necessary to disrupt and transform the imposed identitary and behavioural boxes, yet it is not required for our communities to imagine themselves *sui generis*. This characteristic crucially separates the alterspace our communities inhabit with a 'third space' theorised by Jameson, Bhabha and Abraham. Our communities claim their origins through varying historical narratives, which may or *may not* have any links with the two analysed hegemonic discourses. Their tapping into these discourses, for instance through performance and re-appropriation, comes usually out of bare necessity, out of a *strategic* choice, rather than out of a heart-felt 'belonging'. Their alterity is thus doubly asserted, as *resistance* and as *incongruity*.

Concluding Remarks

The situation I have tried to grasp and understand here is how the individuals and communities of Muslim faith in Pakistan or Indonesia, who are sexually diverse and/or gender-variant to the extent that they cannot comfortably embrace either a heteronormative or homonormative ethos, cope with the hegemonic discourses on which those two systems rely.

The first such discourse is of Muslim theopolitical reductionism, imbued with (post/neo)colonial logics, yet supposedly centred around politically opportunist '(re)Islamisation' projects, which projects heteronormativity as its prime ideological pedigree and thus *revives* a kind of Victorian worldview, rather than a historical Muslim society of any particular place or time. I have demonstrated how this hegemonic discourse, regardless of whether it comes from the ruling elites or from the oppositional theopolitical establishments, employs the narratives of nation-building, culture and religion – reinforced, in the later instances, by the punitive force of law – to *produce* starkly heteronormative patriarchal models of gender/sexuality and to *reduce* all other expressions and identitary tropes along the sexual/gender continuum.

The second hegemonic discourse is of a (neo)liberal provenance and it endeavours to impose homonormativity as the only imaginable alternative to heteronormative oppression. I have attempted to unpack this current as it presents itself globally and, more specifically, in Pakistan and Indonesia, arguing that it also resorts to controlling the sexual and gender plurality of its targeted communities by means of a forceful production or reduction of sexual/gender matrices. The models it tries to impose on non-heteronormative communities attempt to assimilate or gradually obliterate the asymmetries and compounds of the local sexual/gender subjectivities. In this violent process, the targeted communities are encouraged to 'correct' and redefine themselves in accordance with the liberal ideal of freedom and personal integrity, which often denigrates, marginalises and ultimately negates their spiritual, cultural and other experiences, all of which intrinsically form their individual and collective self.

I have argued that the resistance of Pakistani and Indonesian Muslim gender-variant and sexually diverse communities to the two hegemonic discourses is made possible from an alterspace, which is conceptually and operatively based on *différance*. It allows them to simultaneously perform and disrupt the hegemonic identitary tropes, whilst retaining a conceptual distance from such schemata. It provides them with an inhabitable, autonomous, *inner* locus from which they can contemplate and develop their selfhoods, whilst holding out against the hegemonic *outer* currents.

In a world still deeply contaminated with grand false dichotomies (male/ female, 'hetero'/'homo', 'East'/'West', etc.), the multiplicity of human selfhood and social performance is not always readily apparent. The chance is, in fact, that even if one such crude binary ideological distortion is debunked, the other will remain in place as if it is, almost, an insurmountable part of our social *modus operandi* (and *communicandi*). The counter-hegemonic narratives, however, indicate that the *localities* of alterity may help in contemplating our plurality as a *whole*, that is, beyond the implied compartmentalised binarisms of our sexual/ gender/geo-political/etc self.

References

Abraham, I. 2010. 'Everywhere You Turn You Have To Jump into Another Closet': Hegemony, Hybridity, and Queer Australian Muslims. In *Islam and Homosexuality*, edited by S. Habib. Santa Barbara, CA: Praeger.

Al-Qurthuby, S.A. et al. (eds) 2004. Indahnya Kawin Sesama Jenis. *Justisia* 25: 1–24.

Al-Sayyad, A.A. 2010. 'You're What?': Engaging Narratives from Diasporic Muslim Women on Identity and Gay Liberation. In *Islam and Homosexuality*, edited by S. Habib. Santa Barbara, CA: Praeger.

Altman, D. 2001. *Global Sex*. Crows Nest, NSW: Allen and Unwin.

Asian Human Rights Commission (AHRC) 2010. 23 December. Pakistan: Sharia Court Launches Major Challenge to Protection of Women Act. *Asian Human Rights Commission*. Retrieved from http://www.humanrights.asia/news/ahrc-news/AHRC-STM-268-2010 [accessed 6 September 2012].

Bacchetta, P. 2002. Rescaling Transnational 'Queerdom': Lesbian and 'Lesbian' Identitary-Positionalities in Delhi in the 1980s. *Antipode: A Radical Journal of Geography* 34(5): 947–73.

Bhabha, H.K. 2004 [1994]. *The Location of Culture*. London: Routledge Classics.

Blackburn, S. 2004. *Women and the State in Modern Indonesia.* Cambridge: Cambridge University Press.

Blackwood, E. 1998. *Tombois* in West Sumatra: Constructing Masculinity and Erotic Desire. *Cultural Anthropology* 13: 491–521.

Blackwood, E. 2005. Transnational Sexualities in One Place: Indonesian Readings. *Gender & Society* 19(2): 221–42.

Blackwood, E. 2008. Transnational Discourses and Circuits of Queer Knowledge in Indonesia. *GLQ: A Journal of Lesbian and Gay Studies* 14(4): 481–507.

Boellstorff, T. 2005a. *The Gay Archipelago: Sexuality and Nation in Indonesia.* Princeton, NJ: Princeton University Press.

Boellstorff, T. 2005b. Between Religion and Desire: Being Muslim and *Gay* in Indonesia. *American Anthropologist* 107: 575–85.

Butler, J. 1990. *Gender Trouble: Feminism and the Subversion of Identity.* London: Routledge.

Cohen, S. 1973. *Folk Devils and Moral Panics.* St Albans: Paladin.

Courrier International 2008. 9 October. Indonésie: l'école coranique des travestis. *Courrier International.* Retrieved from http://www.courrierinternational.com/article/2008/10/07/l-ecole-coranique-des-travestis [accessed 6 September 2012].

Cruz-Malavé, A. and Manalansan IV, M.F (eds) 2002. *Queer Globalizations: Citizenship and the Afterlife of Colonialism.* New York, NY: New York University Press.

Derrida, J. 1963. A propos de Cogito et histoire de la folie. *Revue de Metaphysique et de Morale* 68(4): 460–94.

Dowsett, G., Grierson, J. and McNally, S. 2006. *A Review of Knowledge about the Sexual Networks and Behaviours of Men Who Have Sex with Men in Asia.* Melbourne: Australian Research Centre in Sex, Health and Society.

Drucker, P. 1996. 'In the Tropics There Is No Sin': Sexuality and Gay-Lesbian Movements in the Third World. *New Left Review* 218: 75–101.

Duggan, L. 2002. The New Homonormativity: The Sexual Politics of Neoliberalism. In *Materializing Democracy: Toward a Revitalized Cultural Politics*, edited by R. Castronovo and D.D. Nelson. Durham: Duke University Press.

El-Rouayheb, K. 2005. *Before Homosexuality in the Arab-Islamic World, 1500–1800.* Chicago, IL: University of Chicago Press.

Foucault, M. 1978. *The History of Sexuality, Vol 1.* London: Penguin.

Habib, S. 2007. *Female Homosexuality in the Middle East: Histories and Representations.* London: Routledge.

Haider, Z. 2009. 23 December. Pakistan's Transvestites to Get Distinct Gender. *Reuters.* Retrieved from http://in.reuters.com/article/2009/12/23/us-pakistan-transvestites-idINTRE5BM2BX20091223 [accessed 6 September 2012].

Halley, J. 2006. *Split Decisions: How and Why to Take a Break from Feminism.* Princeton, NJ: Princeton University Press.

Hamzić, V. and Mir-Hosseini, Z. 2010. *Control and Sexuality: The Revival of Zina Laws in Muslim Contexts.* London: Women Living Under Muslim Laws.

Hamzić, V. 2011. The Case of 'Queer Muslims': Sexual Orientation and Gender Identity in International Human Rights Law and Muslim Legal and Social Ethos. *Human Rights Law Review* 11(2): 237–74.

Hardjomartono, S. 1962. Rejog, Warok dan Gemblakan di Ponorogo: Tritunggal Jang Tak Dapat Dipisah-pisahkan. In *Brosur Adat Istiadat dan Tjeritera Rakyat*. Jakarta: Departmen Pendidikan dan Kebudayaan.

Imran, M. 2010. *Pakistan: National Composite Policy Index*. UNGASS Report. UNAIDS. Retrieved from http://www.unaids.org/en/regionscountries/countries/pakistan/ [accessed 6 September 2012].

Integrated Regional Information Networks (IRIN) 2005. Pakistan: Focus on Gay Rights. *Integrated Regional Information Networks*. Retrieved from http://www.asylumlaw.org/docs/sexualminorities/Pakistan090605.pdf [accessed 6 September 2012].

Jackson, P.A. 2009. Capitalism and Global Queering National Markets, Parallels among Sexual Cultures, and Multiple Queer Modernities. *GLQ: A Journal of Lesbian and Gay Studies* 15(3): 357–95.

Jameson, F. 2002 [1981]. *The Political Unconscious: Narrative as a Socially Symbolic Act*. London: Routledge Classics.

Kennedy, D. 2002. The Critique of Rights in Critical Legal Studies. In *Left Legalism / Left Critique*, edited by W. Brown and J. Halley. Durham: Duke University Press.

Khan, S. 2003. 'Zina' and the Moral Regulation of Pakistani Women. *Feminist Review* 75: 75–100.

Kramer, M. 2003. Coming to Terms: Fundamentalists or Islamists? *Middle East Quarterly* 10(2): 65–77.

Long, S. 2009. Unbearable Witness: How Western Activists (Mis)Recognize Sexuality in Iran. *Contemporary Politics* 15: 119–36.

Massad, J.A. 2007. *Desiring Arabs*. Chicago, IL: University of Chicago Press.

Maudoodi, S.A.A. 1967. *Purdah and the Status of Women in Islam*. Lahore: Islamic Publications Ltd.

Mullally, S. 2006. *Gender, Culture and Human Rights: Reclaiming Universalism*. Oxford: Hart Publishing.

Naqvi, N. and Mujtaba, H. 1997. Two Balochi *Buggas*, a Sindhi *Zenana*, and the Status of *Hijra* in Contemporary Pakistan. In *Islamic Homosexualities: Culture, History, and Literature*, edited by S.O. Murray and W. Roscoe. New York, NY: New York University Press.

Pal, I. 1990. Women and Islam in Pakistan. *Middle Eastern Studies* 26(4): 449–64.

Pamment, C. 2010. Hijraism: Jostling for a Third Space in Pakistani Politics. *The Drama Review* 54(2): 29–50.

Pelras, C. 1996. *The Bugis*. Oxford: Blackwell.

Puar, J.K. 2007. *Terrorist Assemblages: Homonationalism in Queer Times*. Durham: Duke University Press.

Rajabali, A., Khan, S., Warraich, H.J., Khanani, M.R. and Ali, S.H. 2008. HIV and Homosexuality in Pakistan. *The Lancet*, 8, 511. Retrieved from http://www.aidsallianceindia.net/Material_Upload/document/HIV%20and%20homosexuality%20in%20Pakistan.pdf [accessed 6 September 2012].

Rofiah, N. 2010. *Memecah Kebisuan: Agama Mendengar Suara Perempuan Korban Kekerasan Demi Keadilan (Respon NU)*. Jakarta: Komnas Perempuan.

Rouse, S. 1988. Women's Movement in Pakistan: State, Class, Gender. *Dossier*, 3. Retrieved from http://www.wluml.org/node/241 [accessed 6 September 2012].

Shaheed, F. 2010. The Women's Movement in Pakistan: Challenges and Achievements. In *Women's Movements in the Global Era: The Power of Local Feminisms*, edited by A. Basu. Boulder, CO: Westview Press.

Shirkat G. 2010. 29 December. Shirkat Gah's Preliminary Analysis on Federal Shariat Court Verdict. *Shirkat Gah – Women's Resource Centre*. Retrieved from http://www.shirkatgah.org/news.php?id=247 [accessed 6 September 2012].

Soofi, M.A. 2007. 25 June. Open Secrets: Gay Life in Pakistan. *Pakistan Paindabad*. Retrieved from http://pakistanpaindabad.blogspot.com/2007/06/open-secrets-gay-life-in-pakistan.html [accessed 6 September 2012].

Spivak, G.C. 1988. Can the Subaltern Speak? In *Marxism and the Interpretation of Culture*, edited by C. Nelson and L. Grossberg. Urbana, IL: University of Illinois Press.

Stoler, A. 1997. Educating Desire in Colonial Southeast Asia: Foucault, Freud, and Imperial Sexualities. In *Sites of Desires, Economies of Pleasure: Sexualities in Asia and the Pacific*, edited by L. Manderson and M. Jolly. Chicago, IL: University of Chicago Press.

Valentine, D. 2007. *Imagining Transgender: An Ethnography of a Category*. Durham: Duke University Press.

Walsh, D. 2006. 14 March. Pakistani Society Looks Other Way as Gay Men Party. *The Guardian*. Retrieved from http://www.guardian.co.uk/world/2006/mar/14/pakistan.gayrights [accessed 6 September 2012].

Wibowo, H.J. 1995–1996. Drama Tradisional Reyog: Suatu Kajian Sistem Pengetahuan dan Religi. *Laporan Penelitian Jarahnitra*, 1–58.

Wieringa, S.E., Blackwood, E. and Bhaiya, A. 2007. *Women's Sexualities and Masculinities in a Globalizing Asia*. New York, NY: Palgrave Macmillan.

Chapter 3
Spirituality, Activism, and the 'Postsecular' in the Sisters of Perpetual Indulgence

Melissa M. Wilcox

The 2009 Portland, Oregon Pride parade makes its way through the city's downtown, but the celebratory mood is marred by two noisy religious protestors. One wears a blue shirt with the word 'homo' in white letters, surrounded by a red circle with a line through it. 'If you're wondering why we're judging', he announces through a megaphone, 'we're supposed to judge. That's why we're here'. The crowd boos him, and the parade continues. Then comes the contingent of the Sisters of Perpetual Indulgence. Dressed in everything from ball gowns to sarongs, from brilliant yellow and soft lavender to rainbow colors in honor of Pride, the Portland Sisters wear tall, round coronets draped with flowing veils of all colors. Their faces are painted white and decorated with sparkling, brilliant makeup; many sport beards bristling through the whiteface. They draw cheers from the onlookers. The Sisters stop in front of the protestors, who respond in astonishment: 'What in the world is this?' And one by one, the Sisters collapse in the street as one of their number chants through a megaphone, 'Words kill! Words kill!' Some in the crowd take up the chant, while friends of the Sisters run from one fallen nun to the next, chalking their outlines on the pavement. The noise of the crowd begins to drown out the protestors. Finally, the die-in is over, and the Sisters arise from the pavement, cheering with the crowd. The parade moves on.[1]

The Sisters of Perpetual Indulgence are an international charity organisation and network of community activists that was founded in San Francisco in 1979. They raise money for causes related to sexual health, LGBT community needs, and other local charitable organisations, through a wide variety of events that include their famously riotous 21-and-over Bingo nights. Funds are distributed through annual grant competitions. In addition, the Sisters often participate in or provide volunteer workers for fundraising events such as AIDS Walks and Red Dress parties, and they take part in marches for awareness of issues such as domestic violence and sexual assault. They are also community activists in small, everyday ways: each Sister carries with her a purse full of safer-sex supplies and information (in many chapters, packets designed both for men and for women), which she

---

1   Several of the Portland Sisters told me about this event. Footage of it can be found online at http://www.youtube.com/watch?v=gM9xbLUt9Is [accessed 5 May 2011].

hands out at events or in bars, and Sisters are always available with a listening ear or a shoulder to cry on. Finally, some chapters (or 'houses', as the Sisters call them) engage in religion-focused activism such as the die-in described above. The founding house in San Francisco has been especially active in this arena, for instance by performing an exorcism on Pope John Paul II when he visited their city, and by taking communion in a Roman Catholic church while in full habit.[2]

A further aspect of the Sisters' activism is their imitation, and parody, of Roman Catholic nuns. On the one hand, most of the Sisters whom I have interviewed to date seriously consider themselves to be nuns – that is, 'nuns for the twenty-first century'. They explain that they perform the same functions for their community that Catholic, Episcopalian, and Buddhist nuns perform for theirs; the Sisters are simply reaching out to people whom other nuns are less likely to serve, and in ways that other nuns are less likely to reach out. On the other hand, the combination of coronets and veils, white bibs and scapulars, with makeup, eyecatching dresses, and platform boots cannot help but be viewed as parody. Imitation may be the sincerest form of flattery, but what is imitation when combined with parody? Both flattery and critique, perhaps, of which more below.

The final aspect of the Sisters that I find intriguing is the number of them who identify as spiritual (usually not religious) and who consider their work with the Sisters as in some way related to that spirituality. These are the people who register in surveys as part of the vague category of 'nones' – with no religious affiliation, but not necessarily without spiritual beliefs and practices. Given the common image of spirituality in both popular media and the social scientific literature as individualistic, anti-communal, and socially disconnected, this is a surprising finding. I would argue that we can use the example of the Sisters to explore the ways in which spirituality, parody, and politics are intertwined. This paper suggests that scholars take seriously the Sisters' self-definition as twenty-first century nuns, and argues that in the Sisters we can see the breakdown of the secular-religious dichotomy, and the force of parody and irony, in contemporary religious and political phenomena. Studying religion from the margins of sexuality and gender offers to scholars of religion a new angle of vision on contemporary religious phenomena; studying sexuality through the lens of religion offers to sexuality studies a new angle on themes of queerness, parody, and performance.

Secular, Spiritual, Post-secular

In a timely talk given just shortly after the New York terrorist attacks in 2001, Jürgen Habermas 'pronounced that the world had entered a "postsecular age"' (Gorski and Altinordu 2008: 56). For Habermas, as Gorski and Altinordu explain (2008: 56), this meant a time 'in which religious and secular worldviews could

---

2   The Sisters who took communion in habit were not intending this to be an act of religious activism, but I would argue that it is such in impact, even if not in intent.

coexist and even enter into dialogue with one another'. I would suggest that we push this idea further, in line with other 'post' terms that suggest not the end of a phenomenon but its development into a related successor (see Frisk and Nynäs 2012 for an insightful reflection on this question). I suggest that we think of the 'postsecular' as blurring the lines between the secular and the religious. 'Postsecular' religion and 'postsecularization' sociology might then centre in part on the religious 'nones': those who are 'spiritual but not religious', believing but not belonging, agnostics, and religious bricoleurs. 'Postsecular' phenomena might be those that are neither traditionally secular nor traditionally religious, those that smack of the religious and yet are not such by standard definitions. In both ways, the Sisters of Perpetual Indulgence are a case in point.

Methodological Account

My work on the Sisters of Perpetual Indulgence is part of a multi-year study of the organisation, underway since 2009, that includes extensive participant observation in the US and to a lesser extent in Europe, as well as in-depth interviews with over 60 Sisters (US, Canadian, Swiss, English, Scottish, and French) to date. I rely on both fieldwork and interview data below, and for the purposes of this paper I focus on the Sisters from the US. Interviews were semi-structured and usually lasted between 60 and 90 minutes; they covered demographic questions, questions about each participant's involvement with the Sisters, and questions about religion and spirituality (as the participant defined these terms). For ethical reasons that I discuss in depth elsewhere (Wilcox 2009: 223–4), in my research I offer participants several options regarding naming, ranging from complete anonymity to complete disclosure. All of the Sisters interviewed so far have elected to use their real 'Sister names', if not their real 'secular names'.

Post-secular Spiritualities: The None Nuns

The term 'spirituality' as it is commonly used in the US is only vaguely defined, although in popular usage it seems to refer to an individual relationship with the sacred that can take place either within or beyond formal religious settings. For the purposes of this study I will focus on one, particularly post-secular form of this spirituality: beliefs, experiences, and practices that are voluntaristic, individualistic, sometimes experienced in community, and yet rarely associated with formal religious membership or identification. Despite their clear reference to Catholicism, many of the Sisters of Perpetual Indulgence hold to such post-secular spirituality. Others are strict atheists. Thus, the Sisters generally fall into the increasingly complicated category of 'nones': those who hold no formal religious affiliation.

During the course of my interview with a Sister, I ask her whether she considers herself 'religious or spiritual or both or neither'. A few have responded that they are neither, or are atheists. Sista' Anita Lynchin', for instance, has an extensive background in Christianity, including serving as a choir director with a Church of God in Christ congregation. Referring to that time, she said, 'Then I was growing up; now, I know. You know, and I feel like I can achieve the same thing in my life without being part of that organised setup'. Yet, one can perhaps hear in the voices of those claiming outright atheism the echoes of social opprobrium – one possible explanation for the low number of Sisters claiming to be neither religious nor spiritual. Sister Helen Baak told me:

> I don't go to church; I don't really consider myself religious or spiritual in a lot of ways. I'd sort of borderline consider myself atheist. Although that's a really hard thing for me to even admit. Just from all those years of, you know, all that stuff being pounded into you and drilled into you, at forty that's like forty years of all that stuff. It's not so easy just to dismiss it all and say that there is no god and that whole thing.

Sister Polly Amorous answered my questions with 'I really don't know', and then added, 'I'm atheist; this [the Sisters] is not a religion to me'. To clarify, I followed up: 'Do you consider yourself spiritual at all, or just atheist period?' Sister Polly's response was interesting: 'There's a higher power, maybe ... Do I believe that there is somebody out there maybe listening, probably. But it's not something that is in my life'.

Of the 25 members of the Sisters interviewed to date, only three have had any current association with Christianity. One, Novice Sister Cherry Poppins,[3] described herself as 'confused', and elaborated, 'I think I can answer yes to both of those, religion and spiritual, and I can answer no to both of them .... If I sit here and reflect on it, I think I haven't made a decision. I think I have arguments and valid points for both sides, spiritual and religion'. She added later, 'if I were to commit to religion, it would be a Christian one. I don't think I could handle the philosophies of another one'.

Novice Sister Glory Glory Hole-leluja, or G.G., identifies as Christian, though she added the qualification that 'I can't say that that won't evolve as time goes on'.[4] She also considers herself

> more spiritual than religious, because I really feel like there's a big, fat – it's not a fine line – I think there's a big, fat line between spirituality and religion. One of the reasons that I started going to the last church that I went to was because they

---

3　Novice Sister Cherry was elevated to be a fully professed Sister a few months after this interview was completed, but later withdrew from the order.

4　Novice Sister G.G. was also elevated to be a fully professed Sister.

had this sign out in the front and it said – bright bold letters – right underneath their cross it said, 'God isn't the problem; Christians are'.

Sister Krissy Fiction is the third of the Sisters identified with Christianity, and her answer to my question differed from that of both Novice Sister G.G. and Novice Sister Cherry. 'I joke and say I'm a spiritual slut', Sister Krissy told me. 'I've struggled quite a bit with the whole labeling thing. So nowadays, depending on who I'm talking to, I'll say I'm a Christian, sometimes I'll say I'm a Gnostic Christian'. Sister Krissy, before encountering the Sisters, spent about a decade of his life in the ex-gay movement, and served as a youth pastor in the conservative Wisconsin Synod Lutheran Church. Upon leaving that church, coming out, and moving to Portland, he explored liberal Protestantism and eventually began serving as a youth minister with the United Church of Christ. He has pursued interests in other religions, as well. Krissy explained to me that religion is 'like language. It gives us a vocabulary to speak about something which we ultimately can't describe. And so I say I'm fluent in Christianity and fluent in neopaganism, [and] I can kind of ask where the bathroom is in Buddhism, you know'.

Despite her firm and ongoing connections to Christianity, Krissy is quite a bit like many of the other Sisters in her religious multilingualism. Indeed, the vast majority of US Sisters interviewed to date[5] identify as spiritual or agnostic, and many of those draw on aspects of different religions to create distinctive sets of beliefs and practices. Sister Dixie Rupt explained:

> Technically, I think I'm an omniversalist. Which basically means I pick whatever I want from any religion that I like. So for me, predominantly, it's really based on, I would say, *The Secret* [Byrne 2006], and Kabbalah, and Christianity to the extent of looking at Jesus' life and trying not to judge people. But expecting that the universe can provide you what you want, if you believe that you will get it and that you need it and all that stuff.

'Seems to work', she added. 'For me, anyway'. Sister Stella Standing likewise selects from a number of religions to create her own spirituality. 'I'm what you would call a grazer', she explained.

> You know, I pick and choose belief systems from different places. There are some things about Buddhism that I really enjoy, there are some things from Hinduism that I really enjoy. There are some things from paganism that I enjoy. And even sometimes, I hate to admit it, there are things of Christianity that I would hold on to. But I will not subscribe to one. I have such an aversion to religion.

---

5   I have not yet interviewed a sufficient number of European Sisters to enable me to identify patterns in their spiritual or religious self-descriptions.

Sister Stella went on to explain that, from her perspective, religion 'has been the root of so many evil things'. She also objects to proselytising: 'Personally, I don't care what anybody does, or whatever they enjoy. But my whole thing is, don't push your shit on me. You know, whatever your security blanket is, I don't need to cuddle with it. It's got your slobber on it, it's yours'.

Sister VixXxen, too, is a mixer of religions. Having come from a background in the Jehovah's Witnesses, she now identifies as 'definitely spiritual; mildly religious, to a degree'. She continued, 'my actual faith is kind of based in Gnosticism and quantum physics and witchcraft. A blend of those three, with maybe a little sprinkle of Buddhism in there. It kind of all blends in together very, very well'.

Agnosticism is another significant pattern among the Sisters who have participated in interviews. Sister Irma Geddon, who explicitly told me that she dislikes the term 'spiritual but not religious', explained that 'I guess I would have to consider myself agnostic. I definitely believe that there is a divine power, and there's an energy that goes through everything, and we are all connected, bad and good, it is all part of the same thing. We are all part of the same thing'. Sister Daya Reckoning firmly stated, 'I am spiritual, not religious'. When I asked how she explains her spirituality to other people, she replied, 'I tell them I have a belief system that I feel strongly in. I believe in the possibility of God or gods. But that is not defined. And I believe in the possibility of many things. And I think that's where my spirituality dwells, is the possibilities'. And Novice Sister Betti Crotcher, who also considers herself spiritual, is still working out the details. She described her spirituality as follows:

> I believe that we're all here on earth to learn lessons. I don't know if there's a thing in reincarnation. The more I read about it, the more I believe it, because it makes more sense to me. Like I read this book, *Many Lives, Many Masters* [Weiss 1988]. That made a lot of sense to me. A lot of sense. So it's one of those things, I think if you do good on earth, you're going to be able to progress and do the next life, or wherever we're supposed to go. I still don't even know where we're going. There may not be anything. I'm just, I guess I'm more agnostic than anything. I think there's a higher power, I just don't know exactly what's happening.

On further reflection, Novice Sister Betti added, 'I don't know, I'm just, I wouldn't say that it was just really religious or even highly spiritual, I just think that everyone should just be nice to one another'.

It has often been remarked (e.g. Roof 1999) that such 'Golden Rule' spirituality is a common part of religious individualism, and therefore a part of the pattern of what I am terming 'postsecular religion'. Indeed, several Sisters explicitly mentioned the Golden Rule, and others evoked a similar ethos through their focus on love. Sister Anna Wrecks-Ya, for instance, described herself as 'incredibly spiritual', and added:

and more so every day, because I realized that there is something. And I've been calling it the universe because I don't like gods and goddesses and, you know, Muhammads and Buddhas and such. So I call it the universe. It's a good generic term, it seems to be all-encompassing enough. And it's something that guides us to live right and to do unto others as you would have them do unto you, that whole bit. I think that a lot of that was based on some fundamental truths that just got bastardized over the years.

'For me', said Sister Reva Lation, 'my spirituality is love. If you love yourself, you're going to love others, and that love will empower others to take that forward. Religion confuses things. It's not as simple. It's very convoluted'. She went on to say that her spirituality 'kind of goes along the lines of the Golden Rule. But it's not easy to do that [live out the Golden Rule]. But if everything you do comes from a place of love, you'll be fine'. And Sister Ohna Fuckin' Tirade hesitated when I asked whether she considered herself spiritual or religious. 'Um', she replied, 'I think I want to be spiritual, but I have a lot of questions that I haven't answered yet. And may never be answered, but I'm always learning, and sinning, and so yeah, I think I'd go with spiritual. Hopefully spiritual'. When I asked her to describe her spirituality, she paused, then answered, 'You know, I don't really know. I think that everything I do comes from love, and that is a very big word for me. Love. That's my spirituality for now'.

With the exception of a few atheists, all of the members of the Sisters whom I've interviewed consider themselves spiritual; almost none would use either the word 'religious' or the word 'secular' to describe themselves. Even those with some ongoing connection to Christianity experience that connection in an individualist way, or as part of a spectrum of religious beliefs and practices. Many Sisters practise this sort of religious eclecticism, and many are also agnostic. Finally, for some the Golden Rule and a focus on love are all one needs for a fulfilling spiritual life. These characteristics establish most individual Sisters as postsecular. But is their activism a spiritual enterprise?

Spirituality and Politics

During the interviews, I asked each participant whether she/he saw any connection between her/his religion, spirituality, agnosticism, or atheism and being a Sister. A few said this was not the case, including all of the atheists. Novice Sister Edna Daze,[6] who identified as 'between spiritual and neither', said of spirituality and the Sisters, 'they're separate for me. You know, if I felt like it was a religious organisation, I probably wouldn't have had any interest in it'. Guard Lance

---

6   Novice Sister Edna was elevated a few months after this interview, to become Sister Edna Daze.

Boyles[7] offered a similar opinion: 'I don't really see a correlation between the two. You know, I just kind of believe in what the mission is, and I'm there to help make sure that the Sisters carry out that mission'. Guard Noah Shame, on the other hand, saw an 'indirect' connection between the two: 'I think one complements the other. I think the sense of a grounding that I have as Brian [Noah's secular name] serves me better as Noah, and I think it helps me assess situations and helps me have clarity'.

Most of the Sisters who identified as spiritual, however, said that their spirituality and their work with the Sisters are closely connected. Sister Golden Hair Surprise, or Goldee, who likens her religion to a 'fondue' and also has strong leanings toward the Radical Faeries,[8] replied to my question about the connection between spirituality and the Sisters: 'Absolutely. Because for me, being a Sister is about trying to show people how it works for me. Might not work for you, but you can learn something from this, I hope, and process it, and do your own'. For Sister Goldee, being a Sister of Perpetual Indulgence is much like being any other kind of nun: as part of one's work, one offers spiritual guidance through example.

When I asked Sister Babylon Anon whether she considers herself spiritual, she replied:

> Absolutely. In fact, you have to be to be a good Sister. Because you have to be able to feel what that feels like; it's so hard to put into words, and that's where I think it gets mixed up in religion. The type of things we're talking about are so basic and esoteric and miraculous and indescribable that they're not meant to be understood or put into words, they're meant to be felt.

Sister Stella Standing spoke above about the evil caused by religion. Yet when I asked whether there was any connection between her spirituality and her work with the Sisters, she responded immediately. 'Oh, God. It's been the most spiritual experience of my life. I mean, it feeds my soul more than anything anybody could ever do'. As she reflected further, she added: 'You know, it's funny. It's coming to me now with these questions and everything, I guess my religion would have to be the Sisters. That's one of those things that would be the closest thing to my religion is being a Sister'.

The Sisters are engaged in a number of modes of civic involvement that serve to better their communities; one of those modes is political activism. Sometimes this is the activism of the die-in described in the opening paragraph of this chapter;

---

7   In addition to Sisters, there are also Guards in the Sisters of Perpetual Indulgence. These dress in black, often in leather, and generally remain on the sidelines except in cases where a Sister needs assistance.

8   The Radical Faeries were founded in the same year as the Sisters, and in fact some early Sisters were also early members of the Faeries. This Neopagan religion is largely made up of gay men, although some circles now include people of all genders and sexualities.

at other times it is more subtle. One of the early events I attended with the Portland Sisters, for example, was a bar crawl on World AIDS Day.

The evening had begun with a vigil at Portland's Metropolitan Community Church, part of a denomination with a specific mission to lesbian, gay, bisexual, and transgender communities. The Sisters were present to offer a blessing to those assembled. Having made a short introduction, the MC invited the Sisters to the front of the church, where Sister Krissy (chosen for her extensive religious background) introduced each of the 10 Sisters present, along with the one Guard. After a brief blessing, Sister Krissy asked the participants in the vigil to stand, hold hands, and call out the names of people whose presence they wished to invoke. Voices from around the sanctuary spoke the names of loved ones for over a minute, then Sister Krissy asked everyone to invoke the conception of higher power or deity, God or Goddess, that s/he wished to have present, and affirmed that the collectivity blessed the space and turned it into a sacred, set-aside place for the duration of the vigil. The Sisters remained in the audience for most of the vigil, but left before the end because they needed to begin their bar crawl.

World AIDS Day (1 December) landed on a Tuesday in 2009, so there were relatively few patrons in any of the bars we visited. Yet the Sisters were greeted warmly, if sometimes with stares, in each bar they entered. Their purpose was not only to bring awareness of World AIDS Day and sexual health, but also to conduct a special ritual that takes place each year on this day: the writing of the Veil of Shame and the Veil of Remembrance.

The Veils of Shame and Remembrance are long swathes of white cloth worn by a fully professed Sister. As Novice Sisters traditionally wear white veils, it is unusual to see an 'FP' in white. This year, Sister Krissy wore the veil of Remembrance, and Sister Maya Poonani the Veil of Shame. Each carried a permanent marker. As they explained to me and to the patrons in each of the six bars they entered, the purpose of the Veil of Remembrance was to carry the names of people who had died from AIDS; the Veil of Shame carried the epithets that had been used against people in LGBTQ communities over the years. The veils began the night blank, but by the end of the evening they were covered in writing. While some of the names on the Veil of Remembrance were well-known figures, most were personal remembrances, sometimes listed only by first name. The epithets on the Veil of Shame included typical slurs used against LGBT people, but also other slurs, serving as a reminder that people in LGBT communities often deal with intersecting oppressions. At one point during the evening, for instance, someone asked Sister Maya whether he could write 'Go back to your country' on the veil, a request she honored.

During events like these the Sisters also often serve as a listening ear. This evening it was Sister Ohna who was approached by a woman outside of one of the bars. When Sister Ohna, in response to the woman's questioning, explained who the Sisters were and that they were observing World AIDS Day, the woman told Sister Ohna about her father, who had died from AIDS, and her mother, who had kept his illness a secret. The family, including the woman's siblings, all believed that he had died from cancer. This woman shared with Ohna how difficult it was to live with such a secret, and Ohna was clearly moved when she told me the story later that evening.

At the final stop of the night, after everyone had an opportunity to write on the two veils, it was time for the final ritual: the burning of the Veil of Shame. While the Veil of Remembrance is deposited each year into the Portland Sisters' archives, the Veil of Shame is destroyed before the end of the evening. All of the Sisters went out to the sidewalk for this ritual, and one of the bartenders brought a large metal tub. Sister Maya had changed into a different veil and was carrying the Veil of Shame, which she placed in the tub as Sister Krissy started the whole group in a chant rejecting oppression. The bartender poured alcohol on the veil and lit it, and the chant continued while the fabric burned.

Though the Portland Sisters are less politically-oriented and more service-oriented than some houses, such as the founding San Francisco house, they nonetheless have their own forms of activism, and World AIDS Day is one of those forms. By offering a permanent – archived – form of remembering the loved ones of the Portland community who have died of AIDS, and by offering a ritual whereby participants can reject stigma and claim pride in their identities, the Sisters present a discursive form of activism to their community.

The Uses of Parody

The diametrically opposed reactions to the Sisters point to another important form of Sisterly activism. Though events such as the die-in at the 2009 Pride parade are fairly infrequent, simply by appearing in public the Sisters are engaging in a form of religious activism. Witness the response of traditional Catholics, who have gone so far as to call the Sisters' activities a form of 'hate speech' against the church (Glenn 2003: para. 46). And witness the popularity of the Sisters among many (though not all) LGBTQ people, especially those who were raised Catholic but no longer identify with the Church. During the 2010 Pride parades in Seattle and Portland, I was struck by how much the energy and volume of the crowd increased as the Sisters approached – even in the cold drizzle that met Portland's Pride that year. And as we wended our way through downtown Portland, one woman stepped out of the crowd and called out, 'Where were you when *I* was in school?' Perhaps she had attended a Roman Catholic school, and would have preferred the Sisters as teachers rather than Roman Catholic nuns.

As I have argued elsewhere (Wilcox 2010), the Sisters practise a kind of 'parodic politics'. My argument draws, in part, from Cathy Glenn's analysis of the Sisters as resignifying 'the symbol and identity of "nun"' (2003: para. 39). I want to push Glenn's argument further, however; the key to doing so is recognising the unusual combination of parody and seriousness that the Sisters represent.

On the one hand, the Sisters of Perpetual Indulgence are clearly parodying Catholic nuns. They wear veils and coronets; some wear bibs and scapulars, and some houses have formal uniforms that are indistinguishable from nuns' habits. In fact, the Sisters got their start when three men wore retired Roman Catholic habits for a turn around the gay district of San Francisco in 1979. Sisters of Perpetual Indulgence in the US often wear crosses and rosaries. And some do claim to be enacting a form of parody. For instance, when I asked Sister Alma Children whether she considers herself a nun, she told me, 'At first, I really sort of felt like I was mocking that. Because of my own personal take on religion. And I was proud to do that, and I'm not particularly ashamed'. Sister Babylon, whose parents are ex-Catholics, admitted, 'part of me, wickedly, deep down, loves the fact that they [Catholics] see us as a mockery'.

Parody, as Fredric Jameson has noted, is 'the imitation of a peculiar or unique, idiosyncratic style, … [with] ulterior motives' (1991: 17). One might frame the ulterior motive of the Sisters' parody as combating the homophobia of the Church through subversive performance. After all, one half of the Sisters' mission statement is 'expiating stigmatic guilt', and many Sisters have explained to me that organised religion is an important source of such guilt. Bringing sexuality – meaning both human sexuality and sexual orientation – into the portrayal of nuns not only challenges the definition of the sacred 'by sanctifying … the queer bodies of the Sisters' (Glenn 2003: para. 44), but also strips the Church of some of its power by blending the secular into some of its religious symbols. Further, the Sisters do something fairly unusual in US culture: they connect religious practice and sexuality in a positive way. Interestingly, a number of the Sisters whom I have interviewed are influenced in their spirituality by Neopaganism, one of relatively few religions in the US with branches that embrace the intersections of religion and sexuality.

Yet there is another side here. Despite the negative opinion that many Sisters hold of the Roman Catholic hierarchy, they often express great respect for nuns and are eager to tell stories of positive reactions they have received from Catholic nuns. And the Sisters do consider *themselves* nuns, as well: 'nuns for the twenty-first century'. When I asked why this was the case, I received similar responses from most Sisters. Tellingly, these responses separate individual nuns from the male hierarchies of their religions, casting nuns as sacred even among Sisters who are openly hostile to organised religion.

Sister Anna Wrecks-Ya, for instance, explained:

> Historically I have had a passionate, vehement disrespect for religion and all those who practice it. And so at first it was a little distasteful to refer to myself as being a Sister. But it was one of those things that, fortunately enough, took hold really fast and, a great deal, because of the [Seattle Sisters] being [the Portland Sisters'] mentor house. [They said,] "You're a nun. You're serving people. People will come up to you and pull you to the side and they will pour their hearts out. Good or bad. And they're only doing it because you're a nun. They didn't pull somebody, some other stranger off the street, they didn't walk up to anybody else, any other stranger in that bar. They walked up to you. 'Cause they

identify you as something safe. Something larger than themselves. Something, something that they can trust, something warm they can wrap up in. And you'll become that.

Many Sisters gave similar answers to Sister Anna's, albeit without the same difficulties in adjusting to the role. Here, again, is Glenn's 'resignification' of an existing discourse. The role of 'nun' (usually meaning Roman Catholic) is well known in the US. People who have learned that they are unapproachable by Roman Catholic nuns, once they learn that the figures in whiteface and colorful veils are also nuns, gravitate toward them and seek from them the same comfort they might otherwise seek from other religious figures.

Sister VixXxen had a more unusual take on her identity as a nun, but one that nonetheless encompassed the same sense of the sacredness of the female renunciant:

> There are various different perspectives of sacred women throughout all different societies and cultures, and among my tribe I see myself as a sacred woman. And this is just living true to that. I mean, I will be the first one to admit, I am human, I totally make mistakes all the time. But I try, I try my best. And I try to make that interaction I have with people at least as positive as possible. You know, and – well, I don't know about the nuns that were in school that taught people, 'cause I hear some stories about them – but most of the nuns that, like the Buddhist nuns that I've encountered always tend to try to leave you feeling a little bit better about yourself, like you could be more than you thought you could be. Yes, I see myself as a sacred, powerful woman.

Furthermore, the Sisters eagerly tell stories of the approval some Roman Catholic nuns have offered them. Sister Stella, for example, told the following story about her time in San Francisco during the Sisters' thirtieth anniversary party:

> We're walking through Golden Gate Park and we're doing some readings and literally doing a walkabout in Golden Gate Park. And there's a Catholic nun, as we're walking to the Japanese Tea Garden. There's a Catholic nun, stops, and Mary Timothy and her locked eyes. And the Sister just looked directly at Mary Timothy and bowed at her. Clasped her hands like a nun would, and bowed. It was one of the most beautiful and powerful experiences. Because here is a representative of one of the most oppressive and disgusting organizations out there, that is also the root of so many people's happiness and faith and freedom. Here's a representative of that recognizing us. And not just standing there in awe and dumbfounded, literally recognizing and acknowledging. And it was almost like a moment of atonement. It was almost like, it was almost like she blessed us while Mary Timothy was blessing her. It was one of the most beautiful experiences I've ever had [the] pleasure to be around.

None Nuns, Parody, and the Postsecular

The political activism of the Sisters of Perpetual Indulgence comes in many forms. The Sisters hold protests against religious oppression and march in solidarity with causes related to sexual health, sexual assault, LGBT communities, and other groups and issues. They work with local governments to develop HIV testing programs, and put on numerous events throughout the year to raise money for nonprofits in their communities. They educate about safer sex and encourage people to practise it, handing out safer-sex kits in bars and at other appropriate events. They serve as confidants to their communities. And, above all, they strive to fulfill their mission: 'To promulgate universal joy and expiate stigmatic guilt'. This is not your mother's political activism, and these are not your father's nuns.

In other writing (Wilcox 2009), I have argued for the usefulness of the 'exemplary case study' in examining contemporary religious trends. The Sisters of Perpetual Indulgence offer such a case study of what I have termed here the 'postsecular' – not, as Habermas suggests, a dialogue between the religious and the secular, but a melding of the two until, at least at the margins, each becomes indistinguishable from the other. By their own definition the Sisters are not a religious order; yet, also by their own definition, they are twenty-first-century nuns. Most individual Sisters would not define themselves as religious; most, at least in the US, would also not define themselves as secular in their outlook. As 'nones' and as nuns, the Sisters are betwixt and between, working in the postsecular gray area that is both secular and sacred, neither secular nor sacred.

The serious parody which the Sisters enact is part and parcel of their postsecularism. Parodying a religious institution that has proven increasingly unwelcoming of and actively harmful to LGBTQ people, at the same time the Sisters co-opt one aspect of that institution – the figure of the nun – with respect that occasionally borders on reverence. They enjoy telling stories of their acceptance by Roman Catholic nuns, and the vast majority of Sisters whom I have interviewed take their roles as nuns extremely seriously. A Sister is a nun for life, vowed permanently to serve the LGBTQ community in ways both material and emotional. The Sisters' serious parody is, on the one hand, secular, an often sexualised, highly embellished parody of the Roman Catholic nun that appears most often in what some would consider to be the most secular of secular locales: gay men's bars on Friday and Saturday nights. On the other hand, the Sisters' serious parody is also religious, in that they enact a traditionally religious role that some Sisters even see as sacred: serving the community for no reason other than a calling to serve and care for others.

The shift from twentieth-century religiosity (and nuns) to twenty-first-century postsecularism (and nuns) is neatly encapsulated in a comment the Sisters are fond of making when comparing themselves to Roman Catholic nuns: 'They serve the community; we serve the community. They raise money for charity; we raise money for charity. They take a vow of celibacy, we ... serve the community'. The same as other nuns yet different in important ways, these 'none nuns' offer a new way of thinking about religious/secular/postsecular activism in light of the breakdown of yet another dichotomy.

References

Byrne, R. 2006. *The Secret*. New York: Atria Books.
Frisk, L. and Nynäs, P. 2012. Characteristics of Contemporary Religious Change: Globalization, Neoliberalism, and Interpretative Tendencies. In Nynäs, P., Lassander, M. and Utriainen, T. (eds), *Post-Secular Society* 53–70. New Brunswick, N.J.: Transaction.
Glenn, C. 2003. Queering the (Sacred) Body Politic: Considering the Performative Cultural Politics of The Sisters of Perpetual Indulgence. *Theory and Event* 7(1): n.p.
Gorski, P.S. and Altinordu, A. 2008. After Secularization? *Annual Review of Sociology* 34: 55–85.
Jameson, F. 1991. *Postmodernism, Or, the Cultural Logic of Late Capitalism*. Durham, N.C.: Duke University Press.
Roof, W.C. 1999. *Spiritual Marketplace: Baby Boomers and the Remaking of American Religion*. Princeton, N.J.: Princeton University Press.
Weiss, B.L. 1988. *Many Lives, Many Masters*. New York: Simon and Schuster.
Wilcox, M.M. 2009. *Queer Women and Religious Individualism*. Bloomington: Indiana University Press.
Wilcox, M.M. 2010. Parodic Politics. *The Immanent Frame*, 6 August.

Chapter 4

Hindu, Muslim and Sikh Young Adults: Gendered Practices in the Negotiation of Sexuality and Relationship

Sarah-Jane Page and Andrew Kam-Tuck Yip

Introduction

Young adult Hindus, Muslims and Sikhs living in the UK are at a key crossroads, negotiating formative issues in relation to intimate life, such as prospects for marriage. This is situated in a context where family, close-knit extended kinship networks and communities (including religious networks) feature highly. Indeed, although Hinduism, Islam and Sikhism have different conceptualisations and understandings of appropriate sexuality and intimate relationships, and the theologies within each religious tradition vary considerably, in terms of actual lived experiences, these young adults share many similarities regarding the important part that family and associated communities play in informing ideals and expectations about sexuality and relationship. At the same time, this negotiation of family, religion and community has a gendered dimension.

Gender is politically constituted through the body (Weitz 2003). Scholars have highlighted how women's bodies become symbolic of nation and community (e.g. Nagel 2003, Saigol 2008, Shalhoub-Kevorkian 2008). For religious young adults from South Asian backgrounds, such as the vast majority of participants this chapter covers, the gendered body has historically been understood in a particular way. As Shain (2003) highlights, Asian girls are constructed as shy, timid and hard-working, invoking a discourse of restriction and even repression, with the cultures of home constructed against the secular-liberal environment of school (Cressey 2006, Dwyer 1998). Similarly, Asian men have been constructed as compliant and weak (Lei 2003, Saigol 2008) but those who identify as Muslim are often perceived in terms of militancy and aggressiveness (Archer 2001, 2009). These stereotypes are not lived realities, but inform dominant impressions. Gender differences arise in these constructs as it is women's bodies which are invoked as markers of 'community' respect (Hall 2002, Saigol 2008).

In this chapter, gender is conceptualised as embodied and lived. Thus, gender is more than a social category; it is also processual and negotiated in the everyday context. Understanding the body as a political site highlights embodied regulation and governance. Feminists adopting a Foucauldian perspective have emphasised the relationship between bodies, discourses, power and choice. Bordo (1997) views the body as a site of power and control, where appropriate displays and performances of femininity and masculinity are enacted to achieve wider political ends. The person is not passive in this process – rather, the body is a site of contradiction and conflict, influenced by numerous discourses. Its socialisation is never complete; while it acts as an arena for power, the body also acts as a form of resistance (Bailey 1993). Choices and agency underpin the management of bodily rules, giving space for strategies to be utilised in adopting and resisting dominant political scripts. However, bodily agency is only ever enacted within particular discursive conditions. Although individuals remain agentic, (in that they always have *a* choice), discursive manifestations of power can engender great constraint (Sawicki 1991).

Roof defines lived religion as 'religion as experienced in everyday life, [which] offers a model for integrating the official, the popular, and the therapeutic modes of religious identity' (1999: 41). In addition, McGuire has argued that 'The term "lived religion" is useful for distinguishing the actual experience of religious persons from the prescribed religion of institutionally defined beliefs and practices' (2008: 12). This concept of lived religion helpfully articulates the way our participants have shaped their lived and embodied religious identity in conjunction with religious scripts, carving out their own interpretation and making active choices. For the young adults studied, interaction is occurring simultaneously with wider youth culture, but it will be beyond the remits of this chapter to go into detail about this. It is important to highlight, however, that for the young adults we studied, 'white' culture was often used as a reference point, invoking a particular idea of a homogenised identity existing outside of the remit of their own religious community. It was used as a strategic othering device in order to highlight community difference, supporting the findings of Phillips' (2009) research of Muslims living in Northern England, where 'white' was evoked as a separate space. It remains important, however, to recognise all cultures and communities as multi-layered, complex and diverse, even if reification serves as a useful strategy in how participants described their lives (Baumann 1996).

The chapter will start with a methodological account of the study, followed by a consideration of the first theme – the structural framework of family and community within which young adults negotiate sexuality and gender. Sexuality and gender will then be examined though two further themes – heteronormativity and marriage, and virginity. It will be emphasised that understanding these interrelated themes cannot be uncoupled from reference to family and community expectation.

Brief Methodological Account

This chapter is based on a wider project that sought to capture the management of sexual and religious identities among adults aged 18 to 25, who self-identified as Buddhist, Christian, Hindu, Jewish, Muslim, Sikh or a combination of one or more of these faiths, for example, 'Muslim-Christian'[1] (for more details about the overall research and key findings, see Keenan et al. Forthcoming, Page et al. Forthcoming, Yip et al. 2011).

This chapter specifically focuses on those individuals who identified as Hindu, Muslim or Sikh, who were primarily of South Asian heritage. Broadly speaking, these three groups share a particular location and heritage in the UK context, influenced by similar migratory patterns, as well as correlating factors that shaped settlement, resulting in a tendency for all groups to facilitate social life through close-knit communities and kinship relationships (Becher 2008, Parekh 1994, Rait 2005). A total of 188 participants comprised this particular sample: 115 Muslims (61.2%), 47 Hindus (25%), and 26 Sikhs (13.8%) respectively. Each of these participants completed an online questionnaire. In addition, 23 were interviewed, and eight of the interviewed participants also recorded a video diary respectively. Overall, 134 (71.3%) were women, 54 (28.7%) were men. In terms of ethnicity, the majority of participants identified as Indian (69; 36.9%), followed by Pakistani (40; 21.4%), other (21; 11.2%), and Bangladeshi (19; 10.2%). Further, 56% had completed A levels (or equivalent) and 25.5% had completed a degree. The vast majority of participants were single (151; 80.7%) and 157 (85.3%) identified as heterosexual, 14 (7.6%) did not define their sexuality, and 13 (7.1%) identified as bisexual, lesbian, gay or homosexual. To protect participants' identities, we use pseudonyms throughout. All participants were living in the UK at the time of the study. A small minority were resident in the UK as students. The majority, however, were British-born.

Family Connection, Community Identity and Religious Belonging

Religious and ethnic/cultural communities – particularly in the case of minorities – often serve as important spaces within which identity is constructed and reinforced. Within the British context, the Sikh, Muslim and Hindu communities – primarily

1   The project, entitled *Religion, Youth and Sexuality: A Multi-faith Exploration*, was funded by the Arts and Humanities Research Council/Economic and Social Research Council *Religion and Society* Programme (Award no. AH/G014051/1). The research team consists of Prof. Andrew Kam-Tuck Yip (Principal Investigator), Dr. Michael Keenan (Co-investigator) and Dr. Sarah-Jane Page (Research Fellow). More details of the project can be found at www.nottingham.ac.uk/sociology/rys. The research team is grateful for the funding, as well as the invaluable contribution of the respondents, individuals and groups who helped with the recruitment of the sample and the members of the advisory committee.

of South Asian heritage – are significant in the production and distribution of social and cultural capital (Anthias 2007). Such community belonging can act as an inclusive space in a wider context of exclusion. Drawing on the 2005 data from the Home Office Citizenship Survey, Gale and Hopkins (2009) highlight that Muslims, Sikhs and Hindus are more likely to be religiously practising than Buddhists, Christians or Jews. Our participants' high regard for their religious and cultural communities was clearly demonstrated in their responses to the questionnaire statement, 'My religion gives me a connection to my community'. Overall, 141 (75%) of all participants – 98 (73.1%) women and 43 (79.6%) men – across all the three religious groups 'strongly agreed' or 'agreed'. Specifically in terms of religious groups, the percentages were 78.3% (Muslims), 70.2% (Hindus), and 69.2% (Sikhs). Table 4.1 shows a more detailed picture by gender, emphasising that women were less supportive than men regarding the issue of religious community connection.

Table 4.1   Participants who strongly agreed or agreed with the statement, 'My religion gives me a connection to my community', by gender and religion

Muslim		Hindu		Sikh	
Women n = 91	Men n = 24	Women n = 26	Men n = 21	Women n = 17	Men n = 9
76.9%	83.3%	69.2%	71.4%	58.8%	88.9%

Note: n = Total number of valid responses.

'Community' was treated as a space in which politics were lived and negotiated, providing a framework for individual action. Therefore, talking of '*the* community' was a strategy in understanding young adults' lives and how they fitted into the wider culture. There was an understanding amongst participants that 'the community' had to, in one way or another, be negotiated, even if this was in terms of an eschewal of the community. Indeed, although it was discursively useful to discuss 'the community' in monolithic terms, in reality, it was a concept that was highly complex and multi-layered in the lives of young adults. To many participants, 'community' referred to a diffuse network of individuals, particularly extended-family members, often with a place of worship at its heart. Adala, a Muslim woman of Pakistani heritage emphasised in interview that 'people that attend the mosque will always see you as the community … it's like a unity and you're always seen as part of the community'. In the same vein, Surjit said,

> I've got a few aunts and uncles that live nearby … because we were in the same town, we'd often have a lot of social interactions with them and go to their house, they'd come to ours. (Sikh woman of Indian heritage, *Interview*)

Participants often utilised the terminology of 'community' when relaying their experiences, with a recognition that something called 'community' impacted on their lives (Baumann 1996). 'Community', however, was a contingent and shifting notion, invoked in particular contexts, sometimes including extended-family members, and other times directly implicating the worshipping community. Many saw great benefits attached to community membership in facilitating a supportive network, as Parminder said:

> Community is everything, family is everything ... my dad's friends, I don't call them, oh you know, 'Sam is on the phone' or whatever, it will be 'Oh uncle is on the phone' ... even though you know they have got no blood relation to me, family is very much the focus, you know, extended family, you know I see my cousins, brothers and sisters as my brothers and sisters. (Sikh woman of Indian heritage, *Interview*)

Parminder not only demonstrated respect toward elders through giving them familial titles, but in this linguistic connection to family, the bonds between friends, family and kin were strengthened.

Community support often precipitated the expectation to conform. In order to benefit from the support of community membership, young adults felt certain rules had to be adhered to, especially around codes relating to gender and sexuality (Drury 1991). Sexuality was often regulated at the community level, to ensure the continuation of a coherent and bounded collective identity; in this process, western-style individualism could be downplayed (Chan 2004). Discourses such as 'honour' and 'shame' could be invoked, and as Bradby (2006) asserts, such concepts have great currency within South Asian communities, acting as a surveillance mechanism in relation to individual behaviour. However, it is important to emphasise the diversity in how this is played out in different contexts. *Izzat* is a term that underscores these personal and collective responsibilities around discourses of shame and honour – as Din argues, 'Respect is personal: *izzat* is a more general accolade for the whole family' (Din 2006: 66). Jaspal (Forthcoming) highlights that *izzat* is multidimensional, constituted in a variety of ways for different South Asian communities, with elements being drawn from religious discourses, family and community to varying degrees. In addition, Imam (2005) emphasises that in relation to Muslim cultures, shame and honour do not exist as salient concepts in all societies. It is also important to note that discourses of shame and honour are prevalent in other ethno-religious communities. Sharma (2011) argues that shame and guilt are emotions that operate in predominantly white Christian communities, where women regulate not only their own behaviour, but also that of their friends, with transgression having a community consequence. Indeed, such articulations pinpoint the ways in which a concept such as *izzat* taps into the prominence of emotions in underlying action (Riis and Woodhead 2010). Shame, honour and guilt are emotions embodied through gender practices, and become significant in shaping the management of the gendered body. We shall elaborate on this in the following themes.

Heteronormativity and the Negotiation of Marriage

Heteronormativity is a systemic cultural ideology, practice and institution that privileges heterosexuality, requiring social actors to toe the heterosexual line in all aspects of life (Ahmed 2006). The family, as well as cultural and religious communities, are all significant agents in performing, concretising and legitimising heteronormativity. This implicates bodily performance and life choices of not only lesbian, gay, and bisexual (LGB) religious actors whose sexualities fall outside of the normative framework; it also affects heterosexuals who fail to live up to cultural ideals, one of which is marriage. Indeed, the cultural and religious expectations of marriage were widely acknowledged by many participants as a significant rite-of-passage that they needed to negotiate with their family as well as the broader kin network. Dharam, a Sikh man of Indian heritage, argued that the expectation from parents would be 'to find a nice Sikh girl' but stressing that he was 'only 23', his parents had not put pressure on him yet. Meanwhile, Isma, a Muslim woman of Pakistani heritage, had been left 'sleepless on quite a lot of occasions', with pressure arising not only from parents, but also through the intensive number of weddings occurring in the neighbourhood of young women who had recently graduated from university.

This anxiety was intensified for lesbian, gay and bisexual participants. As Jamil, a bisexual Muslim in a relationship with another man, narrated:

> I can delay it for so long, I can say I have studies ... but when it comes to a certain age the community will look at my parents and think why aren't they getting him married, then they will figure it out ... I know if it did get out into the community it will just hurt my parents, and I know it will be hard for me to face the community again. (Muslim man of mixed heritage, *Interview*)

Thus the negotiation of heteronormative expectations were conditionally thwarted through diversionary tactics, such as education and work, but future conflicts were very much in the minds of LGB individuals (for more details, see Page et al. Forthcoming). Among heterosexual participants, gender differences were salient. In general, the men appeared to brush off the expectation, for instance, asserting they were too young (as we see in Dharam's quote, above). Meanwhile, the women seemed to take the issue more seriously, even to the extent of suffering from sleepless nights.

Rashida discussed the consequences for women in her video diary, a method which offers opportunities to participants to reflect on the day-to-day negotiation of faith, friendship and relationship). Rashida (a Muslim woman of Pakistani heritage) had met an old school friend who had experienced a broken engagement.

Her friend felt that this break up 'brought shame onto her family because, in the Asian culture, breaking engagements, the repercussions tend to be with the woman and her family, and there is a lot of shame involved'.

Greater pressure was exerted onto women to conduct themselves impeccably during relationship negotiation. Any breaches result in repercussions for her, not him. Young women were reminded in everyday negotiations of the costs of transgression. Women's bodies were prioritised as the sites upon which community morality was inscribed (Din 2006, Imtoual and Hussein 2009, Rait 2005). Thus, rather than their embodied actions being of personal or even familial concern, they had community consequences.

This meant that female bodies were more heavily scrutinised than male bodies, with Navreet saying,

> When I was 17, my brother's age, I had to be back at home by 9 o'clock; he comes home late ... closing the door quietly ... there are double standards when it comes to boys and girls. (Sikh woman of Indian heritage, *Interview*)

Indeed, while there are undoubtedly liberatory and emancipatory currents within contemporary sexual cultures, discrepant cultural scripts continue to be structured and stratified by gender (Drury 1991, Green 2008, Johansson 2007).

Young adults learned the necessary cultural scripts early in life. As already indicated, most had a sense that marriage and having children were community and familial expectations, and it has been specifically emphasised how young women were implicated in this. But young men too felt a distinct expectation. This was Vishaal's formative experience:

> The one thing that will always stick with me is what my mum said to me. 'Don't get married if you haven't got a job and you can't look after a family. There's no point ruining someone else's life because you've ruined your own' and she's said that to me about five times now ... So I mean that's always stuck with me. It was powerful ... there was always pressure, like I'll end up lonely if I don't make it. (Hindu man of Indian heritage, *Interview*)

Vishaal had internalised the necessity of professional success in order to fulfil his obligations as a family provider. A breadwinning role, validating his placement in a heterosexual relationship, was thus the goal, endorsing appropriate masculinity.

Marriage was consistently referred to as mediated through the community, particularly in terms of arranged marriages. The situations and processes surrounding arranged marriages are multifarious, sometimes invoking community involvement at a local, national or international level. Many were supportive of arranged marriage, seeing it as a dating service facilitated through parents, often saving time for busy professionals:

It's a good way to get introduced to someone. If you don't like them, you're not under pressure. That's what my parents said. Some parents may be different. This is how I know of it ... My parents will accept if you say no to someone. (Ajeet, Sikh man of Indian heritage, *Interview*)

Meanwhile others were more critical, as is typified by the following quote:

[My friends say] nowadays it's not really an arranged marriage; you meet the person beforehand, and I'm like but the parents still choose, and if the parents aren't happy they'll say no, even if you get on brilliantly with that guy. (Uma, Sikh woman of Indian heritage, *Interview*)

Indeed, gender differences did emerge regarding the resources available in choosing a partner. A number of men discussed the benefits of meeting a spouse from another country:

Girls [from Pakistan] appreciate you more. When you bring them over here they appreciate you and look after you and look after your parents and everything ... Girls here are more stuck up; more show off, not that nice to their parents. (Aalim, Muslim man of Pakistani heritage, *Video diary*)

Meanwhile, the women were hesitant in marrying someone from abroad:

There's pressure on the boys to get married in Pakistan. So it's really, really difficult for the girls to find somebody here ... I couldn't understand somebody from Pakistan or how to talk to them ... even if I'm 35, I'm not going to Pakistan to get married. Never, ever. (Adala, Muslim woman of Pakistani heritage, *Interview*)

This could facilitate feelings of despair as women worried about whether they would find a British man of the right caste, occupation and education (Imtoual and Hussein 2009).

In addition to finding a marital spouse, there was also the politics surrounding the wedding itself. The community was at the centre of this negotiation, with Ranjit, a Hindu man of Sri Lankan heritage, highlighting that the whole community needed to be invited to his impending brother's wedding – resulting in 1,000 invites – to ensure that no one was offended.

Weddings were key social occasions where community approval was paramount. Individuals were on display and women's bodies were once again utilised in signifying respect:

Women would never, ever drink at an Indian wedding ... I know I drink and the majority of women here probably do drink, but they don't drink out in public like that because it's disrespectful ... if you're necking loads of alcoholic drinks back and you make like a show of yourself it seems [you are] disrespecting your family and your family's honour. (Parminder, Sikh woman of Indian heritage, *Interview*)

Community dictums were not always adopted without challenge. Some participants disassociated themselves from family and community, such as Uma, who despite financial consequences and the community gossip generated by her departure, deliberately moved out of the geographic locality of her community:

> We wanted to be out of it, that's why we left home, because of all the like pressure … people were talking about the two sisters that left home in the community … my mum must have been very embarrassed, it's all about face value and we brought shame to the family. (Sikh woman of Indian heritage, *Interview*)

For the majority, gender obligations were accepted, with the trade-off being community support and acceptance. But in other situations gender discrepancies were not taken lightly. Akin to Drury's (1991) research with young Sikh women, the costs of opting out completely were often considered too great, but religion could be utilised as a resource in challenging gendered practices (Phillips 2009). Although the power to change things at a communal level was minimal, the women did discuss how they imparted gender-equal policies in their home lives. For example, Isma, a Muslim woman of Pakistani heritage, highlighted that the women in her family would only eat their meal after all the males had eaten. She argued this was 'a silly cultural thing … We just eat all together now because of my ranting … it has no religious basis … people misinterpret their religion to suit their needs'.

Noticeable in Isma's tackling of gender inequality was the strategic separation of culture and religion – because this norm was not religiously endorsed, it could easily be challenged. A number of young people used such a strategy in effecting change in their own lives, with Ajeet, a Sikh man of Indian heritage, telling his parents that he did not want a lavish community wedding where 'you have 2,000 people … you probably wouldn't know half of them. So personally I think I would want to keep it fairly immediate, fairly small. Keep it religious'. The wedding therefore became focused on the religious space of the temple. By emphasising and retaining the strictly religious element of a wedding, the superfluous trappings of extravagance and wealthy display could be eschewed. Religion was therefore a resource used in challenging the gender and sexual politics constituted through the community. As Bradby asserts, in this respect:

> The coincidence of secular traditions of honour and religious expectations can make it very difficult for behaviours to be renegotiated, but where traditions are not considered to have a religious justification, moderation of constraint is possible and religion can offer the means whereby loosening of restriction is achieved. (2006: 133)

For the young adults, negotiating the various communities and individual interests took a number of different forms. Some postponed decision-making to some future point, once education had been completed, for example. Others strategically accepted adherence to norms in certain situations, such as not drinking alcohol in public. Others flatly refused to participate in practices that were negatively perceived, such as marrying a foreign spouse. For some, this entailed challenging norms and values from within; for others, distance was sought and entailed a move away from families and communities, often into non-religious spaces. Finally, some utilised sacred, as opposed to community, authority as a means of challenging community norms.

Virginity: Gendered Perceptions and Practices

Overall, 24.9% of the participants were sexually active, with men being more likely to be so (31.5%) than women (22%). Table 4.2 shows this statistic in more detail.

Table 4.2   Percentage of participants who said they were sexually active, by gender and religion

Religious identification	Gender	Percentage	Total number of valid responses
Hindu	Women	29.2%	24
	Men	28.6%	21
Muslim	Women	17.2%	87
	Men	29.2%	24
Sikh	Women	37.5%	16
	Men	44.4%	9

Carpenter (2005) has articulated that virginity loss can be conceptualised in numerous ways, especially when accounting for the experiences of LGB individuals. However, our heterosexual participants tended to utilise a traditional understanding of sex and virginity loss, with sex often seen as pertaining to penetrative vaginal sex. The way women's bodies were politically situated in virginity discourses meant that their bodies held the repercussions. Sabrina's assessment of a woman losing her virginity was stark:

> It would be very bad, somehow people will find out and it will be very bad, people gossiping and it will cause a lot of problems in that family ... He may not be a virgin ... that wouldn't be an issue at all ... But if she wasn't then it would

cause a lot of uproar in the family and the neighbours and stuff. (Muslim woman
of Pakistani heritage, *Interview*)

In this discourse, it was clear that there was an understanding that a woman losing
her virginity was very different to a man losing his virginity. As Hall asserts in
relation to the Sikh community,

> The ideology of family honor finds its expression as it is embodied in restrictions
> and disciplinary judgments and actions focused toward controlling female
> sexuality – toward protecting the 'gift' of female purity and virginity until it
> can be given away at marriage. The bodies of unmarried women are the sites
> on which the dynamic struggles of sociocultural reproduction within Sikh
> communities are fought. (2002: 168)

Hastrup (1993), utilising Mary Douglas's (2007) work on community boundaries
and bodily markers, has articulated that societies operate through the establishment
of borders. Boundaries are sites of potential danger as they represent liminal
crossing-points, thus causing ambivalence. The (female) virgin represents such
an ambiguity – her 'intact' status is often revered, but full womanhood is not
achieved until she becomes sexually active. However, the conceptualisation of
virginity will vary, depending on context. As Dialmy (2010) has asserted in the
context of predominantly Muslim countries, those with few resources (such as
money and education) will still prioritise virginity status as a form of capital that
can be bargained with. Virginity becomes less important in the context of the UK,
where individualised understandings come to dominate over community benefits,
so that virginity loss becomes a personal matter for the woman herself (Cregan
2006, Hastrup 1993). However, in situations where a population has a minority
status, the boundary markers of the group can become important, endorsed through
mechanisms such as marrying within the group, as well as monitoring the bodies
of women. Virginity loss thus becomes a concern of the whole community. As
Sabrina's quote illustrates, for a man, the prevailing discourse is that one cannot
tell whether he is a virgin or not. But for women, sex marks them. However, some
unmarried female participants did have sex. So how was this managed? Shalini
emphasised the tension:

> In Hinduism they say that sex should be between a man and a woman in marriage
> … so yeah, I guess I've committed wrong there really, but I don't think that my
> religion hates me for it … What would my mum say if she knew I'd had sex?
> She would like, cry … she'd think bad for me because she'd actually think oh
> the person I do actually marry may not respect me as much … a lot of friends I
> have as well that are Hindu and they're male, they all say the same thing, you
> know, they prefer their girls to have only been with no one, or one or two people.
> (Hindu woman of Indian heritage, *Interview*)

Shalini highlighted that religiously, she felt that she had done wrong but her actions were redeemable. However, the consequences were felt to be much more community-oriented – what future spouses and family members would think if they knew she had already had sex. Vishaal, a Hindu man of Indian heritage, also shared this thinking, saying, 'it's always going to be in the back of your mind and someone has, I can't say this right, but someone's been there before'.

However, this was explicitly gendered – Vishaal had had sex already but he expected his future bride to be a virgin. The quantitative data offered further insight. As Table 4.3 indicates, women were more in favour of remaining virgins until marriage than men. Interestingly, when asked whether it was important for one's partner to be a virgin on marriage, the numbers of women agreeing or strongly agreeing went down (whatever religious tradition) whereas for the men, the expectation that their partner should be a virgin only decreased for Muslim men – for Sikh men, the figures stayed the same and for Hindu men, the figure slightly increased. Thus some men had greater expectations of women than women had of men. The qualitative data indicated that, on the whole, the young women were more accepting if potential spouses had already had sex. Rather than privileging his sexually active status, Sabrina, for example, expressed greater concern with a future husband's ability to be a good provider and father, thus prioritising the norms of breadwinning masculinity.

Table 4.3   **Participants who strongly agreed or agreed with the statements, 'It is important that I am a virgin when I get married' and 'It is important that my partner is a virgin when I get married'**

Religious Identification	Gender	'It is important that I am a virgin when I get married'	Total number of valid responses	'It is important that my partner is a virgin when I get married'	Total number of valid responses
Hindu	Women	42.3%	26	23.1%	26
	Men	33.3%	21	38.1%	21
Muslim	Women	70.1%	87	60%	85
	Men	60.9%	23	52.2%	23
Sikh	Women	52.9%	17	25%	16
	Men	44.4%	9	44.4%	9

Some men shared the view that if they were expecting their future wives to be virgins, then they must remain virgins themselves, such as Iqbal, a Muslim man of Pakistani heritage, who said that, 'Girls get more of [a] name if they do it ... [but] I would expect my wife to be a virgin so I have to be one myself. ... There is no way of telling with me but I can with her, so it is only fair'. Iqbal thus had greater leverage in choosing to remain a virgin, creating his own religiously-inspired virginity pledge, where religious and community edicts were seen to apply to each gender equally. There was, however, a recognition that any failure in living up to this ideal would result in few repercussions for him.

There were two different ways in which women's virginity was understood in these narratives. One was as a boundary transgressor that threatened community and relationship cohesion (Cregan 2006, Hastrup 1993, Shalhoub-Kevorkian 2008). A woman was seen as marked by her virginity loss – something intrinsic changed – whereas for a man, his virginity loss was considered inconsequential. This fed into wider discourses about virginity as transgressing a boundary for women in a way that such a boundary was not transgressed for men. The boundary marker – the hymen – represented the intact community to which the participant belonged. If it was illicitly broken (outside the bonds of marriage), the boundaries of the community were transgressed (Douglas 2007, Hastrup 1993).

The intact hymen thus became a marker of respectability, with the hymen constructed as an indicator of proof of virginity when it is broken and blood is produced. This was perhaps what Iqbal meant when he confidently asserted that one could 'tell' whether a woman was a virgin or not. The problem with this virginity indicator is that it is a flawed one. Hymens routinely break, often well before sexual contact. But when the breaking of the hymen is held up as a necessity, it can lead to women seeking hymen repair, even after a rape (Dialmy 2005, Imtoual and Hussein 2009, Lindisfarne 1994, Shalhoub-Kevorkian 2008). Some women participants also endorsed this idea of intrinsic bodily change when virginity loss occured, asserting, as Isma did, that virginity was 'a completely different thing' for women, or as Sabrina did when she asserted 'it's obvious when a girl's a virgin and you can't tell whether a guy's a virgin or not ... the task is really easy for them, whereas the girl will bleed'. Thus myths perpetuate about the necessity of a first-sex bleed, putting enormous pressure on young women to protect their bodies.

The other way of understanding virginity loss was through an 'out of sight, out of mind' discourse. So long as the knowledge of virginity loss was concealed, all will be well. In such a narrative, the goalposts move, and rather than scrutiny coming through a (hymen-focused) virginity loss, the marking of the woman's body would only occur through pregnancy. Thus the pregnant body becomes the marker of sexual activity, and the bodily focus for virginity shifted. Therefore, pregnancy became something to be avoided at all costs. Shalini had already had sex and had rationalised this in her own mind, but on being asked whether she would have children outside of marriage she said very definitely:

No, never. Never. No … That probably would be the worst thing that I could do, for my children like to be outside of wedlock, like people would talk … I like the idea of having a relationship and be … supported with a child. (Hindu woman of Indian heritage, *Interview*)

Despite a relaxing of attitudes in wider British society regarding pregnancy outside of marriage, for these young women, the visible presence of sexual activity through pregnancy was untenable. While sexual activity could be hidden, pregnancy could not. Pregnancy had to be avoided as it became the marker of non-virginity. In this way, young women who had had sex could enact a level of respectability through silence about sexual activity and the avoidance of marking their bodies through pregnancy. Indeed, in discussing the pregnant body, the 'community' was again invoked as a presence casting judgement and comment. At the same time, if a child was born in the context of a married relationship, the rewards of community support were plentiful. It was too costly for this to be breached.

Those who did have penetrative sex had two options: the first, taken by the pre-maritally sexually active young women in this sample, was to move the goalposts, and to redefine the meanings of virginity. Virginity loss became unimportant so long as it was concealed, and one did not invite another marker of sexuality, such as pregnancy. Some participants also expressed that they would conceal previous sexual activity from future husbands. The other alternative, as detailed in other studies, where importance is given to an intact hymen, was through having a surgical procedure to reinstate the hymen (Dialmy 2010, Shalhoub-Kevorkian 2008). However, it was women's bodies that were politically implicated as potential sites of shame and 'community' respect. Meanwhile, men's behaviour was rarely policed and it was only when, like Iqbal, they took a personal stand to remain a virgin that virginity was endorsed. Dharam, a Sikh man of Indian heritage said he'd had a six-month relationship with a girl which had dissolved but 'it was never an issue at home … I think being a boy it is a lot easier'. Instead of expectations of virginity, men were managing expectations of being future family providers. Therefore, in their formative educational years girlfriends were overlooked (so long as they were not impeding one's studies), but expectations were high for young men to do well in their educational and work-based achievements.

Concluding Remarks: Resisting, Recasting, Challenging

As we have shown, our participants took the notion of the 'community' seriously. The community was a salient reality in one's life, even if community values and norms were contested in some contexts. Indeed, community values infused the management of their everyday life. On many occasions, despite the difficulties in accommodating community norms, many young Hindus, Muslims and Sikhs expressed the values and benefits of community belonging, and could be critical of their 'white' friends who never interacted with cousins and did not know the names of members of the extended family. At the same time, what they meant by 'community' was fluid and shifting, invoking a multi-layered entity, implicating the immediate family, neighbours, the extended family and religious connections.

The gendered expectations of community, however, were problematic, especially for young women who felt the restrictions most. When sexist beliefs and practices were challenged and resisted, one strategy utilised that met with success was seeing these practices as cultural rather than religious, and therefore open to question. Many emphasised their religions as vehicles of gender equality, and a means through which monolithic community views could be challenged. Hence, religion, rather than secular culture, was invoked as the space in which action could be realised. This strategy worked as it appealed to a higher authority, such as a sacred text. Meanwhile, others utilised secular spaces, moving out of the boundaries of communities into spaces not governed by their community or religion. Secular spaces were invoked as being freer and less rule-bound. Therefore, for some, official scripts (such as sacred texts) came to be the best space from which to argue a case, and was therefore an important strategic resource, as it carried sacred authority. Meanwhile others eschewed religious cultures, and endorsed a secular positioning. For both groups, culture and religion were strategically separated out, used as a bargaining tool in asserting one's identity. At the outset we argued that 'lived religion' was a useful concept in understanding young people's negotiations of religion – religion as it is lived not through merely following official narratives and authorities but through the active recasting and negotiation of such scripts. In this conceptualisation, religion is understood as being embedded as a cultural practice, endorsing official narratives to varying degrees. Even though participants were making strategic distinctions between religion and culture, we still maintain that lived religion is the best means of understanding these processes, for in navigating life, 'culture' impacted on pious individuals (and had to be navigated accordingly) and those who moved into secular spaces did not entirely remove themselves from their communities and religious scripts (as illustrated for example in negotiating with the community at key moments, such as funerals).

The 'community' thus became the site for political negotiation, the space in which gender and sexual scripts were lived out and endorsed, but also the space where meanings and rules were challenged, sometimes leading to the re-writing of such scripts. The gendered body was very much implicated in this, as the body was often used as the political site upon which norms and values were embedded. Young adults were actively resisting, challenging and recasting community norms and values, emphasising the benefits of some practices and challenging others that were experienced as limiting potential. For example, many saw arranged marriage as a suitable mechanism for meeting future spouses, sometimes casting this in superior terms to a western system where the advantage of free choice is qualified by the fact that people could get badly hurt. The costs and benefits of belonging were weighed up. While young women felt at a disadvantage in terms of freedoms, this too was being actively negotiated. Thus familial and community respectability is still coded on the woman's body – but this is not accepted without a challenge. As Shain articulates:

> Asian girls, rather than being the passive recipients of fixed cultures, are actively engaged in producing new cultural identities by drawing on residual elements of their home cultures and reinterpreting them in the local cultural spaces they inhabit ... cultures are not fixed but historically variable and ... Asian girls play an active role in confirming and transforming the cultural spaces they inhabit. (2003: 129)

This chapter has sought to highlight the ways in which gender is lived, positioning men in this frame, as well as women. The gendered body becomes crucial in understanding how the politics of gender are lived out. It can be articulated that women's bodies encounter more regulation, but men's bodies too are politically inscribed, as the bearers of traditions and expected norms such as economic success and heterosexuality.

By considering the politics of the gendered body and how this intersects with sexuality and religion, this chapter has attempted to detail the commonalities in primarily South Asian experiences – a commonality understood through the way in which community is similarly utilised in the UK context, despite great differences in theology, religious practice, sexual ethics and gendered norms. Indeed, religion as a monolithic entity is rejected; rather, religion has been formulated as a set of practices that interact with other factors, such as the family and community. The presence of a bounded 'community' in existence at some spatial level impacts on the ways in which young people negotiate their decision-making around sexual choices and action, using lived religion as the frame of reference. Thus, the gendered sexual body is brought into play in the context of the community as a site of political action, the body being utilised as representative of the boundaries of the politics of community. But this was not passively accepted. Rather, the body was used in enforcing as well as challenging perceived community norms.

References

Ahmed, S. 2006. *Queer Phenomenology*. Durham: Duke University Press.

Anthias, F. 2007. Ethnic Ties: Social Capital and the Question of Mobilisability. *Sociological Review* 55(4): 788–805.

Archer, L. 2001. 'Muslim Brothers, Black Lads, Traditional Asians': British Muslim Young Men's Constructions of Race, Religion and Masculinity. *Feminism and Psychology* 11(1): 79–105.

Archer, L. 2009. Race, 'Face' and Masculinity: The Identities and Local Geographies of Muslim Boys, in *Muslims in Britain*, edited by P. Hopkins and R. Gale. Edinburgh: Edinburgh University Press.

Bailey, M.E. 1993. Foucauldian Feminism: Contesting Bodies, Sexuality and Identity, in *Up Against Foucault*, edited by C. Ramazanoglu. London: Routledge.

Baumann, G. 1996. *Contesting Culture*. Cambridge: Cambridge University Press.

Becher, H. 2008. *Family Practices in South Asian Muslim Families*. Basingstoke: Palgrave Macmillan.

Bordo, S. 1997. The Body and the Reproduction of Femininity, in *Writing on the Body*, edited by K. Conboy, N. Medina, and S. Stanbury. New York: Columbia University Press.

Bradby, H. 2006. Understanding Honour and Religion as Resource and Constraint for Young British Asians, in *Theorising Religion*, edited by J.A. Beckford and J. Walliss. Aldershot: Ashgate.

Carpenter, L.M. 2005. *Virginity Lost*. New York: New York University Press.

Chan, C.S. 2004. Asian-American Adolescents: Issues in the Expression of Sexuality, in *Sexualities*, edited by M.S. Kimmel and R.F. Plante. New York: Oxford University Press.

Cregan, K. 2006. *The Sociology of the Body*. London: Sage.

Cressey, G. 2006. Muslim Girlswork: The Ultimate Separatist Cage? *Youth & Policy* 92(1): 33–45.

Dialmy, A. 2005. Sexuality in Contemporary Arab Society. *Social Analysis* 49(2): 16–33.

Dialmy, A. 2010. Sexuality and Islam. *The European Journal of Contraception and Reproductive Health Care* 15(3): 160–68.

Din, I. 2006. *The New British*. Aldershot: Ashgate.

Douglas, M. 2007. *Purity and Danger*. Abingdon: Routledge.

Drury, B. 1991. Sikh Girls and the Maintenance of an Ethnic Culture. *New Community* 17(3): 387–99.

Dwyer, C. 1998. Contested Identities: Challenging Dominant Representations of Young British Muslim Women, in *Cool Places*, edited by T. Skelton and G. Valentine. London: Routledge.

Gale, R. and Hopkins, P. 2009. Introduction: Muslims in Britain – Race, Place and the Spatiality of Identities, in *Muslims in Britain*, edited by P. Hopkins and R. Gale. Edinburgh: Edinburgh University Press.

Green, A.I. 2008. The Social Organization of Desire: The Sexual Fields Approach. *Sociological Theory* 26(1): 25–50.

Hall, K.D. 2002. *Lives in Translation*. Philadelphia: University of Pennsylvania Press.

Hastrup, K. 1993. The Semantics of Biology: Virginity, in *Defining Females*, edited by S. Ardener. Oxford: Berg.

Imam, A.M. 2005. The Muslim Religious Right ("Fundamentalists") and Sexuality, in *Good Sex*, edited by P.B. Jung, M.E. Hunt and R. Balakrishnan. London: Rutgers University Press.

Imtoual, A. and Hussein, S. 2009. Challenging the Myth of the Happy Celibate: Muslim Women Negotiating Contemporary Relationships. *Contemporary Islam* 3(1): 25–39.

Jaspal, R. Forthcoming. 'I Never Faced Up to Being Gay': Sexual, Religious and Ethnic Identities among British Indian and British Pakistani Gay Men. *Culture, Health and Sexuality*.

Johansson, T. 2007. *The Transformation of Sexuality*. Aldershot: Ashgate.

Keenan, M., Yip, A.K.T. and Page, S. Forthcoming. Exploring Sexuality and Religion Using an Online Questionnaire, in *Innovative Methods in the Study of Religion*, edited by L. Woodhead. Oxford: Oxford University Press.

Lei, J.L. 2003. (Un)necessary Toughness? Those 'Loud Black Girls' and those 'Quiet Asian Boys'. *Anthropology and Education Quarterly* 34(2): 158–81.

Lindisfarne, N. 1994. Variant Masculinities, Variant Virginities: Rethinking 'Honour and Shame', in *Dislocating Masculinity*, edited by A. Cornwall and N. Lindisfarne. London: Routledge.

McGuire, M. 2008. *Lived Religion*. Oxford: Oxford University Press.

Nagel, J. 2003. *Race, Ethnicity and Sexuality*. Oxford: Oxford University Press.

Page, S., Yip, A.K.T. and Keenan, M. Forthcoming. Risk and the Imagined Future: Young Adults Negotiating Religious and Sexual Identities, in *The Ashgate Research Companion to Contemporary Religion and Sexuality*, edited by S. Hunt and A.K.T. Yip. Farnham: Ashgate.

Parekh, B. 1994. Some Reflections on the Hindu Diaspora. *Journal of Ethnic and Migration Studies* 20(4): 603–20.

Phillips, D. 2009. Creating Home Spaces: Young British Muslim Women's Identity and Conceptualisations of Home, in *Muslims in Britain*, edited by P. Hopkins and R. Gale. Edinburgh: Edinburgh University Press.

Rait, S.K. 2005. *Sikh Women in England*. Stoke on Trent: Trentham Books.

Riis, O. and Woodhead, L. 2010. *A Sociology of Religious Emotion*. Oxford: Oxford University Press.

Roof, W.C. 1999. *Spiritual Marketplace*. Princeton: Princeton University Press.

Saigol, R. 2008. Militarization, Nation and Gender: Women's Bodies as Arenas of Violent Conflict, in *Deconstructing Sexuality in the Middle East*, edited by P. Ilkkaracan. Aldershot: Ashgate.

Sawicki, J. 1991. *Disciplining Foucault*. New York: Routledge.

Shain, F. 2003. *The Schooling and Identity of Asian Girls*. Stoke on Trent: Trentham Books.

Shalhoub-Kevorkian, N. 2008. Towards a Cultural Definition of Rape: Dilemmas in Dealing with Rape Victims in Palestinian Society, in *Deconstructing Sexuality in the Middle East*, edited by P. Ilkkaracan. Aldershot: Ashgate.

Sharma, S. 2011. *Good Girls, Good Sex*. Halifax & Winnipeg: Fernwood Publishing.

Weitz, R. 2003. The Social Construction of Women's Bodies, in *The Politics of Women's Bodies*, edited by R. Weitz. New York: Oxford University Press.

Yip, A.K.T., Keenan, M. and Page, S. 2011. *Religion, Youth and Sexuality*. Nottingham: University of Nottingham.

Chapter 5

Coping with Religious and Cultural Homophobia: Emotion and Narratives of Identity Threat among British Muslim Gay Men

Rusi Jaspal

In Britain, the social, political and legal positions of individuals who identify as lesbian, gay or bisexual have improved, which has generally led to greater tolerance and acceptance at the social level. However, there is evidence that ethnic and religious minority non-heterosexual individuals can continue to face discrimination from within their ethnic and/or religious communities (Yip 2007). For instance, representations of homosexuality within ethnic and religious minority communities in Britain can often be negative and stigmatising (Yip 2012), which may in turn result in decreased willingness to 'come out' (Jaspal and Siraj 2011), as well as psychological 'conflict' (Bhugra 1997). Given that their religious and cultural groups can prescriptively advocate heteronormativity and compulsory heterosexuality, non-heterosexual ethnic and religious minority individuals may opt to remain 'invisible' (Murray 1997). Collectively, these factors can have profoundly negative social and psychological outcomes for those affected. This chapter focuses upon the narratives of British Muslim gay men[1] (BMGM) of Pakistani descent, who may face homophobia from both their ethnic *and* religious ingroups (Jaspal in press).

There is now a growing tradition of research into the interface of religion and sexuality among BMGM (Jaspal and Cinnirella 2010, 2012, Yip 2004a, 2004b). Our research has examined the socio-psychological implications of being Muslim and gay for the self-concept, with a particular focus upon identity threat and coping. A principal contention within this body of work has been that religious and cultural homophobia seems to encourage the perception among BMGM that their religious and sexual identities are entirely incompatible. This may have

---

1   It is acknowledged that some ethnic and religious minority non-heterosexual men reject the sexual category 'gay' due to its 'White' connotations (e.g. Carlson 1997). Our studies have always been presented as investigations of 'being gay, Muslim and Pakistani' and participants have endorsed the category 'gay' (rather than 'bisexual' or 'straight') for sexual self-definition. Therefore, the term 'British Muslim gay men' seems appropriate here.

negative social, psychological and emotional outcomes. The present chapter makes a contribution to existing research by elucidating how BMGM may cope with religious and cultural homophobia.

The chapter begins with an overview of identity process theory (Breakwell 1986), a socio-psychological theory of identity construction, threat and coping, and the conceptual inter-relations between religious/cultural homophobia, identity and emotion among BMGM. The methodological account is followed by a detailed discussion of the following empirical themes: (i) identity dissonance and feelings of shame and guilt; (ii) ingroup norms, God's norms and the experience of fear; and (iii) managing interpersonal relations and anger. The chapter attempts to theorise the potential effects of homophobia for identity and how individuals cope with threatened identity. Furthermore, it addresses the role of emotion in meaning-making *vis-à-vis* religious and sexual identities and the phenomenological aspects of emotional experience when identity is threatened.

Identity, Threat and Coping

In seeking to explore the socio-psychological implications of self-identification as gay and of religious faith, we have drawn upon tenets of Breakwell's (1986) identity process theory (IPT) (Jaspal and Cinnirella 2010, 2012, Jaspal and Siraj 2011). IPT integrates identity construction, threat and coping, while synthesising the social and psychological levels of analysis. The theory proposes that the structure of identity should be conceptualised in terms of its content and value/ affect dimensions and that this structure is regulated by two universal processes, namely (i) the assimilation-accommodation process and (ii) the evaluation process. The assimilation-accommodation process refers to the absorption of new information in the identity structure (e.g. 'I am gay') and to the adjustment which takes place in order for it to become part of the structure (e.g. 'I am gay so maybe I cannot be a Muslim'). The evaluation process confers meaning and value upon the contents of identity.

IPT outlines seven identity principles which define the desirable end-states for identity. These principles guide the aforementioned identity processes. It is argued that the individual needs to perceive appropriate levels of self-continuity across time (*continuity*); uniqueness and differentiation from relevant others (*distinctiveness*); competence and control over their lives and future (*self-efficacy*); feelings of personal worth (*self-esteem*); significance and purpose within their lives (*meaning*); belonging within social groups (*belonging*); and compatibility and coherence between elements of their identities (*psychological coherence*). There is evidence that many of these principles are vulnerable to threat among BMGM. Pervasive homophobia within their religious and cultural groups can make it difficult to derive feelings of self-esteem on the basis of their gay identity and a sense of belonging in relevant ingroups, for instance (Bhugra 1997, Jaspal and Cinnirella 2010).

IPT suggests that, when the individual is unable to perceive appropriate levels of salient identity principles, identity is threatened and the individual will engage in coping strategies to alleviate the threat. A coping strategy is defined as 'any activity, in thought or deed, which has as its goal the removal or modification of a threat to identity' (Breakwell 1986: 78). Some strategies function at the intrapsychic level, such as *denial* that one is actually gay, or *re-conceptualisation* of what it means to be gay. Others function at a social level, such as *isolation* of oneself from others, or *social denial* of homosexuality, that is, accepting that one is gay but refusing to acknowledge this publicly.

Experiencing Religious and Cultural Homophobia

Homophobia is a contentious term which has been the object of much scholarly debate (Yip 2012). It has typically been defined as 'the dread of being in close quarters with homosexuals' (Weinberg 1972: 4), and has been expanded to include feelings of disgust, aversion, anger, anxiety and discomfort towards homosexuals (Hudson and Ricketts 1980). More recently, Herek (2004) has challenged the largely psychological, individualistic conceptualisation of homophobia and therefore advocated a more pluralist approach, encompassing the individual, socio-structural, cultural and ideological dimensions of homophobia. Accordingly, in this chapter, religious and cultural homophobia is broadly conceptualised as encompassing those ideas, norms and representations from one's religious and cultural ingroups, which actively undermine and stigmatise homosexuality and thereby render gay identity a socially and/ or psychologically de-valued component of the self-concept. The perception among BMGM that their salient (i.e. religious, ethno-cultural) group memberships are homophobic may be psychologically damaging, inducing stress and negative general mental health outcomes (Rosario et al. 2002).

The mainstream Islamic stance on homosexuality seems to be fundamentally negative. Islam emphasises the complementarity and unity of the two sexes, with distinguishable gender roles associated with either one (Yip 2004b). Given that homosexuality can undermine this patriarchal social structure, Islamic ideology strictly opposes it (Duran 1993), and homophobia is said to be prevalent in Islamic societies (Siraj 2009). It is acknowledged that there is an emerging 'reverse discourse' concerning the Islamic position on homosexuality, with some scholars arguing that there is indeed scope for the theological accommodation of homosexuality (e.g. Hugle 2010, Jamal 2001). However, such theological accommodation is still in its infancy, given that 'there are at present limited efforts in Islamic theology which offer non-heterosexual Muslims resources to construct a reverse discourse' (Yip 2005: 50). Furthermore, religious identity has been described as 'core' among most British Muslims. For instance, in a survey study, 74% of Muslims saw their religion as 'very important', while only 46% of Sikhs and 43% of Hindus did (Modood et al. 1997). Thus, the dominant Islamic stance on homosexuality may affect how BMGM themselves construct their gay identity.

Pakistani ethnic culture is closely entwined with Islam[2] (Haqqani 2004), but there are distinctive elements of Pakistani culture which may be characterised as homophobic. Anthropological studies have described the 'silencing' of homosexuality within Pakistani culture, due to the cultural processes of heteronormativity and compulsory heterosexuality (Khan 1997). Pakistani culture attaches importance to the concept of *izzat* (personal and cultural honour), which is strictly enforced (Shaw 2000). An essential tenet of maintaining familial *izzat* is the fulfilment of the cultural expectation of heterosexual marriage, which in many cases is arranged by the family (Yip 2004b). Any contravention of cultural norms concerning sexuality (e.g. being gay) can be regarded as a threat to the ethno-cultural group as a whole, potentially resulting in negative consequences ranging from ostracisation to psychological or physical abuse (Jaspal and Siraj 2011). Therefore, homosexuality may be seen as threatening for Pakistani culture, resulting in a *cultural* homophobia.

Empirical research has demonstrated the socio-psychological challenges faced by BMGM of Pakistani descent due to the perceived incompatibilities associated with being Muslim, Pakistani and gay (Yip 2004a). In an early study of 'coming out' among British South Asian gay men, Bhugra (1997) found that most participants disclosed their gay identities to non-South Asians in the first instance. Moreover, he noted feelings of regret, self-deprecation and self-hatred among many of his participants, given the 'traumatic discrepancy' between being Asian and gay. Bhugra (1997: 556) located the problem in the Asian gay man's difficulty in constructing 'a coherent sense of self from the two identities he seeks to attain: Asian and gay'. This alludes to threats to psychological coherence. Similarly, in terms of the belonging principle, he has described individuals as having 'a foot in each culture, without feeling a complete sense of belonging in either' (p. 555). This elucidates how identity may be affected among BMGM.

Homophobia and Emotionality

The management of Muslim and gay identities and the experience of homophobia from salient ingroups can expose BMGM to hyper-threats to identity, that is, threats to several principles at once (Jaspal in press). For instance, perceived homophobia from one's religious and cultural ingroups can inhibit a positive self-conception on the basis of one's gay identity, jeopardising self-esteem, and it can induce the perception that being gay and Muslim are incompatible and contradictory, potentially threatening the psychological coherence principle. However, there is

---

2   Pakistan was established as a homeland for the large Muslim minority in British India. Between 95–98% of Pakistanis are Muslims. Moreover, studies demonstrate the 'core-ness' and centrality of Muslim identity among British Pakistanis (Modood et al. 1997).

no existing knowledge concerning the emotional consequences of this atypical identity configuration or concerning the experience of religious and cultural homophobia. Emotion constitutes an important area of investigation because it can influence perceptions, shape memories, contribute to the development of interpersonal relations and regulate behaviour (Massey 2002).

Emotion can be conceptualised in terms of 'a reaction to personally significant events, where "reaction" is taken to include biological, cognitive and behavioural reactions, as well as subjective feelings of pleasure or displeasure' (Parrott 2004: 6). Markus and Kitayama (1991) have proposed a conceptual dichotomy of emotions, whereby 'ego-focused' emotions (e.g. anger, frustration and pride) are experienced by independent and autonomous individuals, while 'other-focused' emotions (e.g. shame and sympathy) are generally experienced by interdependent, collectivistic individuals. Both the intrapsychic level of cognition (e.g. thinking about the compatibility of being Muslim and gay) *and* the social level of human interdependence (e.g. thinking about whether other Muslims will accept their gay identity) are important (Jaspal in press). Thus, it is necessary to explore both ego-focused and other-focused emotions among BMGM.

Previous research into BMGM suggests that the emotions of shame, guilt, anger and fear can be stimulated by experiences of discrimination and homophobia from their religious and ethnic groups (Jaspal and Cinnirella 2010, Yip 2004a). *Shame* is the emotional response to perceived inadequacy of oneself and to potential self-exposure to disapproval from others (Broucek 1991). The cultural representation among many Pakistanis that being gay is 'immoral' may induce the emotion of shame, for instance. *Guilt* focuses on one's perceived wrongdoing and is more associated with one's private conscience than the risk of public exposure (Tangney and Fischer 1995). To that extent, shame is more 'social' than guilt. *Anger* usually arises when one interprets another's actions as a deliberate and unjustified transgression of normative standards (Averill 1982). For instance, Jaspal and Cinnirella (2012) have found that some BMGM may exhibit anger at the perpetrators of forced marriage, which may be regarded as an unjustified contravention of 'British standards'. *Fear* is an emotional response to a perceived risk of threat or danger (Öhman 2000). BMGM may perceive a risk of physical abuse from their homophobic ethnic and religious communities, for instance. Given that these emotions are invariably negative experiences for human beings, their arousal may induce defensive coping behaviours (Turner 1999), such as those described in IPT.

Emotional experience needs to be investigated in terms of its social and psychological dimensions. It is acknowledged that human culture impacts emotional experience by influencing the ways in which a given situation or stimulus will be evaluated and thus responded to emotionally (Harré and Finlay-Jones 1986). Furthermore, individuals' reflective narratives are always imbued with emotional experience (Eatough and Smith 2006), which highlights the feasibility and necessity of exploring emotion from the socio-psychological perspective of the individual. This chapter provides such a perspective among BMGM.

Methodological Account

The Study

The data presented in this chapter are drawn from four exploratory, qualitative interview studies conducted between 2008 and 2011. Collectively, these socio-psychological studies have explored various issues concerning the management of religious, ethnic and sexual identities (Jaspal in press, Jaspal and Cinnirella 2010), interpersonal relations (Jaspal and Cinnirella 2012) and perceptions of 'coming out' among BMGM (Jaspal and Siraj 2011).

This work is characterised by (i) a psychological focus upon how BMGM perceive and cognitively manage their identities; (ii) a sociological concern with the development of relationships with other gay men of similar and different ethno-religious backgrounds; and (iii) a social focus upon the management of relationships with ethno-religious ingroup members. More generally, our approach acknowledges the reciprocal relationship between the intrapsychic level of cognition and the social contexts in which individual cognition is embedded.

This chapter is concerned with participants' responses to religious and cultural homophobia with identity threat and emotion as central foci. Throughout our interview studies, participants have manifested potent emotions and reflected upon their emotional experiences when thinking about the socio-psychological implications of being Muslim and gay. This chapter builds upon existing work on BMGM by providing preliminary insights into the general tendencies regarding threat and emotion, which are observable in our studies.

Participants

It is typically very difficult to obtain a representative sample of hidden populations such as BMGM (Heaphy et al. 1998), particularly because many BMGM avoid public disclosure of their sexual identity and choose to remain 'invisible' (Jaspal in press). Furthermore, our research has usually been concerned with those BMGM who are not affiliated to gay affirmative religious support group networks (e.g. *Imaan*[3]). Our work suggests that the implications for identity and social relations seem to be somewhat different among BMGM who are not affiliated to these networks. In order to gain access to this population, we have habitually employed a snowball sampling strategy with initial participants recruited from within our own social networks. This has facilitated the construction of a convenience sample. In total, 47 BMGM between the ages of 18 and 28 have participated in our interview studies.

---

3   *Al-Fatiha UK*, which was established in 1999, was the first UK-based support group organisation for gay, lesbian and bisexual Muslims. In 2004, the organisation changed its name to *Imaan* (the Arabic word for 'faith').

Analysis and Procedure

The data were analysed using qualitative thematic analysis, which has been described as 'a method for identifying, analysing and reporting patterns (themes) within data' (Braun and Clarke 2006: 78). The study aimed to capture participants' attempts to make sense of their personal and social worlds, with particular foci upon identity threat and emotion. Consequently, the analysis adopts a realist, epistemological approach in that participants' talk is viewed as a fairly reliable reflection of their cognitions. Interviews were digitally recorded and transcribed verbatim. It is noteworthy that data from the four interview studies have been re-analysed for the purpose of the present chapter. In the quotations from participants, an ellipsis indicates where material has been excised; and other material within square brackets is clarificatory.

Analysis

Identity Dissonance and Feelings of Shame and Guilt

The perception of dissonance between religious and sexual identities among BMGM can threaten the psychological coherence principle of identity. In reflecting upon the emotional implications of this discordance, participants have manifested both shame and guilt:

> It's [homosexuality] against Islam, it's wrong, a sin and I know I'm probably going to go to hell ... I feel so ashamed of myself. I'm doing wrong and I know I shouldn't be. I'm letting myself down, it's against God, my religion, my community ... it makes me feel really just bad inside, like bad about myself. (Asif)

There is a clear sense of shame manifested in Asif's account. This arises from the perceived sinfulness of homosexuality, which could allegedly result in the wrongdoer's condemnation to hell. The perception that being gay equals 'doing wrong' in the eyes of 'God, my religion, [and] my community' seems to induce feelings of shame and guilt. Crucially, this negative, discriminatory representation from religious sources engenders the perception that Muslim and gay identities are incompatible, threatening psychological coherence. Like Asif, participants seem to experience unease at the intrapsychic level, as their private conscience dictates that being gay is wrong. This can induce feelings of guilt, which is reflected in the participant's sense of inadequacy and regret. Furthermore, there is a clear sense of *social* wrongdoing, which is tied to the perception of public disapproval. This reflects the emotion of shame (Broucek 1991). Collectively, these emotions may be conducive to a negative self-conception.

There is an entwined sense of shame and guilt, given the intermeshed social and psychological consequences of being gay and Muslim:

> It feels pretty painful to be honest with you because it goes against everything I
> believe in … I just close my eyes sometimes and keep them closed, slap myself,
> I don't feel like opening them when I think about it … Sometimes I can't like, I
> can't face the Imam at the mosque because it's the shame of it, even though he
> don't know that like what I've done. (Faisal)

On the one hand, being gay is perceived as contradicting one's psychological worldview and, on the other, it is regarded as an example of *social* misconduct. The discrepancy between the 'ideal' self and the self which encompasses the seemingly incompatible Muslim and gay identities seems to jeopardise psychological coherence. The perceived incompatibility of these identities is clearly grounded within negative social representations of homosexuality disseminated by religious sources (Duran 1993). Faisal's account highlights the emotional consequences of perceiving dissonance between sexual and religious identities. His desire to 'close my eyes sometimes and keep them closed, slap myself' seems to highlight feelings of guilt, since his private conscience induces both symbolic self-withdrawal and self-flagellation. Moreover, despite Faisal's acknowledgement that his gay identity is unknown to significant others, such as the imam of his local mosque, he nonetheless feels unable to 'face' this human representative of his religious identity. The entwined emotions of guilt and shame may induce an isolationist strategy, whereby the individual decides to avoid facing others who render salient threatening stimuli (i.e. the incompatibility of one's identities) (Breakwell 1986). Indeed, religious figures such as the imam may be said to render salient threatening stimuli; in our research BMGM have attributed the illegality of homosexuality to Koranic interpretations offered by religious scholars (Jaspal and Cinnirella 2010). It is noteworthy that the participant himself attributes this strategy of self-withdrawal to feelings of shame which ensue from the co-existence of his Muslim and gay identities.

The negative emotion of shame due to perceived incompatibility seems to result from individuals' private conscience:

> I just prefer to forget about it, like switch off, that helps … I just don't think
> about it when I'm with a guy, I just switch off, don't think about being a Muslim.
> I know that sounds really bad but how can I think of that if, if Islam says you kill
> a gay? I know I'll get my punishment afterwards, believe me, I do know it …
> When I look back, I feel even more shit about myself than I did before. (Imran)

The emotion of guilt is manifested by Imran's strong belief that his sexual 'wrongdoing' will be punished in the afterlife; there are clear feelings of culpability and inadequacy at work here. In addition to the negative outcomes for psychological coherence, religious homophobia, of which most participants expressed acute awareness, can impede a positive self-conception, resulting in decreased self-esteem. It is possible that among BMGM, threats to these principles, in particular, induce the negative emotions of guilt and shame.

In our research, BMGM have typically manifested intrapsychic strategies for attenuating the emotions of shame and guilt. In order to cope with these negative emotions, Imran seems to engage in the intrapsychic strategy of denial by simply suppressing knowledge of any dissonance between his religious and sexual identities. This can be achieved by attenuating Muslim identity in those social contexts in which gay identity may plausibly be regarded as 'core' and in which conflict between Muslim and gay identities may occur. Imran describes a social context in which his gay identity seems to be 'core', namely during romantic/sexual encounters with other gay men. The psychological practice of attenuating one identity in favour of another in particular social contexts has been referred to as compartmentalisation (Breakwell 1986). Although there is evidence of compartmentalisation among some BMGM (see also Yip 2004a), religious identity tends to be construed as pervasively 'core' (and sometimes as a 'meaning system') by many Muslims (Norcliffe 1999). This may decrease the efficacy of compartmentalisation as a coping strategy, as suggested by Imran's acknowledgement that compartmentalising Muslim and gay identities 'sounds really bad'. The coping strategy itself seems to be potentially threatening (Jaspal and Cinnirella 2010). Nonetheless, the strategies of denial and compartmentalisation, though potentially problematic given the 'core-ness' of Muslim identity, may be construed as necessary when thinking about the perceived incompatibilities of Islam and homosexuality.

Ingroup Norms, God's Norms and the Experience of Fear

Religious homophobia encourages the perception that Islam and homosexuality are incompatible and irreconcilable, while cultural homophobia indicates the incongruity of membership in the ethno-cultural group and self-identification as gay. In both cases, homosexuality is represented as a contravention of ingroup norms. This can have adverse outcomes for the belonging principle of identity, since being gay can itself hinder acceptance and inclusion in the religious and ethno-cultural groups. In our studies, BMGM have consistently manifested fear as an emotional response to public exposure of their non-normative ingroup behaviour:

> I live my life in fear, I'm scared, 'cause if my brothers found out, they'd kill me, serious ... trust me, you don't know them. The topic has come up and they threatened me ... My mum caught me watching a gay channel and like they don't chat about it no more but my brothers threatened to kill me ... It's 'cause it's wrong in Islam so it's like saying 'I ain't a Muslim' and it's like an honour thing too really like how would my family show their face in the community or go to Pakistan? (Omar)

Omar construes homosexuality as contravening the norms of both his religious and ethno-cultural ingroups. According to Omar, homosexuality is stigmatised because, on the one hand, homosexual practice equates to apostasy, that is, the rejection of Islamic faith (Rahman 2006). This simile suggests that being gay radically impedes a sense of belonging within the religious group. On the other hand, it jeopardises the ethno-cultural construct of honour. Non-conforming individuals may be seen as threatening the integrity and social position of the family as a whole (Yip 2004b). Indeed, Omar suggests that a gay son could involuntarily cause ostracisation of the entire family. Given that religion and ethnic culture can constitute primary sources of belonging among many BMGM (Jaspal in press), this principle may be particularly vulnerable to threat.

The perception that homosexuality constitutes a severe contravention of norms associated with these group memberships can accentuate fear of sexual disclosure. More generally, religious and cultural homophobia renders 'coming out' a threatening prospect. Omar was not alone in highlighting the possibility that 'coming out' as gay could result in psychological and even physical abuse from members of his family (Jaspal and Siraj 2011). He was convinced that his brothers might kill him for being gay, a hypothesis which was grounded in previous experiences of discussing homosexuality with his family. Given the enforced 'silencing' of homosexuality within the family and cultural ingroup more generally (Murray 1997), fear of exposure and open allusion to his gay identity continue to induce fear.

Religious homophobia encourages the notion that God will punish individuals who engage in homosexual acts (Duran 1993). Like 'coming out', this too can induce the emotional experience of fear, as outlined in participants' reported experiences in 'gay space':

> I sat down [in Heaven, a gay nightclub in London] and I kept thinking the roof
> was going to fall in any minute and that we'd all die there and then ... I knew
> it was a bad place with bad stuff going on around me. I hated that night. (Aziz)

The perceived sinfulness of homosexuality from the perspective of his religious identity seems to induce a fear of divine retribution (Jaspal and Cinnirella 2010). Aziz regards his participation in 'gay space' as a contravention of the social and sexual norms associated with his religious identity. This engenders fear of an act of God to 'punish' him and other gay men in what is described as 'a bad place'. Given the centrality of Muslim identity, Aziz employs this identity as the interpretive lens through which gay space is evaluated: 'I knew it was a bad place with bad stuff going on around me'. More generally, the potent emotional experience seems to induce a highly negative evaluation of gay space. This is unfortunate, given that gay space may constitute an important means of constructing 'social capital' among BMGM (Jaspal and Cinnirella 2012). In some contexts, the emotion of fear may be alleviated by ensuring that one's sexual identity remain secret and *socially* denied, that is, 'silenced' as exemplified above. However, the fear manifested in Aziz's account seems to be less easily escapable. The fearful stimulus is located at the intrapsychic, rather than social, level. He perceives his behaviour to be in conflict with the norms established by God's word, which therefore concerns his *spiritual* relationship with God, rather than a social relationship with the institution of religion (e.g. Berger et al. 2008). Thus, 'social' denial of one's gay identity is unlikely to constitute an adequate coping strategy.

In our work, this 'intrapsychic' fear of contravening God's norms seems to impede the development of personal and sexual relationships with other men:

> Mohammed: I don't meet that many guys off the internet but if I do I just regret it afterwards ... 'cause it's like, it feels wrong afterwards and I just get scared, like really worried about what's going to happen to me ... I can lie to my parents and that but God knows what I'm doing.

> Interviewer: Has it affected your relationships with, I mean, how has it sort of affected your relationships with guys?

> Mohammed: Just silly things like after being with a guy, he's like talking to me and I'm coming out with my own thing like making some excuse to leave or just telling him I don't do it much. It's stupid I know but the strong feelings just take, come over me.

Mohammed notes that, although he can conceal his homosexuality and feign heterosexuality in social contexts, 'God knows what I'm doing'. It seems that the emotional experience of fear can seriously impede the development of positive interpersonal relations, and thereby jeopardise sufficient levels of 'social capital' among some BMGM (Yip 2004a).

Fear of contravening God's norms, as described in relation to the accounts of Aziz and Mohammed, may be alleviated by engaging in the strategy of repentance:

> I just go home and I pray, after each one [sexual encounter], each sin, I pray to God and ask for forgiveness ... then I feel better because God is a just god. We call him *Rahim* [merciful]. (Jamal)

The construal of homosexuality as 'wrongdoing' implicitly constructs repentance as the 'appropriate' response. Participants who manifested the emotion of fear when thinking about the implications of being gay for their Muslim identity reported praying and seeking God's forgiveness. This may be regarded in terms of an accessible and effective strategy for alleviating this negative emotional experience, since Islam constructs *Allah* (God) as merciful towards Muslims (Gould 2008). In fact, Jamal cites one of the ninety-nine Arabic names for God, *Rahim*, which means 'merciful'.

More generally, both socially and psychologically induced fear (i.e. fear of ostracisation and fear of God, respectively) could be alleviated by hoping for an eventual change in sexual orientation:

> It scares me when I think about my future, everything about being gay is scary ... I'll be alone at the end, I know it ... Being gay goes against Islam completely, I know, but I try to resist it. I want to get married some day. (Mohsan)

For many BMGM, the prospect of marriage can constitute a short-term strategy for coping with their fear-inducing gay identity, since psychologically it provides scope for change which can remove the source of fear (Jaspal in press). Crucially, this change is consistent with and respectful of the social and sexual norms associated with their religious and cultural ingroups, which are generally averse to homosexuality.

Managing Interpersonal Relations and Anger

BMGM generally attach phenomenological importance to the family (Yip 2004b). The family and religious and ethno-cultural ingroups are said to constitute primary sources of belonging, acceptance and inclusion among BMGM (Jaspal in press). However, disclosure of one's gay identity may disrupt the much-valued interpersonal relations within the family unit. This may be attributed to both religious and cultural forms of homophobia, since homosexuality is socially represented as contradicting the Islamic worldview as well as key norms and customs associated with the ethno-cultural ingroup (e.g. [arranged] marriage).

As outlined in relation to Mohsan's account, some BMGM outline their wish that they were not gay and their desire to change their sexual orientation. This change may be regarded as essential for safeguarding relationships with significant others (Jaspal in press). However, the perceived inability to change can induce feelings of helplessness and anger:

> I just hate feeling so damn helpless, I can't change who I am, I know it's the way I was made but who gets that? Innit? My parents aren't gonna get that when they kill me and that's true my family will kill me ... I feel so fucking mad at myself, like I'm going crazy or something ... I've smashed my hand in the mirror 'cause I get so angry at myself and my life. Why me? ... Why can't I change this? (Ahmad)

Given that Ahmed fears that the disclosure of his sexual identity could result in physical abuse or a threat to his life, his inability to change his sexual orientation is all the more threatening for identity. It does not allow him to shape his future 'self' in accordance with his constructed 'ideal' self. Given that human beings usually have agency in constructing identity (Breakwell 1986), this inability can inhibit feelings of control and competence, which are essential for the self-efficacy principle. This seems to induce the emotional experience of anger, as he feels 'mad' at himself and as if he is 'going crazy or something'. This may constitute a response to this helplessness and perceived inadequacy. Like several other participants, Ahmad described behaviours typically associated with the intense emotion of anger, such as damaging objects and self-harm (Deffenbacher 1992). It is noteworthy that decreased self-efficacy is not universally threatening for BMGM, some of whom actively attenuate self-efficacy in order to reconcile their religious and sexual identities (Jaspal and Cinnirella 2010). However, in this context, the aim seems to be self-construal as a 'good' Muslim, rather than a gay Muslim, as the two identities are perceived as incompatible. Therefore, the self-efficacy principle (that is, the *competence* to change) is salient.

Our research has typically focused upon BMGM who have not publicly disclosed their sexual identities. However, those individuals who did contemplate 'coming out' tended to express anger at members of their family and their ethno-religious ingroup due to perceived homophobia:

> My family is ruining my life and it pisses me off ... I'm gay and it's the way I am, yeah, it's the way I was born and I can't change it ... My folks don't accept it and they have all these stupid expectations. Drives me mad ... It just shakes me up totally and I feel like shouting it out so loud so everyone can hear it but once it's said, it's said and there's no turning back, no more pretending ... denying what's in your face. (Sajid)

Participants who have developed interpersonal relations with other gay men in 'gay space' seem to manifest greater willingness to explore these alternative social networks in order to derive feelings of belonging. As these alternative networks are explored, BMGM may manifest feelings of anger towards individuals within their ethno-religious circles, given that homophobic discrimination is increasingly perceived to be unreasonable. Crucially, BMGM may feel more empowered to criticise the social groups with which they identify, because they have access to *alternative* social groups (Breakwell 1986).

Participants may begin to regard homophobic discrimination from these groups as unjust as they construe their gay identity in essentialist terms as a primordial, innate sexual orientation. The essentialisation of gay identity seems to induce the perception that their parents' expectations regarding sexuality and social life are 'stupid' and unreasonable. While 'closeted' BMGM who do not yet entertain the prospect of 'coming out' may themselves manifest the view that being gay is 'wrong', 'sinful' or a 'chosen' lifestyle (Jaspal and Cinnirella 2010), those who do contemplate 'coming out' seem to perceive this view as a clear example of (unreasonable) homophobic discrimination. Crucially, at this stage of sexual identity development, the perceived unjustness of homophobic discrimination may cause the emotional experience of anger. Sajid states that it 'drives me mad' and 'shakes me up', inducing the desire to 'shout it out loud'. In this case, it seems that public disclosure of his gay identity is construed as a means of alleviating the negative emotion of anger. However, there is a simultaneous recognition that this strategy could have potentially irreversible consequences; it could undermine the *social* denial strategy, which is said to constitute an important social response to homosexuality within ethno-religious circles (Murray 1997).

Concluding Remarks

This chapter makes a novel contribution to research and theory by exploring how homophobic ideas and representations associated with religious and cultural group memberships may affect the self-concept and induce particular emotional experiences among BMGM. Furthermore, there was a concern with the socio-psychological strategies manifested in order to cope with such religious and cultural homophobia.

Throughout our studies, participants have consistently manifested the negative emotions of shame, guilt, fear and anger when reflecting upon being Muslim and gay. These emotional experiences can plausibly be attributed to BMGM's awareness of and exposure to both religious and cultural homophobia. As an example of such homophobia, in January 2012 Derby Crown Court found five Muslim men of Pakistani descent guilty of distributing in the City of Derby anti-gay leaflets calling for the death penalty for gay people (Britten 2012). This incident and reported experiences of discrimination, both implicit and explicit, within religious and cultural settings collectively exemplify the religious and cultural homophobia surrounding many BMGM (Siraj 2009). This can induce both identity threat and negative emotions.

There is some evidence that identity threat can result in negative emotional experiences (Murtagh 2009). Our work has shown that BMGM can perceive dissonance between their religious and sexual identities, which can result in threats to the psychological coherence principle of identity (Jaspal and Cinnirella 2010). Moreover, the general 'core-ness' of Muslim identity *vis-à-vis* gay identity can mean that the negative evaluations of homosexuality according to Islamic ideology are accepted and internalised by BMGM themselves. This may result in threats to self-esteem. This affects the intrapsychic level of cognition, since it shapes how BMGM think about being Muslim and gay, as well as the social level in that it may influence how BMGM relate to others. Challenges to the intrapsychic level seem to be associated with the emotional experience of guilt, since there is an intrapsychic perception of wrongdoing which primarily affects one's private conscience (Tangney and Fischer 1995). Accordingly, participants in our studies have typically reported engaging in intrapsychic strategies for coping, such as denial and compartmentalisation. However, the efficacy of these strategies is limited given that they are transient and themselves fraught with secondary difficulties. For instance, the 'core' position of Muslim identity within the self-concept among many BMGM can undermine the viability of the compartmentalisation strategy (Jaspal and Cinnirella 2010). Possibly due to the imminent failure of deflection strategies, such as denial and compartmentalisation, in the long run, some participants worryingly reported engaging in self-flagellation and self-harm in order to alleviate their feelings of guilt. Conversely, the perception of *social* wrongdoing seems to be associated with the emotional experience of shame due to the perceived possibility of self-exposure to disapproval from others (Broucek 1991). Accordingly, BMGM may engage in interpersonal strategies for coping with negative emotions with social antecedents, such as self-withdrawal from religious circles and general self-isolation.

BMGM may express the belief that their gay identity contravenes key norms and values associated with their religious and cultural group memberships. The anticipated threat to acceptance and inclusion (belonging) in these social groups, which essentially denigrate, undermine and stigmatise gay identity, can induce fear. Furthermore, participants reported their intense fear that their gay identity could be disclosed to members of their religious and cultural ingroups, possibly resulting in ostracisation from the groups or even physical harm (Jaspal and Siraj 2011). In this case, fear has a social antecedent and thus *social* denial (or 'silencing') of gay identity may be regarded as an appropriate coping strategy. Moreover, the emotion of fear could ensue from participants' perception that their gay identity constitutes a violation of God's norms, potentially resulting in divine punishment. This fear is described as intrapsychic given that it ensues from the individual's spiritual connection with an omnipresent God. Accordingly, social denial seems to constitute a less effective strategy for coping, given that participants feel that they cannot conceal their gay identity from God, as they habitually do from members of their religious and cultural ingroups. Consequently, BMGM may engage in divine repentance in order to alleviate their fear.

Due to religious and cultural homophobia, the assimilation and accommodation of a gay identity in the self-concept can be challenging and conducive to negative emotions. Throughout our studies, we have observed that in order to cope, BMGM may construct their gay identity in terms of a mutable behaviour, rather than as an identity, which is consistent with their hope that they may be able to 'become straight'. This may alleviate negative emotions. However, for BMGM who are hopeful that they will be able to change their sexual orientation, the perceived inability (in real terms) to become straight can itself induce anger. This seems to be associated with perceived helplessness, inadequacy of the self and decreased self-efficacy, particularly as individuals recognise that they may have less control and competence over their sexual orientation than originally believed (c.f. Jaspal and Cinnirella 2010). However, there is some evidence that BMGM may begin to contemplate 'coming out' as gay in the long run, provided that they have developed alternative social networks which can provide feelings of acceptance, inclusion and belonging. The perception of an alternative source of belonging can facilitate the assimilation and accommodation of their gay identity within the self-concept, encouraging BMGM to abandon the hope of changing their sexual orientation. At this stage of sexual identity development, some BMGM may begin to manifest anger towards members of their religious and cultural ingroups, as their respective positions on homosexuality are increasingly regarded as being unreasonable and even 'stupid'.

This chapter echoes an over-arching theme in the literature that being Muslim and gay can induce 'hyper-threats' to identity. This may be attributed to the prevalence of religious and cultural homophobia in the lives of many BMGM. This can adversely affect (i) psychological coherence in relation to Muslim and gay identities; (ii) self-esteem due to the negative evaluation of gay identity in religious and cultural group contexts; and (iii) belonging in the family unit and in the religious and cultural groups. Threats to these principles are associated with the negative emotional experiences of guilt, shame, fear and anger. BMGM may cope with identity threat and the experience of negative emotions by deploying intrapsychic and social coping strategies, including denial, divine repentance, self-harm, social 'silencing' of gay identity and self-isolation. Our research suggests that, in addition to identity threat, emotionality constitutes an important dimension of the interface of religion and sexuality. It is hoped that this chapter will stimulate further investigation from additional theoretical, methodological and disciplinary approaches.

Acknowledgements

The author would like to thank the editors for their detailed and constructive comments on an earlier version of this chapter.

References

Averill, J.R. 1982. *Anger and Aggression: An Essay on Emotion*. New York: Springer.

Berger, P., Davie, G. and Fokas, E. 2008. *Religious America, Secular Europe? A Theme and Variations*. Aldershot: Ashgate.

Bhugra, D. 1997. Coming Out by South Asian gay men in the United Kingdom. *Archives of Sexual Behavior* 26(5): 547–57.

Braun, V. and Clarke, V. 2006. Using Thematic Analysis in Psychology. *Qualitative Research in Psychology* 3(2): 77–101.

Breakwell, G.M. 1986. *Coping with Threatened Identities*. London: Methuen.

Broucek, F.J. 1991. *Shame and the Self*. New York: Guilford.

Britten, N. 2012. Muslims Posted 'Nasty and Frightening' Anti-gay Leaflets Demanding Homosexuals 'Turn or Burn'. *The Daily Telegraph*, 18th January 2012. Available at: http://www.telegraph.co.uk/news/uknews/law-and-order/9004998/Muslims-posted-nasty-and-frightening-anti-gay-leaflets-demanding-homosexuals-turn-or-burn.html [accessed 18 January 2012].

Carlson, D. 1997. Gayness, Multicultural Education and Community, in *Beyond Black and White*, edited by M. Seller and L. Weis. Albany, NY: State University of New York Press.

Deffenbacher, J.L. 1992. Trait Anger: Theory, Findings and Implications, in *Advanced Personality Assessment*, edited by C.D. Spielberger and J.N. Butcher. Hillsdale, New Jersey: Lawrence Erlbaum, 177–201.

Duran, K. 1993. Homosexuality in Islam, in *Homosexuality and World Religions*, edited by A. Swidler. Harrisburg, PA: Trinity Press, 181–98.

Eatough, V. and Smith, J. 2006. 'I was like a wild wild person': Understanding Feelings of Anger Using Interpretative Phenomenological Analysis. *British Journal of Psychology* 97(4): 483–98.

Gould, M. 2008. Islam, the Law and the Sovereignity of God. *Policy Review* 149. Available at http://www.hoover.org/publications/policy-review/article/5693 [accessed 22 January 2012].

Haqqani, H. 2004. The Role of Islam in Pakistan's Future. *The Washington Quarterly* 28(1): 85–96.

Harré, R. and Finlay-Jones, R. 1986. Emotion Talk across Time, in *The Social Construction of Emotions*, edited by R. Harré. Oxford, England: Basil Blackwell, 220–33.

Heaphy, B., Weeks, J. and Donovan, C. 1998. That's Like my Life: Researching Stories of Non-heterosexual Relationships. *Sexualities* 1(4): 453–70.

Herek, G.M. 2004. Beyond "Homophobia": Thinking about Sexual Prejudice and Stigma in the Twenty-first century. *Sexuality Research and Social Policy* 1(2): 6–24.

Hudson, W.W. and Ricketts, W.A. 1980. A Strategy for the Measurement of Homophobia. *Journal of Homosexuality* 5(4): 357–72.

Jamal, A. 2001. The Story of Lot and the Quran's Perceptions of the Morality of Same-sex Sexuality. *Journal of Homosexuality* 41(1): 1–88.

Jaspal, R. in press. 'I never faced up to being gay': Sexual, Religious and Ethnic Identities among British Indian and British Pakistani Gay Men. *Culture, Health and Sexuality*.

Jaspal, R. and Cinnirella, M. 2010. Coping with Potentially Incompatible Identities: Accounts of Religious, Ethnic and Sexual Identities from British Pakistani Men who Identify as Muslim and Gay. *British Journal of Social Psychology* 49(4): 849–70.

Jaspal, R. and Cinnirella, M. 2012. Identity Processes, Threat and Interpersonal Relations: Accounts from British Muslim Gay Men. *Journal of Homosexuality* 59(2): 215–40.

Jaspal, R. and Siraj, A. 2011. Perceptions of 'Coming Out' among British Muslim Gay Men. *Psychology and Sexuality* 2(3): 183–97.

Khan, B. 1997. Not-so-gay Life in Pakistan in the 1980s and 1990s, in *Islamic Homosexualites: Culture, History, and Literature*, edited by S.O. Murray and W. Roscoe. New York: New York University Press, 275–96.

Kugle, S.S.A. 2010. *Homosexuality in Islam: Critical Reflection on Gay, Lesbian, and Transgender Muslims*. Oxford: Oneworld Publications.

Markus, H.R. and Kitayama, S. 1991. Culture and the Self: Implications for Cognition, Emotion, and Motivation. *Psychological Review* 98(2): 224–53.

Massey, D. 2002. Emotion and the History of Human Society. *American Sociological Review* 64: 1–29.

Modood, T., Berthoud, R., Lakey, J., Nazroo, J., Smith, P., Virdee, S. and Beishon, S. 1997. *Ethnic Minorities in Britain: Diversity and Disadvantage*. London: Policy Studies Institute.

Murray, S.O. 1997. The Will Not to Know: Islamic Accommodations of Male Homosexuality, in *Islamic Homosexualities*, edited by S.O. Murray and W. Roscoe. New York: New York University Press, 14–54.

Murtagh, N. 2009. Voluntary Occupation Change: A Social Psychological Investigation of Experience and Process. Unpublished PhD thesis, University of Surrey, UK.

Norcliffe, D. 1999. *Islam: Faith and Practice*. Brighton: Sussex Academic Press.

Öhman, A. 2000. Fear and Anxiety: Evolutionary, Cognitive, and Clinical Perspectives, in *Handbook of Emotions*, edited by M. Lewis and J.M. Haviland-Jones. New York: The Guilford Press, 573–93.

Parrot, W.R. 2004. The Nature of Emotion, in *Emotion and Motivation*, edited by M.B. Brewer and M. Hewstone. Malden, MA: Blackwell, 5–20.

Rahman, S.A. 2006. *The Punishment of Apostasy in Islam*. Lahore: The Other Press Sdn Bhd.

Rosario, M., Schrimshaw, E.W., Hunter, J. and Gwadz, M. 2002. Gay-related Stress and Emotional Distress among Gay, Lesbian and Bisexual Youths: A Longitudinal Examination. *Journal of Consulting and Clinical Psychology* 70(4): 967–75.

Shaw, A. 2000. *Kinship and Continuity: Pakistani Families in Britain*. Amsterdam: Harwood Academic Publishers.

Siraj, A. 2009. The Construction of the Homosexual "Other" by British Muslim Heterosexuals. *Contemporary Islam* 3(1): 41–57.

Tangney, J.P. and Fischer, K.W. (eds). 1995. *Self-conscious Emotions: The Psychology of Shame, Guilt, Embarrassment and Pride*. New York: Guilford Press.

Turner J.H. 1999. Toward a General Sociological Theory of Emotions. *Journal for the Theory of Social Behaviour* 29(2): 133–62.

Weinberg, G. 1972. *Society and the Healthy Homosexual*. Garden City, New York: Doubleday.

Yip, A.K.T. 2004a. Embracing Allah and Sexuality? South Asian Non-heterosexual Muslims in Britain, in *South Asians in the Diaspora*, edited by K.A. Jacobsen and P.P. Kumar. Leiden: Brill, 294–310.

Yip, A.K.T. 2004b. Negotiating Space with Family and Kin in Identity Construction: The Narratives of British Non-heterosexual Muslims. *The Sociological Review* 52(3): 336–50.

Yip, A.K.T. 2005. Queering Religious Texts: An Exploration of British Non-heterosexual Christians' and Muslims' Strategy of Constructing Sexuality-affirming Hermeneutics. *Sociology* 39(1): 47–65.

Yip, A.K.T. 2007. Sexual Orientation Discrimination in Religious Communities, in *Sexual Orientation Discrimination: An International Perspective*, edited by M.V.L. Badgett and J. Frank. London: Routledge, 209–44.

Yip, A.K.T. 2012. Homophobia and Ethnic Minority Communities in the United Kingdom, in *Confronting Homophobia in Europe*, edited by L. Trappolin, A. Gasparini and R. Wintemute. Oxford: Hart Publishing, 107–30.

Chapter 6

Sexualities in the Migration Context: Religious Influences on Views on Abortion and Homosexuality

Bernadetta Siara

Introduction

This chapter focuses on sexualities in the context of migration and more specifically on how religion influences views on abortion and homosexuality in the migration space in complex ways. It uses a case study of Poles who migrated to the United Kingdom (UK) after the 2004 European Union (EU) Enlargement.[1] Generally not much research has been done in this respect, especially that of a qualitative nature. Moreover, such an area of interest has not received attention amongst migration researchers, especially those focusing on the recent migration of Poles to the UK. It is interesting to look at these dimensions of sexuality within the migration space, especially in the context of the large number of Poles migrating to the UK within the last few years[2] as these two aspects of sexuality have been actively present in public debates since the democratisation process started in Poland in 1989. This is mostly connected to the Catholic Church's mainstream position and its influence on societal discourses and policies related to sexuality. Both abortion and homosexuality are seen as problematic within the conservative sexuality discourse constructed not only by the Catholic Church's representatives, but also the right-wing politicians and therefore both of these dimensions of sexuality are strongly contested.

Moreover, such focus is important because the new migration environment appears to differ from the one left behind in Poland; that is to say, the position of religious institutions in the UK and their impact on the construction of discourses and policies related to sexuality is different from the position of the Catholic

1   I would like to acknowledge the financial support I received from the Economic and Social Research Council (grant no ES/F008139) in the UK which enabled me to carry out this research for which I am grateful. I would also like to thank all my research participants for all the extremely interesting conversations. This chapter could not have been written without their contribution.

2   It is estimated that over 680,000 Poles have arrived in the UK since the 2004 EU Enlargement (Home Office 2009).

Church in Poland. Moreover, the political scene is also structured differently, with a wider prevalence of conservatives in Poland than in the UK, which results in differences in policy-making surrounding sexuality. Furthermore, not only do laws surrounding abortion (abortion is allowed by law in the UK and is provided by the state health service, whilst it is generally prohibited in Poland with some exceptions, which are discussed later in the chapter) and homosexuality (for example the opportunity to register a civil partnership or adopt a child by same-sex couples which exists in the UK is not possible in Poland) vary in the two contexts, but also societal attitudes to abortion and homosexuality appear to be different. Therefore, it is interesting to look at Poles' views on abortion and homosexuality and see what discourses are constructed in the migration context and how religion influences these constructions. This chapter, therefore, looks at Poles who have arrived in the UK since May 2004 and their attitudes, both to abortion and homosexuality and their perceptions of the differences in approaches to these dimensions of sexuality between Poland and the UK. One more issue requires explanation: why bring analyses of views on abortion and homosexuality together in the same chapter? Firstly, both abortion and homosexuality have been strongly contested aspects of sexuality in Poland. Secondly, they confront the same conservative assumption made in the Catholic Church's discourse, which sees sexuality as being directly connected to reproduction. Abortion contradicts such a view, as it prevents reproduction, and homosexuality is proscribed by the Catholic Church as not leading to reproduction (Sierzpowska-Ketner 2004).

In this chapter sexuality is seen as being socially and culturally constructed, as well as being invoked through the cultural values, beliefs, institutions, and ideologies of the society (Jackson 1996). Sexuality includes a variety of heterosexual, gay and lesbian sexualities (Jackson and Scott 2010). It is recognised that whilst heterosexuality is often constructed as normative, especially in its conservative version (where sexual activity is solely connected to reproduction), homosexuality is marginalised with regards to heterosexuality, and within a heteronormative context it is constructed only within the parameters of sexual activity (Kurpios 2004, Pickett 2011). This research has been guided by feminist theory, which was helpful in recognising various forms of heterosexuality (Jackson and Scott 2010, Seidman 2005) including conservative forms, which connect sexual activity solely with reproduction and therefore disapprove of some anti-reproductive practices such as abortion and more liberal forms of heterosexuality which allow a woman the right to bodily control and to decide about reproductive side of her life herself (Richardson 2000). Queer theory has also been used when looking at the potential to deconstruct heteronormativity, i.e. whilst heterosexuality is constructed as 'normal' and is privileged and institutionalised as such, other sexualities are seen as 'marginal' (Jackson 2005, Richardson 2006). Both theories were helpful in looking at how sexuality is re-constructed in the migration space.

Migration is a 'sexualised' phenomenon and there is a need to recognise the importance of sexuality within the migration context (Siara 2011) as migration has the potential to influence sexualities (Gonzalez-Lopez 2005, Naples and

Vidal-Ortiz 2009). Furthermore, sexual ideologies and beliefs originating in various geographical contexts influence constructions of sexualities in the migration space (Hirsch 2003). These constructions and reconstructions are influenced by state institutions and policies, religious institutions, cultural influences and the general dynamics of migration; they are multiple and shifting (Cantu 2009, Naples and Vidal-Ortiz 2009). Therefore, there is a need to examine the role of sexual ideologies (including views on abortion and homosexuality) and potential changes to them within the migration process (similarly, as suggested by Mahler and Pessar (2006), with regard to gender ideologies). In terms of its structure, this chapter firstly outlines abortion and homosexuality contexts in both Poland and the UK. This is followed by information about methodology and research participants. The subsequent sections set out the research participants' views on abortion and homosexuality and afterwards these views are evaluated within a wider context. This is then followed by some concluding remarks. The following section provides some contextual information about abortion and homosexuality in Poland and the UK.

Sexualities – Setting the Context

Abortion Contexts in Poland and the United Kingdom

Poland has one of the most restrictive anti-abortion laws in Europe (Sierzpowska-Ketner 2004, Wlodarczyk 2010). During communist times, abortion was legalised, but with the growing influence of the Catholic Church on public policies in post-communist times (Hryciuk 2005), a new law banning abortion, called the *Law on Family Planning, Legal Protection of the Foetus, and the Conditions of Permissibility of Abortion* was introduced in 1993. This law prohibited abortion for social and economic reasons (Kramer 2007) and according to this law, abortion can be carried out only in cases when 'the woman's life or health is threatened, when the pregnancy is the result of crime or in cases of severe foetal abnormality' (Nowicka 1996: 24). The proposal for a national referendum on abortion law, before the law was voted in, was rejected (Sierzpowska-Ketner 2004).

Poles, however, appeared to be divided on the issue of abortion. Saxonberg (2000), who analysed the survey data collected around the time when the new anti-abortion law was introduced, found that 55% of the survey respondents supported abortion in the case when the family could not afford any more children and a further 37% supported it in the case when a woman did not want to continue with the pregnancy for personal reasons. In the poll carried out in Poland in 2010 (CBOS 2010a), 50% of respondents were against the right to abortion whilst 45% were pro-abortion, but within this group the majority would impose some conditions before the abortion could be carried out. Within the latter group a quarter of respondents agreed that abortion should be allowed on financial grounds and a further one-fifth claimed that it should be allowed in a situation when a woman does not want to carry on with the pregnancy. Those who were against the right to abortion were predominantly religious (attending church services at least once a week), whilst those who were pro-abortion usually did not attend church services. This poll shows that despite the strict anti-abortion law in place just around half of Poles support it.

The situation around the issue of abortion is different in the UK. The *Abortion Act* allowing the artificial termination of a pregnancy was legalised in 1967 (Pilcher 1999). The implementation of this law led to abortion becoming available on the National Health Service free of charge in 1974. Through this law women obtained the freedom to decide on the reproductive side of their lives themselves, even if the process of organising abortion in the UK seems to be complex and requires counselling before it can be carried out.

Homosexuality Contexts in Poland and the United Kingdom

Graff (2006) alleged that, since circa 2002, there has been a marked shift in the discourse surrounding homosexuality in Poland from a status of 'invisibility' to becoming a 'hotly' debated topic in a political arena. Homosexuality was never prohibited by law in Poland (Sierzpowska-Ketner 2004); however, sexual minorities were suppressed politically during the communist era and by the right-wing politicians in post-communist times. The Catholic Church in Poland has also played an important role in the construction of a negative discourse around homosexuality in Poland (Zielinska 2005), as it does not approve of homosexuality (Sierzpowska-Ketner 2004). In legal terms, although a bill on the registration of same-sex civil partnerships was prepared and submitted by the Left to the Senate in 2003, it has not been passed yet. In a poll carried out in Poland in 2010 (CBOS 2010b), nearly two-thirds of Poles asserted that homosexuality should be tolerated. Those who were tolerant were more likely to be younger and not to attend church services. The report suggested that tolerance levels have increased over the years. However, same-sex relationships were more likely to be accepted by younger Poles, who rarely or not at all took part in church services. This shows that despite the prevalence of conservative and negative discourses around homosexuality in Poland, some people are tolerant of homosexuality and same-sex family practices.

The situation around homosexuality in the UK appears to be different. Whilst lesbian sexuality was never criminalised, gay sexuality was decriminalised in the UK in 1967 (Hall 2000). Attitudes amongst the population in the UK appear to be quite tolerant. According to a poll carried out in 2006, around 80% of the respondents had positive attitudes to homosexuality, including religious participants (Cowan 2007). Moreover, the *Civil Partnership Act* allowing same-sex couples to form a civil partnership was implemented in 2004. This was supported by over two thirds of respondents in the above-mentioned poll[3]

---

3   The sample included just over 2,000 respondents.

(Cowan 2007). Having looked at the context of religion, abortion and homosexuality in this section, I shall proceed to presenting methods and basic information about research participants in the following section.

Methods and Research Participants

The research described in this chapter employed a qualitative approach and in-depth interviews were utilised as a data collection method. The choice of a qualitative approach is very important as it provides an opportunity for people to describe their attitudes to sexuality in their own words. At the same time, research using surveys as a technique, such as the one used in polls carried out in Poland by CBOS and mentioned in the previous section, used pre-determined responses to find out about the attitudes to sexuality and it risked providing quite limited findings.

The research involved interviews with 63 Poles and they were carried out between 2009 and 2010 in three different cities in the UK, namely London, Edinburgh and Cardiff. The majority of participants were between 25 and 34 years old, and this is in line with statistics on migrants from Poland provided by the Home Office (2009). The participants came from various parts of Poland, including cities, towns and the countryside. The majority spoke very good or fairly good English. Just over half had higher education, around a quarter had secondary level education and around one-sixth had vocational level education. Some were students undertaking bachelor or master level courses. Research participants had various occupations. Many experienced de-skilling in the sense that despite having high-level skills they worked in positions requiring lower-level skills. Whilst most of the men had skilled and semi-skilled jobs, most of the women worked in basic jobs.

All the interviews were carried out in Polish, enabling access to all Poles, including those who did not speak English; it also reduced the potential confusion over meaning which is involved in translation. This study involved a relatively small number of individuals, which limits the applicability of the findings. However, it was exploratory and was helpful in identifying a variety of factors that could be useful for a better understanding of constructions around sexuality amongst Poles in the UK and the influence of religion in these constructions. In the following section participants' views on abortion and homosexuality are discussed.

Abortion – A Public Issue and a Woman's Personal Matter

Participants expressed a variety of views on abortion. A quarter of them was against abortion, these being mostly men and unsurprisingly most were religious. A few said they were undecided; they were also mostly men and they were not religious. Just under half of participants would support abortion. Out of those some argued that abortion should be generally allowed. Both women and men expressed this view and interestingly most were religious. Others perceived abortion as a matter for an individual choice. More women than men expressed this view and a half were religious. This non-religious man said:

> It is a normal thing. Not everybody wants to. Not everybody has a financial, health or family situation, there are different reasons [...] abortion should be allowed and this is everybody's private issue. The Church's role should be to educate people that it is not a sin as such but that one should not do it and it should explain it rather than try to prohibit it. Prohibition won't help.

This shows that the role of the Catholic Church may be seen in terms of providing moral guidance but not in prohibiting anti-reproduction practices as there is a need to consider the variety of life situations women find themselves in and in such a way abortion is seen as woman's private matter. Other participants would specifically leave the choice down to a woman to decide whether to undergo abortion. Both women and men expressed this and a few were religious:

> In relation to abortion I think that a woman should decide whether she wants to undergo abortion or not. (man, religious)

> I appreciate the fact that women have a choice here and nobody decides apart from them. (woman, not religious)

This shows that the decision-making power should not only be left to a woman, but that a woman has a right to abortion and the existence of such a right in the UK was seen positively.

Some participants said that religion was very important to them and they attended church services regularly, but they did not agree with everything the Church imposed, namely, prohibition of abortion and contraception. One religious man asserted:

> For me it is sickening to discuss these issues, because it is everybody's individual matter and a concern for everybody's own conscience. Nobody will reach an agreement here, nobody, whether on the religious or state level.

This confirms that abortion may be seen as an individual matter even by religious people and neither the religious institutions nor the state through its laws should have the power to decide on behalf of an individual. Moreover, another religious female participant also suggested that non-religious people's lives should be free from religious influences:

> [The law] that impacts on the lives of people who are not believers should be completely secular [...] abortion should be a matter of choice for people. I am for free choice. I think that you cannot convince somebody that this is a human being with a soul if they don't believe it. If somebody is not a believer, they have a right not to be and nobody can try to convince them that their baby has a soul and call them a murderer [...] if somebody decides that a baby is not a baby for them but a set of cells that doesn't have a soul, they have this right to decide for themselves.

Moreover, this presents a view that religion should not influence the laws of the secular state as is the case with the prohibition of abortion in Poland and people should have a right to make decisions regarding their own lives themselves.

When comparing these findings against the CBOS (2010a) poll quoted earlier, a more complex picture of attitudes to abortion can be seen in research discussed here, where some religious participants were against abortion whilst other religious participants supported it. This shows that religious participants have complex attitudes towards abortion and do not necessarily follow religious rhetoric on this matter. Moreover, women seemed to be more likely than men to support abortion, perceiving it as an individual matter or a woman's choice. This could be down to the fact that abortion is likely to affect women's lives to a greater extent than men's. Such a claim was made by some authors in Poland, who suggested that it seems to be women rather than men who think that abortion is a personal matter for every woman and her basic right (Duch-Krzystoszek 1995, Fuszara 2001). Some religious women and men preferred the approach to abortion in the UK to the one in Poland. Some argued that women have a choice and undergo a consultation with a psychologist before they decide to have an abortion done. This woman said:

> Yes, I am for abortion. I like it that it is legally allowed here [...] but it is not simply that they carry out abortion. You go to the doctor and have a consultation with a psychologist. They want to find out why you want to do it. It is controlled. In Poland there are so many illegal abortions. It is a nightmare. How many women cannot have children afterwards because some kind of poorly skilled doctor used the wrong equipment.

This illustrates that the access to abortion is appreciated and considered to be a better solution than undergoing abortion in the 'underground'[4] in Poland in cases of unplanned pregnancy and that such back-street abortions are associated with health risks.

---

4 Following the introduction of the law banning abortion, the number of abortions carried out in Poland decreased immensely but only officially, as abortions would continue to be carried out in private practices i.e. 'in the underground' (Pascall and Kwak 2005).

However, some participants perceived access to abortion in the UK negatively, as allowing people to be 'irresponsible' for their actions; mostly religious women and men expressed this view. Some argued that abortion in the UK was used as a means of contraception *post-factum* and in their view it was 'overused'. Both women and men expressed this view, but only some were religious. This woman said:

> Abortion is considered to be a method of contraception here ... it is a bit complicated because Catholicism in Poland protects people from behaving like that [...] many women undergo abortions because it is easily accessible and legal. I wouldn't want women in Poland to recognize abortion as a contraceptive method because it is not [...] but I am for people having choice [...] I don't know what limitations could be introduced.

This demonstrates that the 'unlimited' access and use of abortion in the UK can be seen negatively and can be regarded as leading to 'abuse' and such a stance provokes calls for greater control over access to abortion. Some participants, both non-religious women and men, said that there should be limits on the number of abortions a woman can undergo within her life course. This man proposed:

> I am not pro ... I mean I am, but not in a sense of how it is done here ... I've talked to English women and some have had six, seven abortions. It becomes a habit. It becomes automatic. I can go and have an abortion. It is sick. There should be a limit, something should be done about it. It shouldn't be as if there is no tomorrow.

This confirms that whilst abortion can be approved of in principle, it is not simply seen as a way of ending an unplanned or unwanted pregnancy, but as a 'special' event in a woman's life and in the views of some there should be some limitations in terms of access to it.

To summarise, the analysis showed a complexity of attitudes towards abortion amongst participants. Some participants disapproved of abortion; however, some religious participants claimed that the attitude to abortion is an individual matter and only a woman can decide about it. Some also were critical of the Church's views on abortion and the imposition of these views on the whole population in Poland. Some said they preferred the approach to abortion in the UK and this shows that a different policy approach in relation to abortion in the country of migration may be considered positively and may be a platform for critical assessment of the approach to abortion in the country of origin. However, some participants saw the approach to abortion in the UK negatively, as allowing 'irresponsibility' or they saw the procedure being treated as a contraceptive method *post-factum* and said they would impose limits on the number of abortions a woman can undergo. This also confirms that a different approach to abortion in a country of migration may be assessed using the discourses from the country of origin.

Homosexuality – Between the 'Closet' and Life 'Out in the Open'

The majority of participants talked about differences in attitudes to homosexuality in the two countries and only some openly talked about their personal views on homosexuality. Several participants expressed negative views towards homosexuality; they were, unsurprisingly, mostly religious men. A few said they were tolerant of homosexuality and they were, interestingly, mostly religious women. This shows that women seemed to be more tolerant towards homosexuality than men even if most were religious. The gender dimension of attitudes to homosexuality is very interesting and Johansson (2007) has already argued that some men may condemn male homosexuality in a process of reconfirming their own heterosexual identity where gay men may be seen by them as a 'threat' to their heterosexual masculinity (Falomir-Pichastor et al. 2010). Other authors in Poland have also claimed that heterosexual men are more negative towards homosexuality and more homophobic than heterosexual women (Arcimowicz 1997, Sroda 2006).

It was suggested that homosexuality is closely associated with sexual activities and such a perception was criticised. This religious woman proposed that same-sex relationships should be looked at from the point of view of feelings and emotions and not through sexual activities:

> I think that we look at homosexual people only through the prism of sex, through the prism of bed and we see homosexual people like that. It is very wrong. With this couple it was a great love […] I used to hear from them: 'you know, how great it would be if we could hold hands when we were going shopping'. You start visualising such examples and they make you think that it is a feeling. These two people loved each other very much […] and we should look at it like that, from this human aspect; from this human, emotional, spiritual aspect, how these emotions are created and not on whether he is passive or active – this is nonsense and this is how Polish society sees it.

Such narratives show a need to perceive homosexuality in wider than sexual terms. The fact that such a view was expressed by a woman could also be down to the fact that women's interest in the emotional content of relationships may account for their greater acceptance of and sympathy for homosexuality and same-sex relationships (Treas 2004).

Moreover, a few participants said they were supportive of the registration of civil partnerships. Although both religious women and men said this, women appeared to be more approving of registration of civil partnerships than men. This woman said:

> Marriages … if they love each other […] they can be a family in the eyes of the state.

At the same time, some other men were against it and this demonstrates that the acceptance of same-sex relationships is also to some extent a gendered phenomenon.

Some participants said they had changed their views on homosexuality following their migration to the UK. Interestingly, it was mostly the religious women and men who claimed that their attitudes to homosexuality had become more tolerant in the migration context, once they had got to know a lesbian or a gay in the UK. As migration can present lesbians and gays with a chance to 'come out' and live their lives openly (Kosnick 2010), some participants alleged that migration to the UK provided them with the first ever opportunity to get to know a lesbian or gay man personally. This woman said:

> We were shocked, as we must have encountered gay people in Poland, but they were not able to talk about it.

Acquaintance with a lesbian or gay in some cases subsequently allowed a formation of friendship and resulted in a change in attitudes to homosexuality. This religious man said that he used to be against homosexuality, but through talks with his gay friends he became more open and understanding:

> Homosexuality has always existed, but it is not accepted by some religions […] I have superb gay friends […] I talked a lot to them about it because I used to be against such relationships, but I changed my mind […] through talks with them. Conversation is the basis for everything, it is a basis for one's way of thinking, a way of seeing.

This proves that attitudes can change following more intimate acquaintance with a lesbian or gay person, which provides a platform for an understanding of other sexualities than one's own and associated relationship practices.

Participants also compared attitudes towards homosexuality in Poland and the UK and in the latter case they were perceived as being more positive and tolerant and participants appreciated such an approach. Both women and men expressed this view and only some were religious. Some non-religious female and male participants connected intolerant attitudes to homosexuality in Poland with the influence of Catholicism. This man said:

> I think it comes out of the fact that we are a religious nation and many people blindly look to the Bible. I think it comes out of that. That is why we don't tolerate gays.

Such a statement suggests that some Poles may follow religious rhetoric in their attitudes to homosexuality. However, at the same time some religious female participants have asserted that they liked the fact that homosexuality is tolerated in the UK and hoped that tolerance of homosexuality will increase in Poland. This woman claimed:

> Near my house there is a pub where lesbian and gay people come and we sometimes go there with my friends and I think there is a greater tolerance here with regards to these issues. This is how I would like it to be in Poland. Maybe one day ...

This statement illustrates hope for change attitudes to sexuality in Poland in near future. Some participants argued that whilst lesbian and gay people can live their lives 'out in the open' in the UK, where sexual diversity is respected and that this was appreciated, at the same time they have to live in 'hiding' in Poland, because homosexuality is not approved of. This non-religious man said:

> I like it that they can be honest with themselves and with the whole world; two women can walk and hold hands, they can give each other a kiss or go to a party and nobody will be violent towards them. I like it.

This demonstrates that the tolerance and acceptance of homosexuality in the country of migration may be highly appreciated. However, at the same time, some non-religious female and male participants claimed that attitudes to homosexuality in Poland were already undergoing a process of change and becoming more tolerant. This could be associated with a public debate on homosexuality that has been ongoing in Poland during the last decade and a greater number of 'comings-out' by lesbians and gays in Poland. Interestingly, the rise in tolerance has been observed in Poland over the course of the last few years. In a poll carried out in 2010 in Poland nearly two-thirds of respondents alleged that homosexuality has to be tolerated; and the tolerance level has increased since 2008 by 11% (CBOS 2010). Other authors have also argued that as knowledge about homosexuality is increasing in Poland, attitudes to homosexuality are also undergoing a change and becoming more tolerant (Beisert 2006, Kochanowski 2008).

When these findings are compared to the CBOS (2010b) poll quoted earlier, the poll shows more positive findings, actually more tolerant attitudes than the research discussed here, where the attitudes to homosexuality were exemplified more in participants' comparisons of approaches to sexuality in Poland and the UK. In the latter they were seen as more tolerant and participants considered it positively. This is a very important dimension, especially when more tolerant attitudes in the country of migration are appreciated and used as a point of reference when criticising negative attitudes in the country of origin as they may lead to attitudes becoming more tolerant in the longer term.

To summarise, the analysis showed the complexity of attitudes towards homosexuality amongst participants. Some of them, mostly men and not religious, ascribed intolerant attitudes to homosexuality in Poland to Catholic Church's approach to the issue. Some participants liked the tolerance towards homosexuality in the UK and hoped that there would be a widespread tolerance towards homosexuality one day in Poland. Some participants also recognised that these attitudes were already undergoing a process of change in Poland. Both religious women and men liked the ability of lesbian and gay people to live their lives 'out in the open' in the UK. Some had also become more tolerant and understanding through talks with lesbian and gay people. Others had also had an opportunity to get to know personally a lesbian or gay person once in the UK. Having presented the findings, in the following section I will proceed to evaluating them in more general terms.

Complexity around Religious Influences in Views on Abortion and Homosexuality

The analysis showed the existence of various views on abortion and homosexuality amongst religious and non-religious research participants. Some participants supported abortion, including religious participants and some were critical of the Church's views on abortion. The Catholic Church in Poland has been intensively trying to influence policy and public discourse on this matter and it was successful in having the anti-abortion law voted in 1993. However, as both the CBOS 2010 poll quoted earlier and the research findings showed, some Poles support abortion. The views expressed ranged between the public dimension of abortion, as dictated by the Catholic Church's rhetoric and the policy of banning abortion in Poland and the private dimension of a woman's life. It was often stressed that abortion should be seen as a personal matter and should not be decided publicly, and a woman's right to decide about her life was also underlined. Such views are more in line with a feminist approach which privileges women's rights to have control and self-determination over their bodies in relation to reproduction over a state's use of religious rhetoric to decide the issue on women's behalf through the implementation of an anti-abortion law (Petchesky 2000, Plummer 2006).

Some participants talked about their tolerance towards homosexuality and these included some of the religious ones. Some, regardless of their gender or the extent of their religiosity, said they liked the overall tolerance of lesbians and gays and the possibility for them to live their lives out of the 'closet' in the UK and expressed the hope that tolerance towards lesbians and gays in Poland will become greater and more widespread. Some also saw intolerance towards homosexuality in Poland as being rooted in negative discourses constructed by the Catholic Church. However, the findings showed that despite the Catholic Church's attempts to influence the discourses on sexuality negatively, some participants had tolerant views on these issues. The expressed opinions varied between a lack of tolerance and homosexuality being tolerated and accepted. The differences were seen between the private 'closeted' lives (mostly associated with Poland) and the publicly recognised homosexuality (mostly associated with the UK), where lesbians and gays can live their lives openly in public through 'coming out' (Plummer 2006, Richardson 2000). However, such public recognition of homosexuality stretches beyond the right to express one's sexual identity publicly to a full sexual diversity and sexual equality in the public space (Richardson 2000). Moreover, migration might have to a great extent influenced Poles' views, as it offered an opportunity to observe different approaches to abortion as well as more openness and tolerance towards homosexuality in the UK and some participants referred to this during interviews.

Considering the religious influences on the participants' views on abortion and homosexuality, it needs to be added that although the image of Poles as Catholics (Demerath 2000) is well established, it may not actually have strong grounding in social reality. Although, the great majority of respondents (96%) in polls[5] carried out in Poland in recent years (CBOS 2006, CBOS 2009a, CBOS 2009b) described themselves as Catholic, only two-thirds said they believed in God or considered themselves religious. This shows as Demerath (2000) argued that Catholicism can be seen more as a cultural rather than a religious identity, which is to suggest that many Poles may describe themselves as Catholic because they may associate Catholicism with Polishness, but neither they are religiously active, nor do they practise Catholicism in their everyday lives. Findings from this research may be additionally disruptive of such an image, as some participants were critical of the Catholic Church's influence on discourses around sexuality.

Secondly, the analysis showed that although some participants considered themselves to be religious, they appeared to be selectively picking and choosing elements from the Catholic dogma which they found acceptable (Marianski 2001, Zak-Bucholc 2005, Zarzycka 2009) and rejected some of the Church's teachings on sexuality (Borowik 2002). At the same time, they incorporated non-Catholic, more tolerant and democratic elements into their worldviews and merged them with Catholic ones: some were supportive of access to abortion and tolerant of homosexuality, despite the Church's approach to these issues and the attempts to influence their views (Mizielinska 2006). The analysis showed that although the Catholic Church in Poland has been trying to influence discourses on sexuality, some research participants seemed to have more liberal views on sexuality even if they described themselves as religious.

This chapter has shown how religion influences views on abortion and homosexuality in complex ways. In wider terms this research shows that one can be religious and equality minded in relation to sexuality, allowing people to make their own choices with regards to their sexuality and also be tolerant of 'other' than heterosexual ways of loving, living and relationship-making. Therefore, I argue that unproblematic connections between being religious and being conservative, unsupportive of access to abortion or intolerant towards homosexuality should not easily be made, although I recognise that research using surveys as a method have often concluded with such findings (for example, Adamczyk and Pitt 2009, Ford et al. 2009).

---

5   The majority of them use samples of around 1,000 participants.

Concluding Remarks

This chapter has looked at the religious influences on views on abortion and homosexuality among Poles who migrated to the UK in the post 2004 EU Enlargement period. No attention has been paid to such intersections between religion and sexuality within the migration space before, especially in this context and this chapter aims to fill this gap. The analysis presented here shows that conservative religious ideologies only have some impact on people's views on sexuality. It also points out that some peoples' views may undergo a change in the migration space, in which one can encounter a variety of sexual ideologies and practices. The analysis shows that women are especially prone to such changes, but this process of change also involves men. This chapter shows that despite the Church's efforts to try to influence discourses on sexuality, only some Poles subscribe to conservative discourses, whilst many hold liberal views.

In the light of the research findings, the process of recognition of various forms of sexuality, including heterosexuality (in its liberal form, which allows women to make their own choices with regards to their heterosexuality and the reproductive side of their lives) and homosexuality (as being an equally accepted form of sexuality) has been ongoing among Poles. This is in accordance with democratic principles of human rights, tolerance and equality for all, including heterosexual women and both lesbian women and gay men. Saxonberg (2000) has already reported that the Poles appear to be less conservative on moral and sexual issues than the Catholic Church or the right-wing politicians in Poland. Additionally, the migration of Poles to the UK might have influenced this process to some extent. The chapter shows that religion influences sexuality in complex ways. I think that in wider terms this presents a huge potential for change in discourses around sexuality prevailing amongst those people coming from more conservative religious environments and creating greater tolerance, which is more in line with democratic ideals of equality.

References

Adamczyk, A. and Pitt, C. 2009. Shaping Attitudes about Homosexuality: The Role of Religion and Cultural Context. *Social Science Research* 38: 338–51.

Arcimowicz, K. 1997. Wspolczesni mezczyzni. Przeglad problematyki badan (Contemporary Men. The Review of Research Problems), in *Od kobiety do mezczyzn i z powrotem. Rozwazania o plci w kulturze* (*From a Woman to a Man and Back. Deliberations about Gender in Culture*), edited by J. Brach-Czaina. Bialystok: Transhumana, 145–64.

Beisert, M. 2006. Przemiany wspolczesnej rodziny polskiej (Changes in the Contemporary Polish Family), in *Seksualnosc czlowieka: Obszary zainteresowan teoretykow i praktykow* (*Human Sexuality: The Areas of Interest for Theorists and Practictioners*) *Rocznik Lubuski* 32(2) (*Lubuski Annals* 32(2)), edited by Z. Idebski. Zielona Gora, 19–38.

Borowik, I. 2002. The Roman Catholic Church in the Process of Democratic Transformation: The Case of Poland. *Social Compass* 49(2): 239–52.

Cantu, L. (edited by Naples, N. and Vidal-Ortiz, S.) 2009. *The Sexuality of Migration. Border Crossings and Mexican Immigrant Men.* New York: New York University Press.

CBOS (*Centrum Badania Opinii Spolecznej* – Public Opinion Research Centre). 2010a. *Opinie na temat dopuszczalnosci aborcji* (*Opinions on Allowing Abortion*). Warszawa (Warsaw): CBOS.

CBOS (*Centrum Badania Opinii Spolecznej* – Public Opinion Research Centre). 2010b. *Postawy wobec gejow i lesbijek* (*Attitudes towards Gays and Lesbians*). Warszawa (Warsaw): CBOS.

CBOS (*Centrum Badania Opinii Spolecznej* – Public Opinion Research Centre). 2009a. *Wiara i religijnosc Polakow dwadziescia lat po rozpoczeciu przemian ustrojowych* (*Faith and Religion of Poles Twenty Years After the Beginning of Transformation*). Warszawa (Warsaw): CBOS.

CBOS (*Centrum Badania Opinii Spolecznej* – Public Opinion Research Centre). 2009b. *Dwie dekady przemian religijnosci w Polsce* (*Two Decades of Religious Change in Poland*). Warszawa (Warsaw): CBOS.

CBOS (*Centrum Badania Opinii Spolecznej* – Public Opinion Research Centre). 2006. *Znaczenie religii w zyciu Polakow. Komunikat z badan* (*The Importance of Religion in the Lives of Poles. Research Report*). Warszawa (Warsaw): CBOS.

Cowan, K. 2007. *Living Together: British Attitudes to Lesbian and Gay People.* Stonewall.

Demerath, N.J. 2000. The Rise of 'Cultural Religion' in European Christianity: Learning from Poland, Northern Ireland, and Sweden. *Social Compass* 47(1): 127–39.

Duch-Krzystoszek, D. 1995. Malzenstwo, seks, prokreacja (Marriage, Sex and Reproduction), in *Co to znaczy byc kobieta w Polsce* (*What Does It Mean to Be a Woman in Poland?*), edited by Titkow, A. and Domanski, H. Warszawa: PAN, 175–88.

Falomir-Pichastor, J.M., Martinez, C. and Paterna, C. 2010. Gender-roles Attitudes, Perceived Similarity and Sexual Prejudice against Gay Men. *The Spanish Journal of Psychology* 13(2): 841–8.

Ford, T., Brignall, T., Vanvaley, T. and Macaluso, M. 2009. The Unmaking of Prejudice: How Christian Beliefs Relate to Attitudes Toward Homosexuals. *Journal for the Scientific Study of Religion* 48(1): 146–60.

Fuszara, M. 2001. Nowy kontrakt plci (New gender contract), in *Kobiety w Polsce na przelomie wiekow. Nowy kontrakt plci? (Women in Poland at the Turn of the Century. New Gender Contract?)*, edited by Fuszara, M. Warszawa: ISP, 7–12.

Gonzalez-Lopez, G. 2005. *Erotic Journeys: Mexican Immigrants and their Sex Lives*. London: University of California Press.

Graff, A. 2006. We Are (Not All) Homophobes: A Report from Poland. *Feminist Studies* 32(2): 434–49.

Hall, L.A. 2000. Sexuality, in *Women in Twentieth-Century Britain*, edited by I. Zweiniger-Bargielowska. London: Longman, 51–68.

Hirsch, J. 2003. *A Courtship after Marriage: Sexuality and Love in Mexican Transnational Families*. London: University of California Press.

Home Office. 2009. *Accession Monitoring Report May 2004 – December 2008. A Joint Online Report Between the Border and Immigration Agency, the Department of Work and Pensions, the HM Revenue & Customs and Communities and Local Government*. London: Home Office. (Online) Available at http://www.ukba.homeoffice.gov.uk/sitecontent/documents/aboutus/reports/accession_monitoring_report [accessed 1 April 2009].

Hryciuk, R. 2005. *Political Motherhood in Poland: The Emergence of Single Mothers for the Alimony Fund Movement*. (Online) Available at http://www.globaljusticecenter.org/papers2005/hryciuk.htm [accessed 25 June 2008].

Jackson, S. 2005. Sexuality, Heterosexuality, and Gender Hierarchy: Getting Our Priorities Sraight, in *Thinking Straight: The Power, the Promise, and the Paradox of Heterosexuality*, edited by C. Ingraham. Abingdon: Routledge, 11–38.

Jackson, S. 1996. The Social Construction of Female Sexuality, in *Feminism and Sexuality: A Reader*, edited by S. Jackson, and S. Scott. Edinburgh, Edinburgh University Press, 62–73.

Jackson, S. and Scott, S. 2010. *Theorizing Sexuality*. Maidenhead: Open University Press.

Johansson, T. 2007. *The Transformation of Sexuality. Gender and Identity in Contemporary Youth Culture*. Aldershot: Ashgate.

Kochanowski, J. 2008. Seksualnosc w dyskursie politycznym (Sexuality in a Political Discourse), in *Seksualnosc czlowieka i obyczaje a polityka (Human Sexuality, Customs and Politics)*, edited by Szyszkowska, M. Warszawa: tCHu, 20–52.

Kosnick, K. 2010. Sexuality and Migration Studies: The Invisible, the Oxymoronic and Heteronormative Othering, in *Framing Intersectionality. Debates on a Multi-faceted Concept in Gender Studies*, edited by Lutz, H., Herrera Vivar, M. and Supik, L. Aldershot: Ashgate, 121–37.

Kramer, A.M. 2007. The Abortion Debate in Poland; Opinion Polls, Ideological Politics, Citizenship, and the Erasure of Gender as a Category of Analysis, in *Living Gender after Communism*, edited by J.E. Johnson and J.C. Robinson. Bloomington: Indiana University Press, 63–79.

Kurpios, P. 2004. *Inaczej* mowiac o plci (Talking about Gender in *Other* Way), in *Zrozumiec plec: studia interdyscyplinarne (Understanding Gender: Interdisciplinary Studies)*, edited by A. Kuczynska and E. Dzikowska. Wroclaw: Wydawnictwo Uniwersytetu Wroclawskiego, 471–8.

Mahler, S., Pessar, P. 2006. Gender Matters: Ethnographers bring Gender from the Periphery toward the Core of Migration Studies. *International Migration Review* 40: 27–63.

Mariański, J. 2001. Religijność w zmieniającym się społeczeństwie polskim (Religiousness in a Changing Polish Society), in *Katolicyzm polski na przełomie wieków. Mity, rzeczywistość, obawy, nadzieje (Polish Catholicism at the Turn of the Centuries: Myths, Reality, Fears and Hopes)*, edited by J. Baniak. Poznan: UAM, 203–26.

Mizielinska, J. 2006. *Plec, Cialo, Seksualnosc: od Feminizmu do Teorii Queer (Gender, Body, Sexuality: From Feminism to Queer Theory)*. Krakow: Universitas.

Naples, N. and Vidal-Ortiz, S. 2009. Editors' Introduction, in *The Sexuality of Migration. Border Crossings and Mexican Immigrant Men*. L. Cantu, (edited by N. Naples and S. Vidal-Ortiz). New York: New York University Press, 1–20.

Nowicka, W. 1996. Roman Catholic Fundamentalism against Women's Reproductive Rights in Poland. *Reproductive Health Matters* 8: 21–9.

Pascall, G. and Kwak, A. 2005. *Gender Regimes in Transition in Central and Eastern Europe*. Bristol: Policy Press.

Petchesky, R. 2000. Rights and Needs: Rethinking the Connections in Debates Over Reproductive and Sexual Rights. *Health and Human Rights* 4(2): 17–29.

Pickett, B. 2011. Homosexuality, in *The Stanford Encyclopaedia of Philosophy*, edited by E. Zalta. (Online) Available at http://plato.stanford.edu/archives/spr2011/entries/homosexuality [accessed 2 April 2011].

Pilcher, J. 1999. *Women in Contemporary Britain. An Introduction.* London: Routledge.

Plummer, K. 2006. Rights Work: Constructing Lesbian, Gay and Sexual Rights in Late Modern Times, in *Rights: Sociological Perspectives*, edited by L. Morris. London: Routledge, 152–67.

Richardson, D. 2006. Bordering Theory, in *Intersections Between Feminist and Queer Theory*, edited by D. Richardson, J. McLaughlin and M. Casey. Basingstoke: Palgrave Macmillan, 19–37.

Richardson, D. 2000. *Rethinking Sexuality*. London: Sage.

Saxonberg, S. 2000. Polish Women in the Mid 1990s. *Czech Sociological Review* 8(2): 244–53.

Seidman, S. 2005. From the Polluted Homosexual to the Normal Gay: Changing Patterns of Sexual Regulation in America, in *Thinking Straight: The Power, the Promise, and the Paradox of Heterosexuality*, edited by C. Ingraham. Abingdon: Routledge, 39–62.

Siara, B. 2011. Body, Gender and Sexuality in Recent Migration of Poles to the United Kingdom. *Migration Studies: Polish Review* 1, 111–28.

Sierzpowska-Ketner, A. 2004. Poland, in *The Continuum Complete International Encyclopaedia of Sexuality*, edited by R. Francoeur and N. Noonan. London: Continuum, 846–55.

Sroda, M. 2006. Postawy wobec seksu (Attitudes towards Sex), in *Seksualnosc czlowieka: Obszary zainteresowan teoretykow i praktykow* (*Human Sexuality: The Areas of Interest for Theorists and Practictioners*) *Rocznik Lubuski* 32(2) (*Lubuski Annals* 32(2)), edited by Z. Idebski. Zielona Gora, 61–74.

Szukalski, P. 2005. Zachowanie homoseksualne i postawy wobec homoseksualizmu. Analiza porownanwcza Polski i krajow wysoko rozwinietych (Homosexual Behaviour and Attitudes towards Homosexuality. Comparative Analysis of Poland and Well-developed Nations), in *Homoseksualizm: perspektywa interdyscyplinarna* (*Homosexuality: An Interdisciplinary Perspective*), edited by K. Slany, B. Kowalska and M. Smietana. Krakow: Nomos, 75–103.

Treas, J. 2004. Sex and Family: Changes and Challenges, in *The Blackwell Companion to the Sociology of Families*, edited by J. Scott, J. Treas and M. Richards. Oxford: Blackwell Publishing, 397–415.

Wlodarczyk, J. 2010. Manufacturing Hysteria: The Import of U.S. Abortion Rhetorics to Poland. *Genders* (52). (Online) Available at: http://www.genders. org/g52/g52_wlodarczyk.html [accessed 25 March 2011]

Zak-Bucholc, J. 2005 Synkretyzacja wiary katolickiej w okresie przemian w Polsce (Syncretism of the Catholic Faith during Transformation Period in Poland). *Racjonalista*. (Online) Available at http://www.racjonalista.pl/kk.php/s,4184 [accessed 25 March 2011].

Zarzycka, B. 2009. Tradition or Charisma – Religiosity in Poland, in *What the World Believes: Analysis and Commentary on the Religion Monitor 2008*, edited by B. Stiftung. Verlag: Gütersloh, 201–22.

Zielinska, I. 2005. *Who Is Afraid of Sexual Minorities? Homosexuals, Moral Panic and the Exercise of Social Control*. Occasional Paper. Centre for Criminological Research, University of Sheffield.

Chapter 7

Queering Conversion: Exploring New Theoretical Pathways to Understand Religious Conversion in a Western Context[1]

Wim Peumans and Christiane Stallaert

Introduction

On a cold afternoon in October 2010 I arrive at the Rainbow house, which is located in the gay area of Brussels: the Saint-James quarter. Trendy clothing stores, hipster cafés, gay bars and a sauna, specialist shops, a launderette and an organic hairdresser are amongst some of the establishments present. I am here to interview and attend a lecture of the American gay imam and convert Daayiee Abdullah. The door of the Rainbow house is closed and can only be opened from the inside. A note attached to it says: 'We are closed (but still open-minded)'. As I enter, a white young man has just finished an interview with a Belgian TV-station. He gets up from his seat and takes off his kufi. He has a beard and his trousers are just lifted above his ankles. I greet him first, and then he introduces himself: 'Hi, I am Wout'.

Within studies on conversion, sexuality appears to have been relatively less scrutinised in comparison to, for example, gender, which has gained (slightly) more attention (Brereton 1991, Mossière 2009, van Nieuwkerk 2006). The literature which has focused on conversion and sexuality, treats the topic of 'ex-gays', i.e. (often deeply religious) gay men and women who 'convert' to heterosexuality. Although such conversions are not conversions to another religion, they are nearly always linked to the practices of religious organisations (Erzen 2006, Wolkomir 2006).

---

1   The authors would like to thank Wout for sharing his story and reading the first draft. Also we would like to express our gratitude to the participants of the conference *'The Politics of Living Religion/Spirituality and Gender/Sexuality in Everyday Context'* for their insightful comments on the first draft of this chapter; and Andrew Yip and Peter Nynäs, for organizing such a thought-provoking conference.

However, the silence on sexuality within conversion studies is not exceptional, as the religious/spiritual convictions of gays and lesbians appear to have been frequently left out of the picture. LGBTIs are generally thought to be secular or even atheist. According to Alison (2007) and Wilcox (2007) this is a consequence of a general indifference – or even antagonism – of LGBTI scholars towards religion. As a result, studies on homosexuality and religion are scarce and mostly Christian based (Wilcox 2003, Yip 1997).[2]

The objective of this chapter is theoretical and aims to introduce a queer perspective into the study of conversion to Islam and the study of conversion in a Western context in general. We do not wish to make an ethnographical mapping of queer conversion to Islam in a Western context, but focus on one particular narrative and draw more general conclusions from this story in order to queer the study of conversion.

To some, defining queer theory goes against what queer theory stands for. However, for clarity's sake, we see queer as a verb, a set of actions. It is a deconstructive practice, from which one tries to 'challenge the normative – even if that normative is itself' (Goldman 1996: 170). In Giffney's words, queer theory has 'a power to challenge (if not always subvert) all norms relating to desirous identity ... [and] its task lies in visibilising, critiquing, and separating the normal (statistically determined) from the normative (morally determined)' (Giffney 2004: 75). In other words, our project of queering the study of conversion wants to make explicit how knowledge is situated within a social and cultural context and within hegemonic epistemologies, and how our own positionality informs our ways of looking at the world (Haraway 1988). It is an invitation to make explicit both the structures which underline our thinking and our own positionality. Taking this as a point of departure will allow us to consider how a focus on sexuality might open new perspectives for the study of conversion, which has been previously left unexplored.

Let us give an outline of what we will discuss in this chapter. After a short discussion of the notion of conversion, we will sketch out the Belgian context, hereby presenting a concise recent historical overview of the presence of Islam in Belgium and the contemporary status of religion/spirituality in Belgian society. In seeing conversion as a passage, we will then give an analytical description of the narrative of our selected participant, Wout, a white Belgian gay man who converted to Islam, both taking into account the micro and macro context of

---

2   Within the growing – but still surprisingly low number of studies on LGBTIQ Muslims in the West, we have found one example of a white gay man converting to Islam (Abraham 2009). Khan mentions LGBTQ Muslims who ethnically/racially identify as white or African-American, but it is unclear who/how many of them are converts (Khan 2010). The stress in these studies is not on the conversion process *per se*, as will be the case in this chapter.

this process.[3] We look at why Wout specifically converted to Islam and how his sexuality plays throughout this process, hereby we argue it takes up a central role. According to Allievi (1999), studies on conversion often conflate the question of how people convert with the cause of conversion. It would be more correct to answer the question as to why people convert to a specific religion instead of the general question why someone converts (Allievi 1999). Also, we put a particular emphasis on the role of embodied religious practices in the process of conversion. Although religious scholars have taken the body into consideration in recent years (Some notable works include Asad 1993, Coakley 1998, Isherwood and Stuart 1998, Mahmood 2001a), conversion studies have been quite slow to catch up (see, for example, Sachs Norris 2003, Winchester 2008). This is possibly due to existing epistemological and cultural assumptions. To paraphrase Grosz, the body has been a conceptual blind spot in Western thought, especially since Enlightenment and its Cartesian dualism, as it is part of 'a binary opposition between mind and body, reason and passion, thought and extension, psychology and biology', in which the former term in each couplet is being hierarchically ranked higher (Grosz 1994: 3).

Throughout the narrative we will consider how Wout's sexuality plays throughout this trajectory of religious change, with specific attention towards: (1) what place sexuality takes up within the newly constituted religious self; (2) how he manages and negotiates his sexuality and religion in different social relationships and contexts. Lastly then we will try to draw more general conclusions from this case study and look how such narratives allow us to introduce a queer perspective into the study of conversion.

This chapter draws its data from a four-year Ph.D. research project on the intersections of transgressive sexualities, Islam and migration in Flanders and Brussels (Belgium), which is financed by the Research Foundation Flanders and which started in October 2010.[4] Data gathering for this chapter is based on ethnographic fieldwork.

Religious Conversion: What's in a Name?

In spite of the existing literature on conversion, there is no common definition of this phenomenon. Because the study of conversion has long been within the research domain of Christian scholars, the concept was often interpreted along Christian lines. Arabic however has no equivalent of the verb 'to convert'. There is only the idea of 'becoming Muslim', for which the verb '*aslama*' ('to submit') is used (Dutton 1999). While in the contemporary Christian tradition, conversion

---

3   Race is not much used in Belgian academic and public discourse, but I have used it because it is commonplace in Anglosaxon literature. Ethnically speaking, Wout is part of the ethnic majority group.

4   FWO-Vlaanderen (Research Foundation Flanders): project number 1126711N.

is viewed first and almost as an act of faith, an affiliation to a 'community of believers', affiliation to Islam is primarily defined as the adhesion to a community of people who submit to the Islamic law and custom (Leman et al. 2010a, 2010b).

In this chapter we see converting, this turning from and to (Rambo 1995), as a form of 'passage', a concept coined by Victor Turner (1975) – which was brought in connection to conversion by authors such as Birman (1996) and Frigerio (2007) – who prefer the use of 'passages' (*'passagens'*) to denote spaces of interlocution – and Austin-Broos (2003) . We will expand on what is understood by conversion as passage throughout the text.

Aslama as Passage:
A Narrative of Conversion to Islam in Pluri-religious Belgium

In this paragraph we will sketch out the Belgian context, hereby presenting the contemporary status of religion/spirituality in Belgian society and a concise recent historical overview of the presence of Islam in Belgium.

In the post 9/11-world the contemporary social and religious landscape of Belgium, like other North Western European countries, may be characterised as pluri-ethnic and pluri-religious. Although the role of religion/spirituality has not decreased, it has nevertheless become a private, voluntary and individual matter. However, we feel the 'supermarket'-model of religions does not apply completely to Belgium as we learned, for example from previous research on conversion, that converting from one tradition (Christianity) or secularism/atheism to another spiritual/religious tradition is not an easy task, which is often met with negative reactions from kinship and other networks of the converts (Stallaert 2004).

Religion/spirituality still plays a prominent role in political and media debates and social life in general. The issue of conversion takes up a contentious place in these debates. One example is the Flemish TV-program *In God's Name* [*In God's Naam*] which focused on the current state of affairs of religion in Belgium, with an emphasis on conversion by Belgians. Its portrayal of Flemish (young) women who had converted to Islam caused a controversy because of the strict religiosity and pious role these women had taken up, which according to the journalist who made the programme, was 'completely at odds with our values' (2010).

In the 1960s Belgium signed bilateral agreements with Morocco, Turkey, Algeria and Tunisia to control and sustain the flow of 'guest workers' (*'gastarbeiders'* or *'travailleurs étrangers'*) from these countries, who were primarily recruited for the mining industry. During this period family grouping and reunification was made possible. This marked the public presence of Islam in Belgium, which was recognised as an official religion in 1974. In the 1980s the government realised the guest workers were not temporary, but permanent sojourners, which lead to political debate over naturalisation, citizenship and integration policies. Furthermore, the presence of Islam in the public sphere was consolidated through, for example, the opening of Muslim stores, wearing the *hijab* in schools and on the street, and the creation of Qur'an schools (De Raedt 2004, Manco 2000). According to the latest estimates, 6% of the Belgian population is Muslim (Hertogen 2008). While during the guest worker period, Muslims were seen as 'docile, courageous and honest' (De Raedt 2004: 19), over the past three decades they have become the scapegoats of Belgian social problems. From the end of the 1980s, xenophobic and anti-immigration sentiments were, at least in Flanders, incited by the extreme right party, *Vlaams Belang*, which made immigration and Islam key issues in their electoral campaigns and party programme. Since 9/11, Islamophobic feelings and attitudes are on the increase and in international research on negative attitudes towards ethnic minorities, Flanders is ranked amongst the highest (Billiet and Swyngedouw 2009).

'It Fanned a Kind of Fire in Me': The Quest for a New Religious Self

We will now turn to the narrative of our selected participant, Wout, a Belgian gay convert to Islam. We will first look at what drew him to Islam specifically, with particular attention to how his sexuality played throughout this process.

Wout, 34 years old, grew up and lives in a rural area of Flanders. Nominally raised as a Christian, Jesus Christ was a source of inspiration to his mother – who had a strong consciousness of God and tried to bring Christian charity into daily practice through involvement in all kinds of social activities. As a child he had a 'naive, yet intense relationship with God, who of course was a mix between Superman and St. Nicholas' (Wout). Around the age of 14, he discovered science had a more consistent and rational way of explaining the world. At this age he also joined the extreme-left political movement Workers' Party of Belgium ('Partij van de Arbeid'), where he learnt that religion was 'the opium of the people'. Everything concerning religion was old-fashioned superstition and one day mankind would be freed from this nonsense. Around the age of 20, while studying social work in the city of Antwerp, he started to notice how a purely rationalist and scientistic worldview which reduces everything to science had its shortcomings in giving meaning to life. Having read Christian mystical works on negative theology and also Wittgenstein, an analytical philosopher who was preoccupied with arranging facts, while at the same time realising the limits of this activity, knowing there is something beyond factuality, he started searching and reading. From the start of Wout's quest towards a new religious being-in-the-world, the way homosexuality was viewed upon in each spiritual tradition was a breaking point: 'I could never join a Wahhabi movement or a Westboro Baptist Church in the United States, because homophobia is such a structural part of their creed that it becomes impossible [for me to join]' (Wout). His sexuality then became a central part of his conversion.

During the next five years he went to several religious and humanist movements and read the works of different spiritual traditions. Although there was a core in all these texts which appealed to him, he was not entirely convinced:

> Either it was a very complicated theology, which did not fit together well
> and which did not appeal to someone like me who has a reasonably scientific
> outlook, like for example the Christian theology of the Holy Trinity and all the
> dogmas. Or either it was a way of practice: the Japanese Zen Buddhism has a
> certain aesthetics, but at the same time for us non-Japanese this aesthetics is very
> hard to feel and assess. (Wout)

Here we see how conversion as a cultural passage is at first experimental, a
process of trial and error in finding the right path (Austin-Broos 2003). It is a
process of negotiating a place in the world, a search for new forms of subjectivity,
involving a crossing of religious, cultural and ethnic borders. Also we may see
a first reason why he chose Islam: according to Wout it has an uncomplicated
theology which is easy to comprehend and which has a few relatively simple
ways of looking at the world. But at the same time it is felt by Wout as the most
rational of all religions and hence Islam forms no rupture but a passage between
his former secular and current religious self.

When people adopt a new set of beliefs and practices, these are interpreted
according to their pre-existing worldviews and ideas (Sachs Norris 2003). At a
certain moment Wout also read the works of *Ibn Al-Qayim* and *Imam Ghazali* who
endorse the idea of a negative image of God, which suited his scientific outlook
on life. Being able to syncretise these views may mark another reason for being
attracted to Islam.

While reorienting towards a new belief system may be experimental at first,
later the change will become more deliberate with a definite direction and shape
(Austin-Broos 2003). When the following Ramadan came along, 25-year-old
Wout decided to take part in this embodied ritual. As this turned out to be such a
wonderful experience, he was adamant in dedicating the following year to looking
more closely at what Islam could offer him. With 9/11 fresh in his memory, he
could not believe a religion could offer such beauty while at the same time the
news showed such atrocities. During a following travel to Morocco he talked
to many Muslims and learned Islam has both very conservative and very liberal
movements. This aspect of diversity was another characteristic which pulled him
towards Islam:

> Every year the Ramadan is the month in which you get to know more and more
> new Muslims because it is a month in which people are much closer together,
> people will invite each other for dinner much quicker. This was one of the nicest
> things in the beginning, seeing how Islam is universal across the globe and there
> are so many overlaps in all Muslim communities, while at the same time Islam
> is as pluriform as anything and a Muslim from Indonesia or Saudi Arabia or
> Turkey or Gambia is totally different. I felt it was very pleasant to go from a
> Pakistani to a Turkish and to an African *iftar* meal. And to see all those parallels
> and differences at the same time. (Wout)

But from this quote other elements may be elicited which contributed to his conversion to Islam specifically: first there is the element of 'the Other', or the appeal of a religion which originally belonged to another culture than his own; secondly, the new forms of relatedness, the warmth of a shared culture and the collective aspect involved in the communal rituals such as the Ramadan; thirdly, the *Ummah* and its diverse character (Allievi 1999). The discovery of this diversity is a crucial element in his conversion narrative, as it enables him to position himself within Islam as a gay man, as we will see in the following paragraph.

Next then – and like most of the other reasons we list here in accordance to what Allievi (1999) wrote about what Islam has to offer to prospective converts – there is the political aspect, which appealed to a strong adherent of Marxism and Leninism such as Wout. What's more, to him this political character is the spirit of the *true* Islam: 'Legend has it the last words of grandson *Hussayn* [*ibn Ali*] were: "Rather to die for Allah than to live for a dictator"'. We found a similar ideological evolution in our previous studies on anarchist/left-wing activists of the *Liberación Andaluza* converting to Islam in Andalusia, Spain in the 1980s (Stallaert 1998). Islam has helped him to better comprehend his political convictions and vice versa:

> I feel that by becoming Muslim, through allowing religion into my life I can walk on two legs again instead of hobbling around. Where religion is sometimes woolly and esoteric, Marxism is rooted firmly in the ground. And where Marxism limits itself to bare facts, religion is suffused with a spirituality which brings everything to life. (Wout)

Islam's comprehensive ritual praxis also appealed to Wout. We have to note at this stage that as anthropologists we can only construct a conversion narrative as it is rationalised by the convert afterwards. It is instructive to be aware of this as this will allow us to tease out the importance of embodied practices in the process of religious change.

Around the age of 26, he started doing a second ritual (during the Ramadan of 2003), namely *salat*, which he now considers to be his 'spiritual *heartbeat*'. He had read in a book about how to do the prayer ritual, but the first time he actually prayed, he closed all the curtains so no one could see him: 'I felt ridiculous standing on a little carpet, but I had to try, all the other stuff was superstition and nonsense' (Wout). In contrast to historical examples of conversion to Islam, Allah is not mentioned explicitly in Wout's telling of his tale of conversion: there is no divine intervention or heavenly call involved, nor are causes to be found in the world of dreams (Dutton 1999, Garcia-Arenal 1999). Yet what we do see in this narrative is how new embodied religious practices such as *salat* are not merely symbolic of the newfound faith, but constitutive in the process of religious change. Or as Lofland states: 'Embodied religious practices are significant methods through which people go about converting themselves' (1978: 817).

> It [praying] worked and it helped me and *it fanned a kind of fire in me.* So
> I quickly realised: 'I cannot let go of this'. Because at the same time how
> can I explain this? I am still a person who maintains a very scientific attitude
> and I have a very exact worldview ... Not only did I get involved more with
> spirituality, but I became a person who completely behaves as can be expected
> of someone who belongs to a certain theistic faith group... It was so unreal that
> this was something which called me, which pulled me. And at the same time,
> based on my ratio – which I had always been most familiar with – I had to think
> this was some sort of superstition. (Wout)

These practices lead to emotional experiences which only afterwards are
rationalised into words relating to the body ('*spiritual heartbeat*' and '*it fanned a
kind of fire in me*').

Prayer is a primary modality through which Wout developed 'the subjective
dispositions necessary to begin living a new moral way of life grounded in Islam
... [and it is] also related to a sense of humility, an embodied disposition toward
respecting and responding to God's time on a regular basis' (Winchester 2008:
1765–6).

> Our ego does not like to do stuff which we have not decided ourselves to do and
> which will make us better. Doing the same pattern of actions five times a day
> which makes you, certainly in the beginning, feel foolish, is however something
> which tries to diminish your ego again and again ... It kind of transforms you.
> And after a while ... one of the transformations is the way you grow, how
> that rule of something absurd which you have to do or which you believe you
> should do because otherwise you would go to hell or whatever other formality,
> it becomes part of your life so you have to do it because otherwise you would
> miss it. (Wout)

So this desire to pray must be created through 'economies of discipline' (Mahmood
2001b: 832). Wout added Islam is submission in the sense you want to lead your
life according to something larger than yourself. Although in Wout's opinion such
rituals are based on individual choice, founded on a personal relationship between
the believer and Allah, they are however a necessary means for the cultivation
of an ideal virtuous self. What is more is that they are both a means and an end:
'Ritual prayer is an end in that Muslims believe Allah requires them to pray, and
a means insofar as it is born out of, and transforms, daily actions, which in turn
creates or reinforces the desire for worship' (Mahmood 2001b: 834).

What is distinctive here about Wout's narrative however corresponds to what
Sachs Norris (2003: 175–6) wrote on how the reorientation of a person to a new
belief system is based on his pre-existing identity and embodied worldview. In
this sense we may say that conversion as a passage is neither syncretism nor
absolute breach (Austin-Broos 2003). In this case 'ritual requirements must come

from personal meaning, not from authority' and have to be in line with European cultural ideals of individuality and freedom of choice (Sachs Norris 2003: 176).

Conversion as a passage is not diffuse or to be contained in a particular event. 'It is a process of continual embedding in forms of social practice and belief, in ritual dispositions and somatic experience' (Austin-Broos 2003). In this sense the body and its behavioral forms do not only 'have a capacity as a signifying medium, but also as a tool for becoming a certain kind of person and attaining certain kinds of states' (Mahmood 2001b: 837). So gradually Wout integrated more outward embodied practices (such as fasting, dress codes, language learning, body comportment and dietary precepts) into his daily life until he suddenly realised he had 'somehow become Muslim along the way' (Wout). Some of these corresponded to practices from before he was Muslim: for example, he already had a beard and he was vegetarian so he was already used to living according to certain dietary precepts. But it took two years after first taking part in the Ramadan, before he publicly came out as Muslim. Around this time, he also made the *Shahada* at the mosque, the double declaration of faith which in historical terms has been the only way to become Muslim. After doing the *Shahada*, Wout did not however take on a new Muslim name – although some people at the mosque refer to him as *Yusuf*.

The Intersection of Sexuality with Religious Change

Based on the narrative we discussed so far, we would like to argue that Wout's sexuality played a central part in his conversion to Islam. It is because and not despite of his sexuality that some of the crucial elements mentioned in his narrative led him to convert to Islam. In the remainder of this chapter we consider further how Wout's sexuality plays throughout and after his passage to Islam, with specific attention towards what place sexuality takes up within the newly constituted religious self and how he negotiates his sexuality and religion in different social relationships.

Queering the Qur'an:
The Use of Interpretative Strategies to Reconcile Faith and Sexuality

During our conversation Wout many times expressed a need to go back to the original, authentic Islam, which according to him was characterised by openness towards (sexual) diversity and a greater liberalism than is the case nowadays. As converted Muslims are not 'born into' Islam, putting a stress on diversity is a way to negotiate and even justify their conversion to their Muslim and non-Muslim peers. Related to this, he makes a differentiation between 'Islam' and 'Muslims' (c.f. Sultan 1999). In Wout's opinion the current problem is the instrumental use of religion by persons in a position of power or what Hamzić has called in this volume (Chapter 2), 'the discourse of heteronormative Muslim theopolitical reductionism'.

To sustain the argument of an authentic Islam which was more open towards sexual diversity, Wout queers the Qur'anic texts and the *Hadith*, referring to examples from the time of the Prophet, such as the *Mukhannathun*,[5] mentioned in *Sura Al-Nur* (24:31) which discusses the *hijab* and the categories of men in front of whom a woman may dress and behave more loosely. According to hegemonic interpretation, the *Mukhannathun* are said to be men who have become too old to be attracted to women. But, Wout refutes, 'a random check of the elderly people I know tells me straight elders still fancy women and elderly gays take to men with the same intensity as they did when they were sixteen' (Wout).

Here Wout also notes how *Mukhannat* was a culturally and historically specific identity, which does not overlap entirely with the modern and Western idea of homosexuality. Wout then proceeds to historically frame the revolution the Prophet caused, aware of how 'heterodox' his words might sound to other Muslims. Certain gender transgressive behaviours such as cross-dressing were not allowed, which according to Wout can be explained as follows: 'The revolution God's messenger brought about fourteen centuries ago, did only go as far as was possible within that historical context, but not further' (Wout).

Lastly, he mentioned the story of Lut, saying these were heterosexual men who robbed, kidnapped and raped other heterosexual men. If Muslims understand homosexuality to be this kind of sexual behavior, it is due to the *Ulema*, the scholars who are heterosexual and interpret the story according to their heteronormative standards. Wout affirms the actual content of the story, but questions the authority of religious scholars by countering their exegesis through indicating the multivocality of religious texts. This is similar to the findings of Yip (2005), who studied LGBT Christians and Muslims who tried to construct a sexuality-affirming hermeneutics. One of the strategies they used which was similar to that of Wout was to 'critique the credibility of institutional interpretive authority by highlighting its inadequacy and ideology, and relocating authentic interpretive authority to personal experience' (Yip 2005: 47).

To conclude we can say the ability to criticise the hegemonic interpretation and meanings of religious texts is related to the absence of a central authority in Islam and the possibility to exercise *ijtihad*. For someone whose sexuality is not taken-for-granted, studying the theme of homosexuality in the Qur'an and the *Hadith* is crucial as a resource to fend off criticism and possibly offers an advantage since, in Wout's opinion, 'concerning the knowledge of sexuality, I am of the impression most Muslims are not very informed and did not do a lot of homework' (Wout). What's more, as a Muslim he considers it an obligation to share this type of knowledge of Islam with his Muslim brothers, which brings us to the topic of the next paragraph.

---

5   The Arabic term is '*hayri olee al-irbati mina arrijali*' which is literally translated as: 'those servants who do not have the distinctive feature of men'.

Coming-out as 'A Question of Honour':
Living Out Religion and Sexuality in Everyday Life

As many things in his life, sexuality has always been a field for political action and the development of his sexuality was strongly infused with Marxist-Leninist ideology. In his teenage years he joined the *The Pink Action Front* (*Roze Aktiefront* – a left-wing gay movement which was shut down in 2001): 'When I was 16 I used to walk around wearing pink triangles and I would even start to feel frustrated when people did not take offence to what I did' (Wout). Monogamy was considered greedy and a steady relationship was something neurotic and felt like a prison. Promiscuous behaviour was the only viable political alternative and so his love life existed of exchanging one boyfriend for another. Also, in what Wout now calls a naïve Freudian pseudo-Marxism, everyone was considered to be born bisexual, so out of political considerations, he tried to show interest for women in the past, but this remained an unsuccessful enterprise.

In the new moral Muslim self-established through the process of conversion, sexual identity, sexual practices, attitudes towards sexuality and relationships have undergone considerable changes. A steady relationship is considered more important and now he honestly looks for a potential husband in each relationship. In the eight years since he became Muslim, he has been intimate with only a few people. His views of marriage have partly changed: although same-sex marriage is legally recognised in Belgium, in his opinion civil marriage should be abolished ('Whether they have a relationship or not, whether they marry one or seven persons, each individual should be entitled to the same rights'), but a religious marriage should be open for everyone.

The way in which he deals with coming-out has become more subtle than in the past. He does not like it when people think he is straight and postponing his coming-out when meeting people for the first time would only complicate the matter in subsequent meetings. Coming-out is a question of honour and, as has been said before, he thinks it is his duty as a Muslim *and* as a gay man to instruct other Muslims on issues concerning sexuality. He does however feel that towards some categories of people at the mosque – mainly the elderly – performing a coming-out is pointless. In articulating new forms of relatedness as a convert, he became aware of the importance of appropriate behaviour in intergenerational contact with other Muslims. For example, when he wears a *kufi* in public, young Muslims will approach him with respect and treat him like a *sheihk* (an erudite man). So in such contacts he presents himself as a role model towards these youngsters and talks openly to them about sexuality, especially when a closeted gay might be amongst them. The openness about his sexuality has brought about some hostile reactions, for example, from Salafi or Wahhabi Muslims. However, when the people who react in such manners are open to this, he enters a dialogue with them. Or in-between such discussions they just do random activities together which have nothing to do with sexuality (e.g. watching a movie, talking about the Qur'an). Wout mentions an instance where someone who had found out he was gay had threatened a few times to kill him, because in his Salafi line of thought this was the only possible solution of dealing with gay persons. But Wout tried to interact with him on a friendly basis, look past the contradiction between his vision and the one of the fundamentalist, or between his homosexuality and the other one's homophobia: 'To see this human being as a normal *brother* in the mosque with whom I was at variance on certain issues … Now he feels that as a gay man I got a certain luggage which lets me look at things in another way or help him with certain things' (Wout). This way Wout created a social network of people to whom having both taken the *Shahada* and being members of the *Ummah* precedes the differences related to their sexual identity, as in this quote is evidenced for example by the adoption of a kinship terminology.

People reacted in several ways to his coming-out as a convert to Islam. Although he felt his family reacted positively, most hostile reactions came from strangers who deemed him a betrayer of his people and who could not understand why he would convert to such a backward and homophobic religion. The responses he received in the gay world have been more hostile than the ones of Wahhabi Muslims. Often when he gives a lecture at a gay organisation, people ask him a question and use this opportunity to bash Islam and basically call him a bastard and a traitor. Telling the members of the political movement, of which he had been a part since he was 14, about his conversion proved to be a difficult task: he was afraid of their reactions, since they were all academics and Bolsheviks who thought of atheism as the inevitable next stage in mankind's evolution. Although the reactions eventually turned out to be positive, a friend of Wout told me how at a political demonstration a fellow activist once said: 'No problem if he's religious, but does he have to wear that hat [*kufi*]? That's overdoing it a bit' (Hugo).

In romantic/sexual relationships Wout has to negotiate his religious identity as well. At the time of the interview, he was together with another white Belgian man who spiritually identified as 'non-atheist'. The performance of *salat* sometimes makes his partner impatient: not because of the act of prayer itself, but because of the practical consequences – he lying in a cold bed waiting for Wout – which shows the complicated relationship between performing prayer and one's daily activities. Yet at the same time Wout's boyfriend now defends Islam in conversations with others. While Wout respects his boyfriend's preference for an open relationship, Wout wants to remain monogamous. In two previous relationships he dated an Albanian and Bosnian man who were nominally raised as Muslim but did not actively practise their faith. While to the former it did not matter whether Wout prayed or not, the latter felt embarrassed. Although Wout never forced him to pray or take part in the Ramadan, he felt Wout's strong commitment to religious practices as an accusation.

Concluding Remarks

The narrative presented in this chapter touched upon many issues which provide an impetus to queer the study of conversion. Even though we focused on conversion to Islam, we think this narrative is an invitation to open up other directions of research as well. To think with Talal Asad (1995), future research might look at conversion of people with non-normative genders/sexualities from a particular spiritual/religious tradition to secularism (or atheism), or vice versa. Or it could look at conversion from the four types Rambo lay out: apostasy, intensification, affiliation and institutional transition (1995: 13).

The questions we posed in this chapter might be taken up again in such projects: what role does their sexuality play in this religious/spiritual passage? What place does sexuality take up in the newly constituted religious self and how do they negotiate their religious and sexual belongings in their daily life? How do they deal with the possibly heteronormative doctrine of their new religion on the one hand and the new community of believers of which they are now part on the other hand?

As came to the fore when discussing the narrative, we argue that in a project of queering conversion, sexuality takes up a central place. Sexuality is not a thing in itself, but is socially and culturally embedded, produced and constructed. It is not an extra 'add in', but social life is only fully comprehensible by having an analysis of sexuality as central (McDermott 2011: 238). In this sense it is critical to understand processes of conversion.

Queering conversion also stresses the political meanings around sexuality. Sexuality is in this sense very much a public and political matter. This is exemplified in this narrative by a sentence such as 'coming-out is a question of honour' and the instances in which Wout both comes out as Muslim and as gay respectively in different communities of belonging – opening op possibilities to change these communities through these individual acts of coming-out.

We do feel that research on sexuality in conversion processes should not be limited to individuals with transgressive sexualities/genders only. Heterosexuality is too often taken for granted, it is always 'a silent term' (Kitzinger and Wilkinson 1993: 3). Therefore we think it might be fruitful to look at the sexual identities and practices of heterosexual converts as well. This way queering the study of conversion will not only shed light on the sexual subjectivities of LGBT converts, but on those from everyone.

References

2010. *In godsnaam* [Online]. Humo – The Wild Site. Available at http://www. humo.be/tws/tv-tips/19451/in-godsnaam.html [accessed 4 March 2011].

Alison, J. 2007. The Gay Thing: Following the Still Small Voice, in *Queer Theology – Rethinking the Western Body*, edited by G. Loughlin. Oxford: Wiley-Blackwell, 50–62.

Allievi, S. 1999. Pour une Sociologie des Conversions: Lorsque des Européens Deviennent Musulmans. *Social Compass* 46: 283–300.

Asad, T. 1993. *Genealogies of Religion: Discipline and Reasons of Power in Christianity and Islam.* Baltimore: John Hopkins University Press.

Asad, T. 1995. Comments on Conversion, in *Conversion to Modernities: The Globalization of Christianity*, edited by P. Van der Veer. New York: Routledge, 263–74.

Austin-Broos, D. 2003. Introduction, in *The Anthropology of Conversion*, edited by A. Buckser and S.D. Glazier. Lanham: Rowman and Littlefield Publishers, 1–12.

Billiet, J. and Swyngedouw, M. 2009. *Etnische Minderheden en de Vlaamse Kiezers – Een Analyse op Basis van de Postelectorale Verkiezingsonderzoeken (Ethnic Minorities and the Flemish Voters – An Analysis based on Postelectoral Election Research).* Leuven: Centrum voor Sociologisch Onderzoek – K.U.Leuven.

Birman, P. 1996. Cultos de Possessão e Pentecostalismo no Brasil; Passagens. *Religião e Sociedade* 17(1/2): 90–108.

Brereton, V.L. 1991. *From Sin to Salvation: Stories of Women's Conversions, 1800 to the Present.* Bloomington: Indiana University Press.

Coakley, S. (ed.) 1998. *Religion and the Body.* Cambridge: Cambridge University Press.

De Raedt, T. 2004. Muslims in Belgium: A Case Study of Emerging Identities. *Journal of Muslim Minority Affairs* 24(1): 9–30.

Dutton, Y. 1999. Conversion to Islam: The Qur'anic Paradigm, in *Religious Conversion: Contemporary Practices and Controversies*, edited by C. Lamb and D.M. Bryant. London: Cassell, 151–64.

Erzen, T. 2006. *Straight to Jesus: Sexual and Christian Conversions in the Ex-Gay Movement.* Berkeley: University of California Press.

Frigerio, A. 2007. Analyzing Conversion in Latin America: Theoretical Questions, Methodological Dilemmas, and Comparative Data from Argentina and Brazil, in *Conversion of a Continent – Contemporary Religious Change in Latin America*, edited by T.J. Steigenga and E.L. Cleary. New Brunswick: Rutgers University Press, 33–51.

Garcia-Arenal, M. 1999. Les Conversions d'Européens à l'Islam dans l'Histoire: Esquisse Générale. *Social Compass* 46(3): 273–81.

Giffney, N. 2004. Denormatizing Queer Theory. *Feminist Theory* 5(1): 73–8.

Goldman, R. 1996. Who is that Queer Queer? Exploring Norms around Sexuality, Race, and Class in Queer Theory, in *Queer Studies: A Lesbian, Gay, Bisexual, and Transgender Anthology*, edited by B. Beemyn and M. Eliason. New York: New York University Press, 169–82.

Grosz, E. 1994. *Volatile Bodies: Toward a Corporeal Feminism.* Bloomington: Indiana University Press.

Haraway, D. 1988. Situated Knowledges: The Science Question in Feminism and the Privilege of Partial Perspective. *Feminist Studies* 14(3): 575–99.

Hertogen, J. 2008. *In België wonen 628.751 moslims* [Online]. Available at http://www.manavzw.be/dossiers/In_Belgie_wonen_628751_moslims [accessed 20 June 2011].

Hugo. 21.03.2011. Interview with Hugo.

Isherwood, L. and Stuart, E. 1998. *Introducing Body Theology.* Sheffield: Sheffield Academic Press.

Kitzinger, C. and Wilkinson, S. (eds) 1993. *Heterosexuality: A Feminism and Psychology Reader.* London: Sage Publications.

Leman, J., Stallaert, C. and Lechkar, I. Forthcoming. Conversion and Agency: Tradition Transition to and Intensification within Islam, in *Negotiating Autonomy and Authority in Muslim Contexts*, edited by M. Buitelaar and M. Bernards. Leuven: Peeters.

Leman, J., Stallaert, C., Choi, P. and Lechkar, I. 2010a. Crossing Boundaries: Ethnicity and Islamic Conversion in Belgium. *Ethnoculture* 2: 27–44.

Leman, J., Stallaert, C. and Lechkar, I. 2010b. Ethnic Dimensions in the Discourse and Identity Strategies of European Converts to Islam in Andalusia and Flanders. *Journal of Ethnic and Migration Studies* 36(9): 1483–97.

Lofland, J. 1978. Becoming a World-Saver Revisited, in *Conversion Careers*, edited by J.T. Richardson. Beverly Hills: Sage.

Mahmood, S. 2001a. Feminist Theory, Embodiment, and the Docile Agent: Some Reflections on the Egyptian Islamic Revival. *Cultural Anthropology* 16(2): 202–36.

Mahmood, S. 2001b. Rehearsed Spontaneity and the Conventionality of Ritual: Disciplines of "salāt". *American Ethnologist* 28(4): 827–53.

Manco, U. 2000. *Voix et voies musulmanes de Belgique.* Brussel: Facultés Universitaires Saint-Louis.

McDermott, E. 2011. Multiplex Methodologies: Researching Young People's Well-Being at the Intersections of Class, Sexuality, Gender and Age, in *Theorizing Intersectionality and Sexuality*, edited by Y. Taylor, S. Hines and M.E. Casey. Basingstoke: Palgrave Macmillan.

Mossière, G. 2009. *Des Femmes Converties à l'islam en France et au Québec: Religiosités d'un Nouveau Genre.* Ph.D. in Anthropology. Université de Montréal.

Rambo, L.R. 1993. *Understanding Religious Conversion.* New Haven: Yale University Press.

Sachs Norris, R. 2003. Converting to What? Embodied Culture and the Adoption of New Beliefs, in *The Anthropology of Conversion*, edited by A. Buckser and S.D. Glazier. Lanham: Rowman and Littlefield Publishers, 171–81.

Stallaert, C. 1998. *Etnogénesis y Etnicidad en España. Una Aproximación Histórico-antropológica al Casticismo (Ethnogenesis and Ethnicity in Spain. A Historical-Anthropological Approach to Castizo)*. Barcelona: Anthropos.

Stallaert, C. 2004. *Perpetuum Mobile – Entre la Balcanización y la Aldea Global*. Barcelona: Anthropos.

Sultan, M. 1999. Choosing Islam: A Study of Swedish Converts. *Social Compass* 46(3): 325–35.

Turner, V. 1975. *Dramas, Fields, and Metaphors*. Ithaca: Cornell University Press.

Van Nieuwkerk, K. (ed.) 2006. *Women Embracing Islam: Gender and Conversions in the West*. Austin: University of Texas Press.

Wilcox, M.M. 2003. *Coming Out in Christianity: Religion, Identity and Community*. Bloomington: Indiana University Press.

Wilcox, M.M. 2007. Outlaws or In-laws? Queer Theory, LGBT Studies, and Religious Studies. *Journal of Homosexuality* 52(1): 73–100.

Winchester, D. 2008. Embodying the Faith: Religious Practice and the Making of a Muslim Moral Habitus. *Social Forces* 86(4): 1753–80.

Wolkomir, M. 2006. *Be Not Deceived: The Sacred and Sexual Struggles of Gay and Ex-Gay Christian Men*. Chapel Hill: Rutgers University Press.

Wout. 13.01.2011. *Interview with Wout*.

Yip, A.K.T. 1997. *Gay Male Christian Couples: Life Stories*. New York: Praeger.

Yip, A.K.T. 2005. Queering Religious Texts: An Exploration of British Non-heterosexual Christians' and Muslims' Strategy of Constructing Sexuality-affirming Hermeneutics. *Sociology* 39(1): 47–65.

Chapter 8

Body and Sexuality Constructs among Youth of the Ultra-Orthodox Jewish Community

Sara Zalcberg and Sima Zalcberg

Introduction

The significance attributed to conceptions of the body and sexuality is derived from social, cultural and religious contexts (Caplan 1987, Mendlinger and Cwikel 2005/2006, Zalcberg 2007, 2009). In hedonistic Roman society, for example, sex was seen in a positive light. In Europe during the Middle Ages, with the rise of Christianity, the official attitude towards sex took a dramatic turn. It was no longer considered to be a legitimate source of pleasure. Instead, Christianity considered sex to be solely a means of procreation, and any other aspects of sexuality were frowned upon (Boswell 1980, Gardella 1985). From the mid-nineteenth century sexuality became an inseparable part of the modern human being's identity, and the Western world's endorsement of romance and courtship as separable from reproduction gave new meaning to couplehood and sexuality.

At present, Western society allows a relatively high degree of sexual freedom, as long as people do not hurt others or violate the law. In contrast, traditional patriarchal societies consider sexual desire to be a manifestation of unrestrained evil impulses, and their fear of sexual permissiveness, excessive sexual activity, or illegitimate sexual connections can be seen in a variety of ethnic and social settings (McCarthy-Brown 1994). The traditional patriarchal societies carefully supervise their members' sexuality, through gender segregation and restrictions on women's dress and discussions about sex.

McCarthy-Brown (1994) claims that these restrictions are salient characteristics of fundamentalist religious views in the modern world. According to this approach, fundamentalism strives to control the hidden forces of the human body and physical desires, especially sexual desire, which it considers to be a major threat to human spirit and existence. Among these societies are fundamental religious groups such as radical Islam, various Christian sects and the ultra-Orthodox Jewish society.

Jewish society and rabbinic literature feature various types of discourse about sexuality, ranging from negative perceptions of sexual pleasure to an acceptance of its value (Boyarin 1993).

The *halakhic* authorities (*halakha* – the Jewish law)[1] consider sexuality to be an essential component of human existence and appreciate its value – including enjoyment, intimacy, and bodily pleasure (Song of Songs Rabba 1:31). But while the *halakha* permits sexual activity, it also includes many prohibitions of particular types of such activity, particularly sexual intercourse when the woman is menstruating, homosexual activity, and male masturbation.[2] The first two prohibitions are directly stated in the Pentateuch (Leviticus 18:22, 20:3), while the third is considered by the *halakhic* authorities to be based on a biblical verse (Deuteronomy 23:10), as discussed in the Talmud (Ketubot 46a, Avoda Zara 20b), and is considered very serious. Although no Jewish authorities dispute the prohibition of male masturbation, there are those who suggest a more moderate view, due to their understanding of how difficult it is for many young men to deal with it.

The ultra-Orthodox society acts according to social, cultural, and moral codes that are based on the strictest interpretations of the *halakha* (Friedman 1991). These codes affect this society's attitudes to the body and sexuality; it considers sex as intended only for procreation (Aran 2003), and it sees the body and the soul as two polar opposites that are in constant conflict (Hakak 2005). The practical expression of this view includes the imposition of many restrictions and prohibitions on the body, strict rules about women's dress, and gender separation in most areas of life, beginning at a young age (Heilman 1992, Zalcberg 2009). As a result, with the exception of their mother and sisters, young men are isolated from women until marriage; they must fight the desires of their bodies for sexual release. (Hakak 2005).

One of the main ways in which ultra-Orthodox society deals with sexuality issues is to avoid mentioning them and try to keep young people ignorant of them (Aran 2003). Sexuality is supervised in this society by means of enforced isolation from general society so as to avoid exposure to the sexual realm, and by remaining silent and silencing others, with any discussion of sexuality considered taboo (Friedman 2006, Goshen-Gottstein 1984, Heilman 1992, Zalcberg 2009).

Individuals become preoccupied with sexuality during adolescence, when many bodily changes occur (Kalman 2003). The way one copes with these changes and the meaning one ascribes to them are culture-dependent, differing among cultural, ethnic, and religious groups. Accordingly, young people's attitudes toward aspects of adolescence, the body and sexuality, such as the *menarche* (the first period)

---

1   The *halakhic* authorities are the authority of the Jewish law, which is composed from various books and texts that were written over generations by different rabbis, and which are recognised by the Jewish people.

2   Like some other social/religious conceptions of masturbation, female masturbation is often not mentioned, as if masturbation is a male preserve. Regarding 'homosexual activity', prohibition in the Jewish religion refers only to sex between men. Regarding sex between women, Jewish law does not prohibit it, however it perceives it as very inappropriate behaviour.

among girls, masturbation among boys, and the process of reproduction among both, are culturally influenced and differ among the various groups (Marvan and Bejarano 2005, Mendlinger and Cwikel 2005/2006). These differences derive in part from cultural variance in perceptions of the human body and of femininity and masculinity, in attitudes toward sexuality and fertility, and in gender roles, as well as from differences in the sources of young people's knowledge about their bodies and the changes that occur at adolescence.

This leads us to the issue of how the ultra-Orthodox Jewish community constructs its young people's perceptions of the body and sexuality, the socialisation of young men and women with regard to these issues, and the way they acquire their knowledge about adolescence and sexuality.

Our aim is to give a picture of what occurs among the young people in relation to an issue that is generally not discussed in religious groups, by presenting ultra-Orthodox women's and men's personal experiences from their childhood and adolescence, within their own conceptual world and social context.

Methodological Account

The findings presented here are based on two studies. The first concerns a cohort drawn from a study that addresses various sexuality issues among ultra-Orthodox men; the second concerns a cohort drawn from a study that addresses various women's issues among women in one of the most extreme groups within the ultra-Orthodox community in Israel, the *Toldot Aharon Hassidic*.

The common denominator between the group of men who were sampled and the group of women who were sampled is that they are both part of the ultra-Orthodox society with its unique characteristics. It is noteworthy that the group of men included interviewees from several groups within the ultra-Orthodox society, both the more moderate, who tend to lead a modern lifestyle and integrate into Israeli society and the more extreme, who avoid doing so. On the other hand, the women belonged to a particularly extremist group. Some of the men who were interviewed also belonged to this specific group. Despite the heterogeneous nature of the men's group, the interviews with them show that in all matters related to sex and sexuality, they are all guided by a uniform approach which is characterised by silence.

Since the various streams of the ultra-Orthodox community try to isolate themselves from people coming from 'the outside',[3] this makes it particularly

---

3   In this context it is worth noting that when we speak of Orthodox Jewry, we speak of a trend in Judaism that advocates strict observance of the laws of *halakha* as it has developed into the modern age and which is characterised by the belief that social changes have no validity to change these laws. This is in contrast to non-Orthodox movements, such as Reform and Conservative, which believe that Jewish *halakha* must be flexible and adapt to its times. Among the Orthodox Jewry are the ultra-Orthodox and the modern

difficult for strangers to enter its groups. Therefore, making contact with the subjects of the study was a long, slow process of establishing informal relationships and developing trust on the basis of personal contact.

The data about the ultra-Orthodox men were obtained from in-depth interviews (Patton 1990) conducted with 40 ultra-Orthodox men, aged 18–42. The process of locating the interviewees was complicated. At first one of us – Sara – tried to make contact on the street randomly with ultra-Orthodox men in the neighbourhoods where they lived, requesting to speak with them on the subject, but they were reluctant to speak with her, both because the subject is taboo in their society and because she was woman and an ultra-Orthodox man does not speak with women, except for his wife, sisters and daughters. Moreover, our being alien to their community aroused the suspicion that the study would defame the ultra-Orthodox community. Therefore Sara used the snowballing method – she asked people from this group whom she knew from before to refer additional people to her. This method helped win the trust of the interviewees and allayed their apprehensions. At the same time, since ultra-Orthodox society avoids talking about the subjects that were being researched, the people she knew found it hard to refer others to her. Therefore, Sara also devised other sampling strategies, which included: 1) putting out advertisements on internet sites frequently viewed by ultra-Orthodox men and on noticeboards in the area asking them to contact a specified e-Email address; 2) direct appeals to ultra-Orthodox men in areas which were not identified as ultra-Orthodox neighbourhoods, where they were less apprehensive about being seen speaking with women. Furthermore, the contact was made gradually, which is to say that Sara first asked 'Can I ask you something?', and when she received a positive response, she asked in a general way if the person would be willing to take part in the study. When the subject showed interest, she elaborated upon the subject of the study. In this way, she managed to reach the interviewees.

The data on the ultra-Orthodox girls and women were obtained from in-depth interviews with 25 women aged 25–60, from the *Toldot Aharon Hassidic* group. All of them were mothers, and some were also teachers at a school which was attended by most of the women in the group.

Since the *Toldot Aharon Hassidim* are considered the most extreme group in ultra-Orthodox society, studying this issue among the group's women provides a high-contrast illustration of the meaning ultra-Orthodox society ascribes to women's bodies and sexuality.

Orthodox. Secular Jews who observe certain Jewish rituals such as circumcision, religious funeral services and being called up to the Torah at the age of bar-mitzva (13) generally do this according to the rules of Orthodox *halakha*. However, while modern Orthodox Jewry advocates combining traditional religion with modernity (Cohen 2004) and integration into modern society, ultra-Orthodox Jewry advocates closing oneself off from modernity and from secular society, and the scrupulous observance of particularly stringent restrictions aimed at guarding personal modesty.

The first step in the access process to the women included walking around the area where the group lives, visiting stores in the neighbourhood, and the like. However, every attempt to start a conversation with the women in this way was met with hostility and refusal. After many such attempts one of us – Sima – met a woman who recommended that she attend the wedding of the *Rebbe's*[4] granddaughter, which was taking place at that time, and meet the women of the group in this way. Accordingly, Sima's next step was to attend this wedding. At the wedding she was invited to a sabbath meal at the home of a family known for its hospitality. She accepted this invitation, and from then on this home was open to Sima whenever she wanted to go there. This was one of the most important and well-connected families in the group, and Sima continued to visit them. This connection became a vital resource for gathering information about the group and, more important, it was a channel for getting to know many other women. Above all, this connection provided Sima with an acceptable identity among the women and made her 'legitimate' and less threatening.

The interviews included open questions about the formal and informal socialisation of young people with regard to their bodies, sexuality and adolescence, as well as where the young people obtained any information they might have about these issues. During the interviews the interviewees were asked to speak about their own experiences during their childhood, youth and adolescence. Therefore a significant portion of the data is retrospective.

Because of the difficulty involved in making contact with the research subjects and getting them to cooperate, the study is based on 'convenience sampling', that is, approaching potential subjects on the basis of practicability. As the fieldwork progressed, we used the snowballing method, making use of some of the first informants to reach a wider spectrum of group members. For a more detailed discussion of gaining access to the *Toldot Aharon Hassidic* group, see Zalcberg (2007).

The study was based on the phenomenological approach, eliciting information about the world as seen through the respondents' eyes, thus providing insight into their experiences and conceptual worlds (Berger and Luckmann 1967, Denzin and Lincoln 1994). The personal accounts we obtained from the respondents served as the basis for the phenomenological aspect of the research. Since phenomenological inquiry relies as much as possible on pure experience, we presented the personal experiences of the respondents in their own words and in terms of their own conceptual world.

The analysis was based on grounded theory (Glaser and Strauss 1967, Strauss and Corbin 1998). Grounded theory is appropriate when there is a general research question, with no hypotheses to prove or disprove, as is the case in this study. Since people with common life circumstances are assumed to have

---

4   The leader of a *Chasidus* (Chasidic movement) is called a *rebbe*. His followers would address him as 'the *Rebbe*' or refer to him when speaking to others as 'the *Rebbe*' or 'my *Rebbe*'.

common social and psychological patterns, the purpose of the research is to generate categories of theorising about the subjects' experiences. The analysis has two levels. The first is a general thematic analysis, looking for major themes and patterns in the interviews, while the second consists of finding the meanings underlying the more obvious ideas in the data, as well as the meanings of the first-level categories.

We shall now turn the presentation of the findings, organised into three empirical themes: the prohibition of discussions of the body or sexuality; channels of information about sex; and the ramifications of the silence and the silencing. Throughout this chapter, pseudonyms have been used to protect the respondents' privacy.

The Prohibition of Discussions of the Body or Sexuality

The interviewees indicate that the major element in their socialisation process is the construction of silence about sexuality issues. This occurs in both informal settings – within the family, especially the parents – and formal settings, namely, the school. The construction of silence is attested by the remarks of Shifra, one of the teachers in the *Toldot Aharon* community, and members of the community as well: 'We don't talk about it'. Zlota, another teacher, indicated that all the teachers take great care to prevent the girls from discussing reproductive matters:

> If, for example, the girls say that a teacher is pregnant, they are told that this is a private matter, and that it will be very bad for them if they are caught talking about it again. But the girls generally don't want to talk about it; they are embarrassed. And this is one of the things that protects the girls. Because once you talk about it, you don't know where you will get to.

According to Zlota, the avoidance of all talk about the reproductive functions is a way of protecting the girls' spiritual world from exposure to various subjects, which, they believe, would 'contaminate' them – that is, lead them to think about sexual matters. Similarly Yosel said:

> [When I was a little boy and during my adolescence] I knew that there were things I could not talk to my parents about. For example, I could never tell them that I had pain in my sexual organs. Not even the slightest hint, because that would be considered using obscene language.

According to the interviewees' reports about their childhood, unlike the girls, the boys are subject to physical and emotional sanctions for verbal or behavioural expressions of a sexual nature. Regarding verbal expressions, Yitzchak noted that 'At school and at home, when we would say, for example, the word … penis, we would be beaten up for it'. Similarly, Moshe remarked:

When I was 11, one of the boys said 'backside'. When the teacher, heard this, he slapped the boy in front of everyone. The teacher wanted to show the children that it's very bad to use words like that and that there are certain things connected to the body that one is forbidden to talk about.

Tuvia told the following story about the practical results of involvement in sexual incidents:

Once when I was in the eighth grade [age 13], the teacher started to hit me. He said to me, 'Bring your father to see me, otherwise I'm throwing you out of the *yeshiva*!' [*yeshiva* – the educational institution where ultra orthodox boys are educated] I said, 'What did I do? I'm afraid to go to my father'. The teacher told me, 'No. You're going home now'. That was truly hellish. After father spoke to the teacher he hit me and said, 'You touched yourself!' I said to him, 'What did I touch, what are you talking about?' Father responded, 'The teacher said that you touched, you held …' I said, 'I didn't hold anything, I didn't do anything!'

According to Tuvia's description, we see that in addition to the harsh attitude of his father, who hit him without bothering to talk to him or check the facts first, as well as the teacher's humiliating actions, his father, like the teacher, totally disapproved of any touching of his sexual organs.

Another manifestation of the construction of silence is that both our male and our female interviewees tried to avoid using words such as 'sex', 'sexual relations', 'monthly period' and the like throughout the interviews, replacing them all by 'it'. Language is rarely neutral, and the words chosen by the interviewees are a deep reflection of their social norms and cultural values, as well as those of the ultra-Orthodox community as a whole.

This type of speech shows how difficult it is to have an open conversation about sexual topics, and it illustrates the educational and psychological inhibitions of this community with respect to these issues (Samet 2005).

Knowledge about Physiological Changes during Adolescence

This silence creates a situation where young people are ignorant about sex. Eli, for example, said, 'At thirteen-and-a-half I still didn't know anything about sex. When I asked my mother where babies came from, [she would say] "God sends them"'. Srulik reported that until the age of 18 he 'thought that when a man and a woman get married, God places a baby inside her belly'. It seems that even the physiological changes that the interviewees underwent at puberty did not contribute significantly to their knowledge about sex. Srulik, for example, said:

> I woke up at night and I saw that it seemed as if I had wet the bed, at the age of 15. I was frightened, what was happening to me? After all, I wasn't a little boy anymore. I woke up my mother and said to her that I had wet the bed … My mother said, 'Change your underpants and go back to sleep, nothing happened to you'.

Srulik's mother did not explain the meaning of what had happened to him, and he never got any real explanation about sexuality and sexual relations until he got married.

The young men's ignorance makes them anxious. Yaakov, for example, reported that at the age of 11, 'some boy whispered to me once that sexuality is connected with the mother and father doing something together in their bedroom … and even thinking about it terrified me'.

For Avigdor too, the little knowledge he had in this area represented something 'terrible'. As he put it, 'We knew it was terrible but we didn't know why'. This finding about the anxiety that the youth experience is not unique to the ultra Orthodox youths, but was also found among modern Orthodox youths (Avishai Forthcoming a, b).

According to the men's reports – based on their youthful experiences – the boys' lack of knowledge about sex, in spite of the physiological experiences they were undergoing, is explained by the fact that they did not receive any guidance in this area. This is in contrast to the situation in society generally, where the schools are an important source of information about sexuality and adolescent issues (Cohen et al. 2004, Irvine 1994). The girls, too, are ignorant in this area, as described by Hana, one of the teachers:

> When a girl gets married she's like a little child …. I won't say that no one knows, but it's a private matter. The less one says about it, the better.

The girls, however, do get some information and guidance about the physiological changes they are undergoing, at the time of their first period (*menarche*), mainly from their mothers, as in modern Western society (Costos et al. 2002, Cumming et al. 1991). In *Toldot Aharon*, however, the mothers are almost totally responsible for socialising their daughters on this issue. Sheindel explained: 'only the mother tells them … In our family my mother told me about it, and she told it to each one in the greatest of privacy'.

As the mothers in the group are the major channel for providing their daughters with information about menstruation, the kind of information provided is not the same in every case. The information provided by the mothers can be described on a continuum, ranging from a minimal amount of information, which is mainly a technical explanation, to the broadest amount, which includes the significance of the event – that the girl is now fertile.

Feige is among the mothers who believed in presenting the girls with more information, relatively speaking. This is how she explained her position:

> My daughter told me that she had bleeding. I told her what it was. I was happy
> for her; I told her that it is a happy thing, because it is connected with the
> children she will have, but I didn't tell her anything about sex. I would tell all
> of my daughters that what they have is a private thing and that they should not
> talk about it.

Perl represents the less open women. According to Perl, the explanation given
to girls is intended only to prevent them from being terrified by this unfamiliar
phenomenon: 'The mother says that there is nothing to be afraid of, and that's all.
We don't talk about it'.

In spite of the differences among the various mothers' approaches, all of them
indicated that discussing menstruation is taboo, and that they avoided making
any connection between the girl's periods and sexuality. They not only avoided
making any connection between menstruation and sex, but they also said nothing
about the sexual feelings girls might experience during and after adolescence.
They considered this sort of information potentially harmful to the girls

More information was given to the young people just before their weddings.
The girls are instructed by a professional 'bride instructor', and the boys by a
'groom instructor'. Since discussion of the subject among adolescents in the
group is not permitted, the parents assumed that their children had little, if any,
knowledge about sex, and so they took care to provide them with information and
guidance on the subject when they were about to get married. This information
was given by the aforementioned instructors for brides and grooms. The
instruction includes very detailed explanations about reproductive biology, as
well as practical guidance for sexual relations (Zalcberg 2009). The guidance
for the youths before their weddings by the 'bride instructors' and the 'groom
instructors' is not unique to the ultra-Orthodox youths, but also exists in the
modern Orthodox community (Avishai Forthcoming a, b), although the content
is different because modern Orthodox come to this guidance with much more
knowledge about the body and sexuality.

Due to the preparation the girls received, they were not so terrified by the
appearance of the *menarche*, while the boys became deeply anxious as a result
of physiological experiences such as wet dreams and erections. However, at least
some of the girls became deeply anxious when they found out about the facts of
life just before their wedding, as Mindel illustrated: 'When I first heard about
intercourse before my wedding, I had absolutely no idea ... It was very hard for
me when I heard [about it]. I couldn't believe that that's the way it is'.

Channels of Information about Sex

From the retrospective reports of the interviewees, we can see that despite the
silence imposed upon them, most of the ultra-Orthodox adolescents managed to
find out some information about sexual matters. Their knowledge in this area was

drawn from bits of knowledge they gathered from occasional opportunities to look at 'forbidden literature' – secular texts that include references to the body or sexuality.

David reported: 'I am eighteen, and I found out about these topics only four months ago when I accidentally opened an 'undesirable' book [a secular book that mentions or deals with issues related to sexuality] and started reading it'. Even though David is an extreme example, since he was so old when he found out about the facts of life, this is not an isolated case in the ultra-Orthodox community.

According to the women's reports, all the girls' reading material is very carefully selected. They are permitted to read only books that have been approved by their mothers and/or teachers. However, some of the girls may read secular material obtained by secretly going into secular bookstores, while waiting at the doctor's office, or obtained from people in the outside world.

Meeting people on the street outside their community can also provide the adolescents with information in this area. For this reason the girls are forbidden to talk to people outside the group. Perl, one of the mothers, illustrated this situation: 'I would not have allowed my daughter to talk to you before her wedding, because you might tell her all sorts of things that she is allowed to know only after she gets married'.

In recent years, more and more people from the ultra-Orthodox society have begun to use the internet, even though the highest religious authorities (the rabbis) prohibit this activity (Barzilai-Nahon and Barzilai 2005, Tydor Baumel-Schwartz 2009). The advantage of this channel is in the privacy and confidentiality it offers the users. Therefore, the internet became an important illegitimate information channel about issues related to the body and sexuality. Avi says, 'It is not legitimate for us, but I have it'. Another source of information is the *Torah* and *halachic* literature, the religious texts, which are legitimate for the boys, as Binyamin reported:

> An ultra-Orthodox boy suddenly reads about the 'impurity of semen' in the
> *Torah* and the subject of marriage [in the *Talmud*]. Suddenly you realise you're
> in on the 'big secret'. You read this material in *Shulchan Aruch*,[5] *Maimonides*[6]
> and the *Gemara*.[7]

---

5   The *Shulchan Aruch* (literally: 'Set Table'), also known as the Code of Jewish Law, is the most authoritative legal code of Judaism. It was authored in Safed, Israel, by Yosef Karo in 1563 and published in Venice two years later. Together with its commentaries it is the most widely accepted compilation of Jewish law ever written.

6   Maimonides was a preeminent medieval Jewish philosopher and one of the greatest *Torah* scholars and physicians of the Middle Ages. Maimonides's *Mishneh Torah* is considered by traditionalist Jews, even today, as one of the chief authoritative codifications of Jewish law and ethics.

7   The Gemara is the component of the Talmud comprising rabbinical analysis of and commentary on the Mishnah – which is the first major written redaction of the Jewish oral

The girls, in contrast, are kept away as much as possible from the *Torah* texts which contain hints about sexual matters, as Tzirel, one of the teachers, explained:

> In the elementary grades the girls do not read the text [of the Bible], so that they won't look at things that they don't need [to see]. They are absolutely not given a Bible, because you can find all sorts of [passages on sexual] issues in it. In the boys' schools the boys are required to read the text from the Bible, but their teachers read the problematic passages quickly, without explaining them.

Another major source of information is peers. Yitzhak reported that when he was 13, 'A friend tried to tell me how babies are made; he knew quite a bit for someone at the age of 13–14'. Similarly, Yosi reported that only 'at the age of over 17 did I hear for the first time – from my best friend – about ejaculation, sexual relations and things about marriage'. Similarly, Rochel explained that:

> [The girls] won't talk about it in a group of girls, but one girl might talk about it to her best friend as a secret. One day my daughter came home from school and said that her friend told her about not-nice things that a husband does to his wife, and that she was very angry with this friend; the way she was talking. ....

It is important to note that the narratives presented by the mothers construct their situation as they see it, and to some extent, it must be assumed, as they wish to see it. We may therefore speculate that even though the mothers claimed that the girls have minimal knowledge of sexual matters and rarely speak about these things among themselves, we can assume that the girls actually know more than the mothers claim. This speculation finds support in the remarks of the bridal instructor concerning the knowledge possessed by adolescents before their weddings:

> Most of the girls know [about sex], because each one has a mind, and there are things you understand with your mind ... There is a story about a boy whose father locked him in the house until he was 18 years old. One day he left the house and saw a girl. The boy asked his father, 'What's this?' and his father said, 'A *kachkale* [little duck]'. The boy replied, 'I want a *kachkale* like that'. So the adolescents generally know something. I don't know if they know exactly what happens in married life, because they don't watch television ... and their young age at marriage helps them not to know [beforehand]. Some know more and some know less.

---

traditions called the 'Oral Torah'. The Gemara is the major text of the Jewish law that the ultra-Orthodox men and boys learn.

The Ramifications of the Silence and the Silencing

In parallel with the mechanisms of silencing and supervision just described, ultra-Orthodox young people have an internal supervisory mechanism that forms when they internalise the messages and prohibitions instilled in them by various socialisation agents. We learned from the interviews that, due to the differences between the physiological changes undergone by the boys and the girls and the significance ascribed to them by the community, there are some gender differences in the ramifications of the supervisory mechanisms. Even though the monthly period is considered taboo – an impure, polluting event – in many cultures (Costos et al. 2002, Cumming et al. 1991, Houppert 1999), the women in the group did not report any feelings of guilt arising in their daughters due to the changes occurring at puberty, or in themselves as girls. Moreover, Gitel, one of the women insisted, 'They don't know anything and look how happy they are'.

In contrast, the boys' internal supervisory mechanism gives them a sense of profound sin as a result of their preoccupation with sexual matters, especially auto-erotic thoughts and practices. Yaakov described the sense of profound sin he felt throughout his adolescence: 'As soon as you masturbate you become involved in religious conflicts ... at an advanced stage I realised that I was sinning severely – that I was a serial sinner!' Similarly, Eli said:

> All ultra-Orthodox adolescent boys live with a heavy sense of sin. They are familiar with severe texts that tell them that while one can repent for other sins, there is no repentance for this sin! There are texts which state that [masturbation] is worse than murder! Because here you murder sperm, and those are potential human beings. This creates terrible conflicts for the boy *vis-à-vis* his God, but especially *vis-à-vis* his innermost self.

The awareness of sin leaves deep scars on the adolescent boy's psyche, as Yosi said, 'You try to distract yourself from your evil impulses, and you feel like dirt. It destroys the person and it casts a shadow over everything you do. You think you are worthless'.

Beyond the descriptions of deep distress, several of the interviewees openly criticised the way ultra-Orthodox society relates to the whole realm of sexuality. These voices were a minority but cannot be ignored. Michael, for example, contended that the attitude of the ultra-Orthodox community on this subject is 'catastrophic to the point that it is painful'. David explained that, 'I maintain that they did an injustice to religion, because religion would not stop something that is a physiological need, which is natural. Religion is not against nature'. Similarly, Hayim said that, 'It seems to me that something here is not right. I have a theological problem [and] in general, I hate this whole lifestyle'.

Concluding Remarks

The results of the study show that young people in the ultra-Orthodox community are not provided with knowledge in the area of sex. Instead, the community constructs a network of silence and silencing in this area. Thus, while Western psychology views adolescents' sexual involvement as one of the many ways in which they explore and shape their sexual identity (Samet 2005), the ultra-Orthodox community sees it as something that must wait until marriage. The major agents of socialisation try to extinguish interest in and discussion of these topics by avoiding them.

This approach, according to Samet (2005) and Fine (1988), can have undesired consequences, since the lack of discussion of the positive aspects of sexual activity distorts the young people's perceptions of their bodies and the possibility of positive sexual experiences.

The major socialisation agents in the ultra-Orthodox community (parents, teachers and rabbis) consider it a religious obligation to avoid passing on information about sexual matters. From their viewpoint, adolescents should not discuss the subject, as it may endanger their spiritual world. For this reason they avoid such discussions until the young people are about to get married, so as 'to preserve the "purity" of public discourse' (Hartman and Samet 2007: 80)

Prohibitions on knowledge are associated with power. Foucault (1980) claims that society and modern knowledge control the human body. He believes that modern society intervenes to channel natural human instincts, in accordance with the society's requirements, so as to achieve control. One way this control is achieved is by supervising sexuality. The refusal of the socialisation agents in the ultra-Orthodox community to provide adolescents with knowledge about their bodies, their sexuality and what they undergo during adolescence is part of their attempt to control the young people's sexuality in accordance with the community's ethos and norms, and to keep them innocent of sex until they are married off.

This silencing of discourse about sexuality is not unique to the ultra-Orthodox community, but is also prevalent in regular Orthodox schools (Hartman and Samet 2007) and non-religious schools (Phillips and Fine 1992). In these other schools, however, there are at least formal programmes for sex education. Despite the many problems with such programmes, as can be seen in Hartman and Samet (2007), their very existence reflects a degree of openness about sexual issues in these schools.

Yet another finding is that the silence and silencing are a product of the cooperation between the two parties – the agents of socialisation and the adolescents. Both the boys and the girls avoid discussing the topic due to shame, embarrassment and the fear of sanctions from the educational authorities.

The young people fill in their missing knowledge about sexuality, if only partially, through other means, especially their peer groups. In addition, they find out forbidden information from encounters with the general society, reading forbidden material, and even the internet. The fact that the adolescents resort to these means in spite of the various supervisory mechanisms in their community attests to their great need for knowledge in this area.

The findings of this study attest that the boys are subject to much greater psychological conflicts and emotional difficulties than the girls. This is because the external mechanisms of silencing and supervision (Foucault 1980) lead to internal supervision in the boys, giving them a sense of profound sin due to their sexual thoughts and practices – mainly autoerotic. This sense of sin remains with them throughout adolescence and has long-term consequences as well, greatly impacting their functioning as adults in many areas of life (Zalcberg 2009).

The silence and silencing mechanisms that were discussed, and the ramifications they have for ultra-Orthodox youth are in effect a form of coping with what Taussig (1999: 2–3) identified as the 'public secret' that is defined as 'what is generally known but, for one reason or another, cannot easily be articulated'.

Taussig sees the 'public secret' as a mechanism that allows a society to cope with conflicting forces and without which its social structure would collapse. In ultra-Orthodox society, this mechanism allows it continued existence and stability. However, it is not only in ultra-Orthodox society that this mechanism is active. According to Zerubavel (2006), this mechanism serves many societies and is founded on a symbiosis between the individuals who structure and feed it and thus contribute to its perpetuation. The key to this dynamic lies in co-denial, both by the one possessing the information and by the one lacking the information – who does not ask.

The application of this mechanism is expressed both in patterns of formal control as well as in informal strategies of distraction on a range of discourses. The more society is characterised as possessing a hierarchical structure and being more closed, the more it will develop a tendency to encourage silence (Zerubavel 2006). The subjects excluded or included in societies are the product of internalising certain social and political norms. Accordingly we have been witness in recent decades to changes and transformations in modern Western society in all matters that relate to containing issues in the area of sexuality. At the same time, in more traditional, more closed societies, these subjects are still excluded.

References

Aran, G. 2003. The Haredi's body: Chapters of Ethnography in Process, in *Israeli Haredim: Integration without Assimilation?* edited by K. Caplan and E. Sivan. Jerusalem–Tel Aviv: Van Leer Institute–Hakibbutz Hameuchad Publishing (Heb), 99–133.

Avishai, O. Forthcoming a. What to Do with the Problem of the Flesh? Negotiating Orthodox Jewish Sexual Anxieties. *Fieldwork in Religion*, 7(2).

Avishai, O. Forthcoming b. Contesting Sex-Restrictive Sexual Narratives from Within: Jewish Laws of Menstrual Purity and Orthodox Sexual Anxieties, in *Ashgate Research Companion to Sexuality and Religion*, edited by S. Hun and A.K.T., Yip. Farnham: Ashgate.

Barzilai-Nahon, K. and Barzilai, G. 2005. Cultured Technology: The Internet and Religious Fundamentalism. *The Information Society* 21(1): 25–40.

Baumel-Schwartz, J. 2009. Frum Surfing: Orthodox Jewish Womens' Internet Forums as a Historical and Cultural Phenomenon. *Journal of Jewish Identities* 2(1): 1–30.

Berger, P.L. and Luckmann, T. 1967. *The Social Construction of Reality*. New York: Doubleday.

Boswell, J. 1980. *Christianity, Social Tolerance and Homosexuality*. Chicago: University of Chicago Press.

Boyarin, D. 1993. *Carnal Israel: Reading Sex in Talmudic Culture*. Berkeley: University of California Press.

Caplan, P. 1987. *The Cultural Construction of Sexuality*. London: Tavistock.

Cohen, J.N., Byers, E.S., Sears, H.A. and Weaver, A.D. 2004. Sexual Health Education: Attitudes, Knowledge, and Comfort of Teachers in New Brunswick Schools. *The Canadian Journal of Human Sexuality* 13(1): 1–15.

Costos, D., Ackerman, R. and Paradis, L. 2002. Recollections of Menarche: Communication between Mothers and Daughters Regarding Menstruation. *Sex Roles* 46(1–2): 49–59.

Cumming, D., Cumming, C. and Kieren, D. 1991. Menstrual Mythology and Sources of Information about Menstruation. *American Journal of Obstetrics and Gynecology* 164: 472–6.

Denzin, N.K. and Lincoln, Y.S. (eds). 1994. *Handbook of Qualitative Research*. Thousand Oaks, CA: Sage.

Fine, M. 1988. Sexuality, Schooling and Adolescent Females: The Missing Discourse of Desire. *Harvard Educational Review* 58(1): 29–53.

Foucault, M. 1980. Truth and Power, in *Power/Knowledge*, edited by C. Gordon. New York: Pantheon Books, 51–75.

Friedman, M. 1987. Life Tradition and Book Tradition in the Development of Ultra-Orthodox Judaism, in *Judaism Viewed from Within and from Without: Anthropological Studies*, edited by H.E. Goldberg. Albany, NY: State University of New York Press, 235–55.

Friedman, M. 1991. *Ultra-Orthodox Society: Sources Trends and Processes*. Jerusalem: Jerusalem Institute for Israel Studies (Heb).

Gardella, P. 1985. *Innocent Ecstasy: How Christianity Gave America an Ethic of Sexual Pleasure*. Oxford University Press.

Glaser, B. and Strauss, A.L. 1967. *The Discovery of Grounded Theory*. Chicago: De Gruyter.

Goshen-Gottstein, E.R. 1984. Growing up in Geula: Socialization and Family Living in an Ultra-Orthodox Jewish Subculture. *Israel Journal of Psychiatry and Related Sciences* 21(1): 37–55.

Hakak, Y. 2005. *Spirituality and Worldliness in Lithuanian Yeshivas*. Jerusalem: The Floersheimer Institute for Policy Studies (Heb).

Hartman, T. and Samet, B. 2007. Uncovering Private Discourse: Teachers' Perspectives of Sex Education in Israeli Religious Jewish Schools. *Curriculum Inquiry* 37(1): 71–95.

Heilman, S. 1992. *Defenders of the Faith: Inside Ultra-Orthodox Jewry*. New York: Schocken.

Houppert, K. 1999. *The Curse: Confronting the Last Unmentionable Taboo – Menstruation*. New York: Farrar, Straus & Giroux.

Irvine, J.M. 1994. Cultural Differences and Adolescent Sexuality, in *Sexual Cultures and the Construction of Adolescent Identities*, edited by J.M. Irvine. Philadelphia: Temple University Press, 3–29.

Kalman, M.B. 2003. Adolescent Girls, Single-parent Fathers, and Menarche. *Holistic Nursing Practice* 17(1): 36–9.

McCarthy Brown, K. 1994. Fundamentalism and the Control of Women, In *Fundamentalism and Gender*, edited by J. Stratton Hawley. New York: Oxford University Press, 175–201.

Marvan, M.L. and Bejarano, J.B. 2005. Premenarcheal Mexican Girls' and their Teachers' Perceptions of Preparation Students Receive about Menstruation at School. *Journal of School Health* 75(3): 86–9.

Mendlinger, S. and Cwikel, J. 2005/2006. Learning about Menstruation: Knowledge Acquisition and Cultural Diversity. *The International Journal of Diversity* 5(3): 54–62.

Patton, M.Q. 1990. *Qualitative Evaluation Research Methods*. Thousand Oaks, CA: Sage Publications.

Phillips, L. and Fine, M. 1992. Commentary: What's 'Left' in Sexuality Education? In *Sexuality and the Curriculum*, edited by J.T. Sears. New York: Teachers College Press, 242–9.

Samet, B. 2005. Attitudes of Religious Educators towards "Family Life Education". Ph.D. Dissertation, The Hebrew University of Jerusalem (Heb).

Strauss, A.L. and Corbin, J. 1998. *Basics of Qualitative Research: Grounded Theory Procedures and Techniques*. Thousand Oaks, CA: Sage Publications.

Taussig, M.T. 1999. *Defacement: Public Secrecy and the Labor of the Negative*. Stanford, CA: Stanford University Press.

Zalcberg, S. 2007. "Grace is Deceitful and Beauty is Vain": How Hasidic Women Cope with the Requirement of Shaving One's Head and Wearing a Black Kerchief. *Gender Issues* 24(3): 13–34.

Zalcberg, S. 2009. Channels of Knowledge and Information about Menstruation and Sexuality among Hasidic Adolescent Girls. *Nashim: A Journal of Jewish Women's Studies & Gender Issues* 17: 60–88.

Zerubavel, E. 2006. *The Elephant in the Room: Silence and Denial in Everyday Life*. New York: Oxford University Press.

Chapter 9

When God is Not So Good: Corporate Religion contra New Social Movements

Kenneth Houston

Introduction

Weber's contention that modernisation would equate to secularisation and the diminishing importance of religion has come under sustained attack in the last two decades (Norris and Inglehart 2004). Within the study of religion and politics the 'death of God' has been questioned and debated with some energy (Bader 2007, Berger et al. 1999, Bruce 2011, Casanova 1994, Cliteur 2010, Kepel 1995, Strenski 2010, Westerlund 1996). Both the inevitability, and even the desirability, of secularisation have lost their scholarly and normative purchase, replaced instead by a reckoning with religion as a force of political importance. This chapter examines the horizons of meaning and perspectives of religious actors relative to their stances on public policy related to gender and sexuality. Analysis is led by – and primarily concerned with – the conflict that arises between religious and gender-sexuality activism.

The purpose of this approach is to demonstrate the vulnerability of progressive improvements in gender-sexual equality to conservative religion, a point noted by Inglehart and Norris (2003: 50). This is undertaken through an analysis of texts-as-action (Fairclough 2003) in order to demonstrate the intentional pursuit by religiously motivated movements of public policy outcomes that conform to the ideational ends of religious biases. In what follows, we will outline a theoretical trajectory that builds upon Foucault's concept of 'governmentality'. Religiously motivated social movements are here referred to as *corporate* religion (see Westerlund 1996). This is defined as the mobilisation of religion as an interest embodying both the capacity and willingness to engage with political authority in the formulation or implementation of public policy.

This chapter critically engages with the assumption among many political theorists that the inclusion of corporate religion in policy processes will result in unqualified reciprocal acts of recognition of other groups by the religious. This study argues that attention must also be directed laterally across social movements. The contention is that corporate religions embody rationalities that impede a fuller realisation of civil liberties and universal human rights, particularly in relation to social movements and normative perspectives mobilised around gender and sexual equality.

The empirical focus on the two monotheisms of Christianity and Islam emanates from their salience in public social conflict in late modernity. For both Christianity and Islam, political authority should accept the significance – even primacy – of a faith/religious identity in comparison to other claims upon subjectivity. Policy and law should be considered in light of the insights articulated by its ecclesial and religious associational biases. The failure of modern societies to unambiguously recognise these is characterised as a lapse, a deviation from our 'true' human heritage and a failure to fully embody the democratic commitment to equality and freedom. These failures are perceived to harbour potentially malignant if not grave socio-political consequences, through a decline in moral standards, social cohesion and increasing societal dysfunction.

Theoretical Approach

Foucault's study of 'governmentality' provides a fruitful angle of analysis for consideration of the nascent role of religious associations relative to policy on gender and sexuality (Ciccarelli 2008, Dean 1999, 2002, Foucault 2000a, 2007, Hindess 1998, Merlingen 2006, O'Malley et al. 1997, Rose 1999, Sending and Neumann 2006, Walters and Haahr 2005). Rose notes that the term does not equate to the study of governance (Rose 1999: 21). While governance establishes a duality between state and civil society actors (wherein the power of the state is reduced), governmentality sees no transfer of power from the former to the latter, but rather a redirection of state power *through* civil society (Sending and Neumann 2006: 652). Governmentality, in its broadest sense, is concerned with the 'rationalities of government' (Hindess 1998: 63), or the mentality of government (Dean 1999), whereby *non* political agency is harnessed for political (and implicitly 'statist') ends. In a governmentality analysis, the focus is upon the extent to which civil society has become both the subject and the object of rule, where it is the object of state regulation, and simultaneously the source of rule over others (Sending and Neumann 2006: 658). It offers an analytical perspective that asks:

> What authorities of various sorts wanted [what] to happen, in relation to problems defined how, in pursuit of what objectives, through what strategies and techniques [?]. (Rose 1999: 20)

A governmentality approach would ask 'how is the smoker or the obese person "managed" or conducted', or 'how is the drug abuser re-habilitated?' The axis of analysis via governmentality runs from the governing authority right through to a particular facet of individual conduct, seeking to manage or conduct it for the ostensible benefit of the individual and society. Dean (1999: 11) provides us with four key questions that a governmentality approach asks:

- What specific facet or component of the behaviour of the subject is the target of action or policy?
- What techniques are employed in order to actualise the policy programme?
- How, or in what sense, is the human subject imagined or conceived in the policy programme (or what identity is attributed to the subject)?
- What are the policy objective(s) to be sought?

In this chapter the human subject is viewed through two normative lenses – the religious and the gender/sexual – and the point of tension and conflict between each is examined.

In *Governmentality, Omnes et Singulatum,* and *The Subject and Power* (2000a, 2000b, 2000c), Foucault linked the practices of the medieval Christian confessional and the government of souls to modern political rule. It was the practices of the early and medieval church in Europe that sought to administer and govern the 'souls' of Christian believers, which laid the foundations for its secular variant of political rule within the state. This he called 'governmentality'. Pastoral power exhibited two co-extensive features that were translated into secular political rule: its individualising and its totalising tendencies (Foucault 2000b: 308).

It was a form of power, however, that could not be exercised 'without knowing the inside of people's minds, without exploring their souls [...] it implies knowledge of conscience and an ability to direct it' (Foucault 2000c: 333). Foucault then linked this idea of individualising and totalising power, which he considered to be based on the extensive knowledge of individuals established through modern forms of political rule. The pastorate may have lost much of its salience since the beginning of the modern period, but its functional modalities and features spread *beyond* religious institutions (Foucault 2000c: 335). Foucault then goes on to elaborate on the mechanisms of modern liberal governance that expanded, refined and developed the individualising and totalising impetus of the pastorate. The modern state, far from ignoring the individual, was instead 'a very sophisticated structure in which individuals can be integrated, under one condition: that this individuality would be shaped in a new form' (Foucault 2000c: 334). Rather than the otherworldly salvation of Christian pastor-ship, secular governmentality sought to ensure worldly salvation through the improvement of living standards and security across a range of questions (health, education, etc.) that intersected each citizen-subject. In this way, we begin to see liberal governance and political freedoms as means toward the end of rule through *voluntary* compliance. It is, to use a more contemporary term, an *outsourcing* of sovereign political authority to subjective self-reliance, principally through the exchange of transcendent forms of sovereign power for more immanent guidance in the form of self-regulation, self-direction and agency. The explanatory capacity of this perspective has yielded a wide variety of empirical research (see Dean 1999: 3). However, research has tended to embody an analytical perspective that places the governmentalisation conducted *by the state* through community and individual agents in society.

Underpinning the argument presented here is that governmentality is not confined to the state. The idea of *religious* pastoral care, or *religious* governmentality as a contemporary end in itself needs revisiting. Religions in their organised forms are still in the business of government: the government of souls. The tendency to view 'community' associations as passive receptors of state guidance has obscured the role that community – specifically corporate *religious* – associations have in the instrumentation of political governance processes for self-interested ends.

Corporate religions have not only compromised with secular rule; they have made it a means to their own ends. They have adapted their pastoral strategy to accord with, and take advantage of, the imperatives of liberal governance and the normative axioms that underpin them: freedom of conscience, freedom to manifest religion or belief, freedom of association, and even 'community' cohesion and state multiculturalism. Freedom is understood not only as the absence of constraint but also the provision of capacity by political authority through funding and resources.

This pastoral imperative can be conducted through public policy via a bi-directional strategy. First, there is the direct approach through the unmediated pursuit of interests and influence by corporate religious entities within the decision-making process, through shaping or influencing the formulation of policy. This first approach is classic interest representation or lobbying. These include objections to specific policies pursued by national, supranational or international bodies or initiatives that are deemed contrary to 'Christian' or 'Muslim' teaching or morals, usually within the policy consultation or early formulation stage. It may also mean the advocacy or approval of policies that do conform to these foundational ideals. The second mode is where we would note the failure of policies to be successfully or fully implemented due to pressure exerted at the end point of delivery, such as a whole or partial retreat from policy objectives regarded as antithetical to religious sensibilities.

Corporate Religion and Gender-sexual Equality

Europe

Enshrined within the recently enacted Lisbon Treaty of the European Union is an article committing the EU's institutions to 'open, transparent and regular dialogue' with various religious associations (see Houston 2009). This structured dialogue between political authority and religious associations is a reflection of a counter-intuitive practice within 'secular' Europe: the regularised interaction between political and religious actors. While frequently portrayed as a positive move to engage all elements of civil society in the process of governance (Kooiman 2003), in this section analysis will focus on the points of conflict with respect to religion's role in policies around gender and sexuality within the European context.

Within the religious biases considered there are markedly distinct conceptualisations of the freedom-domination dichotomy relative to the role of individual faith and public religion. A succinct example of such tension was evident in remarks made by Pope Benedict XVI when accepting the credentials of the Swedish Ambassador to the Holy See in December, 2008:

> [E]very liberal society has to assess carefully to what extent freedom of speech and expression can be allowed to ignore religious sensibilities. The question is of particular importance when the harmonious integration of different religious groups is a priority. Furthermore, the right to be defended against discrimination is sometimes invoked in circumstances that place in question the right of religious groups to state and put into practice their strongly held convictions, for example, concerning the fundamental importance for society of marriage, understood as a lifelong union between a man and a woman, open to the transmission of life. (Vatican 2008)

The Pontiff, capitalising on the socio-political imperatives of tolerance in the context of *religious* pluralism, sought to limit the freedom to express dissent and criticism of religious faith. Simultaneously, he challenged restrictions on the expression of religious convictions that sought to criticise other lifestyle choices relative to sexuality and gender. In the Pontiff's hierarchy of freedoms, the freedom to believe ranks higher than the freedom to embody subjectivities relative to gender and sexuality that do not conform to the specifically Catholic ideal. Freedoms must be balanced, but balanced in favour of limiting criticism of religious sensibilities, and equally in favour of protecting the right of religious actors to voice negative convictions regarding issues of sexuality and gender. More recently, Pope Benedict drew a connection between the imperatives of ecological conservation and the reform of laws that legislated for same-sex unions (Vatican 2010).

Similarly, a more qualified view of human rights paradigms was evident in remarks made by the Patriarch of the Russian Orthodox Church (2009):

> The weakness of the human rights institution lies in the fact that while defending the freedom of choice, it tends to increasingly ignore the moral dimension of life and the freedom from sin.

Choice, according to the Patriarch, needs to be subordinate to the religious imperative to avoid the specifically religious concept of 'sin', and choices are only valid as long as those made conform to particular ideals. The concept of 'sin' makes no distinction between infractions of the integrity of others and the perceived infraction of the behaviour of the self. For example, homosexuality and 'promiscuity' are considered equal in weight to the violation of the integrity of others.

The contribution of the *Commission of the Bishop's Conferences of the European Union* (COMECE) to the drafting of the Charter of Fundamental Rights of the European Union sought to include a clause that declared that 'every human being has a right to be born of a man and a woman' (COMECE 2000: 3). The Vatican's 2003 *Ecclesia in Europa* opposed the expansion of rights claims on a range of life-style choices. Europe's broad liberalisation of reproductive health is interpreted as exemplifying Europe's 'culture of death' (Vatican 2003a: sect. 9). The legitimate or traditional family is in a state of 'crisis', broken marriages reflect a 'moral disorder', and Europe's declining birth-rate is 'symptomatic of a troubled relationship with our own future' (Vatican 2003a: sects. 90–95). In its 2004 *Letter to the Bishops of the Catholic Church*, the Congregation for the Doctrine of the Faith outlined its position on the consolidation of sexual equality and women's rights (Vatican 2004b). A 'harmful confusion' was identified when the quest for women's equality resulted in an adversarial attitude developing between men and women (Vatican 2004b: sect. 1). Instead, the Letter reiterated the need to recognise the 'genius of women' and their ability to 'elicit life' (Vatican 2004b: sect. 13). The consequences of them failing to embody these ideals are that 'society as a whole suffers violence and becomes in turn the progenitor of more violence' (Vatican 2004b: sect. 13). With regard to homosexuality it is worth noting at length the form of opposition suggested by the Vatican to the laity, including:

> Reminding the government of the need to contain the phenomenon within certain limits so as to safeguard public morality and, above all, to avoid exposing young people to erroneous ideas about sexuality and marriage that would deprive them of their necessary defences and contribute to the spread of the phenomenon. (Vatican 2003b: sect. 5)

Allowing the adoption of children by gay couples amounted to 'doing violence' to them (Vatican 2003b: sect. 7). In the first of his 2006 monographs, Pope Benedict XVI outlined the normative ideal guiding the drafting and completion of the European Draft Constitution. Among other things, a central element that the Pontiff ascribed to European identity was the institution of marriage (Ratzinger 2006a: 76). Consequently, other forms of family, such as the dissolved family through divorce, cohabitation without legal form, and the increasing demands of same-sex couples, all 'fall outside the moral history of humanity' (Ratzinger 2006a: 77). A concession to such claims making would lead to the 'dissolution of the image of humankind bearing consequences that can only be extremely grave' (Ratzinger 2006a: 77). The Pontiff feared that homosexuality, because of the enlargement of anti-discrimination laws, may soon no longer be affirmed as 'an objective disordering of the structure of human existence' (Ratzinger 2006b: 35).

The predominant questions of freedom relative to Islam tend to be primarily concerned with the eradication of prejudice and the right to gain equality in religious expression where Islam is a minority faith. However, nuances have emerged about conceptualisations of freedom as expressed by Islamic associations and their representatives. One such example involves the *Union of Islamic*

Organisations of France (UOIF), the umbrella body of Muslim associations accorded official recognition by the French government. In response to questions about an impending ban on Muslim headscarves (*hijabs*) in French public schools the UOIF clarified its stance. Through its spokesman on Islamic law, it made clear that, while families should not coerce their daughters into wearing the *hijab*, and that women should enter public life, they should do so in compliance with Islamic law. Islamic law, so far as the UOIF is concerned, is clear on the question of the *hijab*: it is *obligatory* for women to wear it:

> Islam requires women to wear the *hijab*, and here all scholars, in the past and today agree [...] Cover the maximum possible with the *foulard*, and not just with a bandanna. Don't focus on the issue of its colour, the point is to cover up. (quoted from Bowen 2004: 885)

Bowen noted the divergence of normative frames evident between French political and religious actors with regard to the *hijab*. Whereas political actors justify their positions from the positive laws of France, the UOIF starts from 'the authoritative interpretations of Islamic norms' (Bowen 2004: 886). The UOIF did state that the laws in question were contrary to the European Convention, and could be challenged on that basis. Bowen noted, however, that the references to secular normative resources were 'purely instrumental'.[1]

In 2007 the *Muslim Council of Britain* (MCB) published guidelines outlining suggested practices in primary and secondary education regarding Muslim pupils that exhibited some gender-segregationist tendencies. These were particularly focused on mixed gender contact sports and swimming (MCB 2007a: 37–8), but also on the provision of sex and relationship education (MCB 2007a: 49). The MCB also withdrew its support for a Muslim multi associational consensus on the drafting of a reformist 'Muslim Marriage Contract' (Muslim Institute 2008). The contract sought, within the perspective of Islamic law, to reform Islamic jurisprudence in order to re-calibrate the rights of women in light of contemporary social reality. This was undertaken, in light of reported instances of abuse and forced marriages, so as to give the woman greater power within a Muslim marriage (Muslim Institute 2008: 5). In a statement issued by the MCB the association made clear that the document represented a 'misinterpretation' of Sharia, which it could not be associated with (MCB 2008).[2] In addition, a UK government proposal to

---

1   As he writes: 'The specific norms invoked are entirely a function of the strategic advantages such citations will produce [...] references to non-Islamic normative sources are secondary to a justificatory discourse *that is based in Islamic jurisprudence*, manifestly transnational, and not European' (Bowen 2004: 887, emphasis added).

2   It was also noteworthy that, notwithstanding the clear egalitarian impulse behind the Muslim Institute's efforts to reform the Muslim Marriage Contract, it also stipulated in the document that violation of its agreed terms 'constitutes a sin' (Muslim Institute 2008: 5).

repeal a law that prohibited the presentation of same-sex unions within secondary education was opposed by the then Secretary General of the MCB. He remarked:

> [support for opposition to] Section 28 … is totally alien to Islam…we are making our position very clear that we cannot be a part of the liberal lobby … that goes against the very principle of existence. (quoted in Modood and Ahmad 2007: 198)

When New Labour's Jack Straw commented on the wearing of the veil by a constituent, several Islamic organisations and scholars signed a joint statement on the veil (MCB 2006). In it they affirmed that the wearing of the veil is an *Islamic* practice, as opposed to a cultural trait, and asserted that its status as a religious obligation is 'not open to debate' (MCB 2006: para 3). Furthermore, those who fail to exercise 'extreme caution' with respect to denying any part of Islam or its practices risk being led into disbelief.

> We recognise the fact that Muslims hold different views regarding the veil, but we urge all members of the Muslim community to keep this debate within the realms of scholarly discussion amongst the people of knowledge and authority within the Muslim community. (MCB 2006: para 4)

For the authors of the joint statement the wearing of the veil by women is less a right to be defended than an obligation to be imposed. Like their French counterparts, the UOIF, the language of rights is instrumental, the ultimate imperative underpinning the wearing of the veil is an imposition upon the subject. In addition, the function of the veil is primarily as a symbolic juxtaposition against 'less widely condemned practices such as sexual promiscuity, nudity and alcohol consumption by other segments of society' (MCB 2006: para 7). Furthermore, the determination of what is and is not 'true' faith and 'true' Islamic stricture is to be determined exclusively by 'people of knowledge and authority', which in Islam is invariably the (exclusively male) *Ulema*. Finally, there is the constructed coherence of an Islamic 'community', where faith is to the forefront of collective identity, and personal identity is mediated through this prism. Deviation is explicitly delegitimised, and characterised as a direct threat to Muslim 'solidarity'. Foucault's 'governmentality', most often applied to the relationship between the state and the human subject, also offers a useful analysis of the governing impulses of social movements. In the examples above, corporate religion has asserted the importance, even primacy, of an individual's religious identity. The human subject is mediated through a religious prism, one over which corporate forms of the faith claim interpretative authority. It is a prism, however, that finds itself at odds with those social movements concerned with the dimensions of gender and sexuality.

International

There have been notable examples of corporate religious pressure on secular political institutions at the inter-governmental level of the United Nations. The International Conferences on Population Development (ICPD) of the mid 1990s, and subsequent special UN General Assembly events, embarked on a coordinated, normatively based policy initiative to realise certain goals around the question of women's empowerment, equality and social justice.[3] The conferences sought to integrate population issues into all development planning policies and programmes (UN-Cairo Declaration 1994: para. 3). In this policy arena, the international organs of the UN had problematised specific elements of human social reality and conduct. They conceptualised the human subject, and particular facets of her conduct, in a specific manner in order to set out remedial objectives to meet particular ends.

Both Christian (primarily Roman Catholic) and Islamic biases dissented from wider consensus reached. During the run up to the ICPD in Cairo, the Vatican along with conservative Islamic institutions (such as the Al Azhar University in Cairo), majority Muslim states and the majority Muslim interstate umbrella body the Organisation of the Islamic Conference (OIC) sought to coordinate their stances. Al Azhar University issued a statement condemning the event, which it viewed as promoting a plural vision of marriage forms, making advice on sexual and family planning matters available to individuals outside marriage and making references to the idea of safe abortions. Al Azhar claimed that these were all contrary to Islamic teaching (Inter Press Service 1994a). Al Azhar and the Vatican, along with several majority Muslim states such as Iran, had found common ground in their attitudes towards abortion in reproductive health (*Washington Post* 1994). In a letter sent to the Secretary General of the Conference, Pope John Paul II made it clear that the forthcoming event's draft proposals were a cause of 'grave concern', and that 'the vision of sexuality which inspires the document is individualistic' (Vatican 1994: para 10). The Pontiff was specifically concerned by the failure of the draft declaration to demand the provision of state assistance for women in order to avoid abortion, and was also keen to ensure that abortion was not envisaged as another form of birth control.[4]

Both Al Azhar University and the Vatican assumed that the specific tenets they embodied regarding sexual conduct and family planning and formation should be considered the norm. Furthermore, for these Christian and Islamic biases, the state should be concerned to regulate sexual relations among its citizens, a certain ideally acceptable form of sexual conduct and family formation was – or should be – the subject of political intervention. While religious biases did reflect the

---

3   On the development of the International Population Conferences from a governmentality perspective, see Sending and Neumann 2006: 658–63.

4   This had been included in the previous Mexico City conference on Population and Development in 1984.

broader appeal to greater respect for individual dignity, they also saw the concept of individual *autonomy* in mainly negative terms.

The caveats emanating from Christian and Muslim bodies at these events tended to centre on several key areas of contention. These included perceived individualistic or 'permissive' interpretations of sexuality, as well as opposition to redefinitions of 'the family' that might include same-sex unions, single parent families, or childless couples. For example, the Holy See delegation made the point that the draft proposals only attempted to limit the impact of 'risky' sexual behaviour, rather than challenge such behaviour at its attitudinal roots. In addition, 'the Holy See strongly rejects any attempts to weaken the family or propose a radical redefinition of its structure, such as assigning the status of family to other life-style forms' (UN-ICPD 1994b: para 4). The family was seen as the nucleus of society, and women, according to Catholic and Islamic perspectives, were attributed a unique and 'privileged' position as mother and homemaker within this framework. Their role is specific and contrary to individualistic self-fulfilment. Womanhood, according to the Pontiff, is a 'gift', insofar as it teaches women to place themselves 'at the service of others in their everyday lives' (Vatican 1995).

At the outset of the subsequent Beijing conference of 1995, the Holy See delegation emphasised that:

> Marriage, motherhood and the family, or adherence to religious values should not be presented only in a negative manner. To affirm the dignity and rights of all women requires respect for the roles of women whose quest for personal fulfilment and the construction of a stable society is *inseparably linked* to their commitment to God, family, neighbour and especially to their children. (UN-ICPD 1995b: para 2, emphasis added)

The OIC, in its *Declaration of Human Rights in Islam* (OIC 1990), in particular Article Six, assigned specific duties to women in accordance with Sharia law, which, while acknowledging their equal *dignity* to men, effectively accorded them fewer comprehensive freedoms (see Mayer 2007: 138–40). The intervention of the OIC at the Beijing conference made the point that women, in the Islamic civilisation, had a 'fundamental role in the entity of the family', which in view of their 'tender and sensitive' nature had specific 'rights and obligations to perform' (UN-ICPDc 1995). The OIC intervention goes on to emphasise that 'we cannot but admit that women's natural disposition made it possible for them to enjoy the honour of upbringing the future generations' (UN-ICPDc 1995). Axiomatic to the Catholic and Islamic perspectives exemplified here is that women are, *by their nature*, subservient to others and duty bound to place the good of others above their own.

In its final statement to the Cairo conference the Holy See made it clear that human life 'begins at the moment of conception', that reproductive health should not include artificial means of contraception, or abortion, and that sexual activity should remain within the confines of a heterosexual marriage (UN-ICPD 1994a:

para 27). It noted the prevalence of 'exaggerated individualism' and it criticised the 'impoverished, libertarian rights dialect' of the final report of the conference (UN-ICPD 1995a: para 11). The Holy See's main intervention at the conclusion of the Beijing event also alluded to the 'disproportionate attention to sexual and reproductive health' (UN-ICPD 1995b: para 11). Echoing this, the OIC emphasised their prohibition on 'aggression committed against the foetus's right to life', and equally stressed the imperative to confine 'sublimated' sexual relations to those of a heterosexual relationship, foregoing the 'adulation of individuals' and the 'institutionalisation of deviation, on the pretext of liberty and realism' (UN-ICPD 1995c). 'Deviance' from a religiously defined 'norm' is a centrepiece of the language employed here. Not all religious biases exhibited solidified positions. In its intervention at the Cairo conference, the World Council of Churches (WCC) offered a more nuanced position concerning the issue of abortion. While concurring with the Roman Catholic and OIC position that abortion should not be a family planning instrument, the WCC made the point that:

> Dogmatic assertions which affirm the sanctity of life but ignore the context in which conception takes place fail to bring that assertion to bear on the real circumstances of life. (UN-ICPD 1994c)

The permeation of normative criteria with regard to sexual relations through the perspectives of conservative corporate religion at the two population conferences continued subsequently into the related Special General Assemblies. In its intervention to the 2001 Special General Assembly on HIV/AIDS prevention, the Holy See reiterated its stance on the question of HIV/AIDS prevention that 'the only safe and completely reliable method of preventing the sexual transmission of HIV is abstinence' (UN-S/GA 2001c: PV.8). Further, it emphasised the '*proper* use of sexuality [and] the values of matrimonial fidelity and of chastity and abstinence' (UN-S/GA 2001b: PV.7 emphasis added). At the same event, the OIC attempted to block a contribution from a civil society organisation that had been invited to contribute to the Special General Assembly. Initially included on the list of accredited NGOs, the International Gay and Lesbian Human Rights (IGLHR) Commission delegation was latterly removed at the instigation of eleven anonymous member states.[5] At the 1999 Special General Assembly on Population, the Holy See delegation expressed its 'grave concern' at the introduction of emergency contraception, as well as efforts by some western states to strengthen the privacy of adolescents over the rights of parents (UN-S/GA 1999: 9th Plenary). In its intervention at the special General Assembly on Children (2002), the Holy See delegation reiterated its insistence that a family be defined as being within a heterosexual marriage only (UN-S/GA 2002: Rec 6). The ideologically based interpretation of optimal government embodied by these Christian and Islamic

---

5   Ultimately the objections of the OIC to their reinstatement were defeated by a vote (UN-S/GA 2002: PV 1).

biases points towards a conflict within one of the four component questions of the governmentality approach: how is the human subject imagined? Furthermore, the policy ends sought differ significantly between non-religious and religious biases. For the UN, the policy objective is the mitigation of social paralysis in (primarily) developing nations due to the unequal social status of women and the corrosive impact of HIV/AIDS and other infectious diseases, as well as poor family planning options with detrimental impact on populations and economic development. For the religious, the vision of the human subject, the problems and remedial measures envisaged to tackle these are very differently conceived, and internationally coordinated policy should endeavour to ensure the correction of 'deviant' human behaviour, and not merely engage with the consequences of behaviour.

Subject-believers and Subject-citizens: Points of Cleavage

These interventions by corporate religions at international level are not without consequence. Health experts, in an article published in *The Lancet* medical journal, have noted that the objectives of the population development conferences in Cairo and Beijing have not been met. Subsequent efforts to realise these aims have been diluted or hampered, and effective interventions aimed at reducing global transmission of infectious diseases, reducing mortality due to pregnancy complications, increasing access to family planning services, and gender equality were omitted or diluted in the subsequent Millennium Development goals (Glasier et al. 2006: 1595). A significant element in this failure is because of the increasing strength of the very conservative religious forces that threatened agreement at the ICPD (Glasier et al. 2006: 1605).

It is also important to note the conclusions of the most recent Millennium Development Goal Report (UN Report 2010). Goal Five (Improve Maternal Health) included several targets relating to reducing the maternal mortality ratio and improving access to reproductive healthcare. The report notes that:

- Progress has stalled in reducing the number of teenage pregnancies
- Progress in expanding the use of contraceptives by women has slowed
- Inadequate funding for family planning is a major failure in fulfilling commitments to improving women's reproductive health (MDG Report 2010: 30–38)

A recent study on the impact of emphasising religious identity in community cohesion policy in London has found that often women are net losers through such policies (see also Patel 2011, 2008). The Southall Black Sisters report into women's lived experience in Ealing, *Cohesion, Faith and Gender*, noted that women tended to emphasise their lived experience above other attributes such as race, culture or religion, that religion was often a source of gender discrimination and that respondents had a deep mistrust of religious leaders (Patel 2011).

One of the key recommendations of the report offers a stark challenge to the prevailing normative assumptions around social cohesion:

> The cohesion approach with its dangerous and narrow assumptions about identity and 'community' reinforces racist, exclusionary and divisive practices, cultural conservatism and religious fundamentalism. It prevents a secular, rights based and democratic public culture from emerging. (Patel 2011: 7)

The current elevation of corporate religion as an organised interest group has clear implications for the state's obligation to uphold the freedom of all its citizens. While religious biases adopt and support the discourse of human rights their support is a qualified one. The underlying corporate religious imperative is pursuit of conformity to fixed normative criteria, which are in tension with the broader pursuit of gender and sexual equality. Not all social movements are progressive. From the highly consequential perspective of studying public policy, the difficulties do not simply rest with the willingness of churches to assert their perspectives openly. The difficulties also lie in the willingness of policy makers to listen sympathetically. By doing so, there is a risk that the subject citizen and the subject believer – two very distinct facets of human subjectivity – become entangled to the point where policy directed towards the citizen becomes suffused with the pastoral objectives of faith associations, to the detriment of wider human freedom.

The concept of governmentality applied to both political and corporate religious interests affords an informative analysis of policy tensions around gender and sexuality. For political governmentality the human person requires protection from deadly infectious diseases, including sexually transmitted diseases, and women need to be empowered to plan families and pursue economic development. For corporate religious governmentality the human person requires moral and spiritual regeneration through education in the proper use of sexuality and the proper bases and obligations of family life. Furthermore, women need to be empowered in order to adopt their essential social roles as mothers and homemakers. The differences are subtle but profoundly important in terms of the divergent political and religious ends of policy. On the one hand the political ends involve the programmatic emancipation of individuals from the risk of deadly infectious disease and the burden of unplanned families that they cannot materially support within a framework of informed choice in conduct. On the other hand *religious* governmentality involves the liberation of both believers and non-adherents from the risk of disease through regulated sexual conduct and the rejection of public regulatory support for deviant family forms through the conformity of individual human conduct with religious strictures.

Concluding Remarks

There is an obvious disparity between the public health and gender equality objectives of both political institutions and social movements on the one hand and the conservative norms embodied most forcefully by some corporate religious interests on the other. Foucault's 'governmentality' approach, applied to the intersection of politics, religion and human subjectivity, throws into relief arguably the most urgent question posed by the contemporary resurgence of faith-based politics, both nationally and globally. Are the rights of women and homosexuals sufficiently protected when religious interests and narratives enter policy debates? By directing attention, as Foucault's suggests, at the rationality behind governing, broadly considered, a cleavage point emerges between the human individual conceived alternately as citizen and 'soul'. The bio-political management of public health, disease control and political empowerment clashes sharply with the religious imperative to regulate morals, normalise gender roles and determine the 'proper' utility of human sexuality. In truth, this is not a new conflict, but the vicissitudes of late-modernity mean that its trajectory has perhaps entered a new phase.

References

Bader, V. 2007. *Secularism or Democracy? Associational Governance of Religious Diversity*. Amsterdam: Amsterdam University Press.

Berger, P. (ed.) 1999. *The Desecularisation of the World: Resurgent Religion in World Politics*. Grand Rapids: Eerdmans Publishing Co.

Bowen, D.L. 1997. Abortion, Islam, and the 1994 Cairo Population Conference. *International Journal of Middle Eastern Studies* 29: 161–84.

Bowen, J.R. 2004. Beyond Migration: Islam as a Transnational Public Space. *Journal of Ethnic and Migration Studies* 30(5): 879–94.

Bruce, S. 2011. *Secularization: In Defence of an Unfashionable Theory*. Oxford: Oxford University Press.

Casanova, J. 1994. *Public Religions in the Modern World*. Chicago: University of Chicago Press.

Ciccarelli, R. 2008. Reframing Political Freedom in the Analytics of Governmentality. *Law Critique* 19: 307–27.

Cliteur, P. 2010. *The Secular Outlook: In Defense of Moral and Political Secularism*. London: Wiley Blackwell.

COMECE 2000. Contribution by the Commission of the Bishop's Conferences of the European Community to the Draft Charter of Fundamental Rights of the European Union 8 February [Online: COMECE website]. Available at http://www.comece.org/upload/pdf/secr_chart1_000208_en.pdf [accessed 22 May 2009].

COMECE 2003. Statement of the COMECE Executive Committee on the Draft Treaty establishing a Constitution for the European Union [Online: COMECE website]. Available at http://www.comece.org/comece.taf?_function=future&_sub=_integ&id=9&language=en [accessed 22 May 2009].

Dean, M. 1999. *Governmentality: Power and Rule in Modern Society*. London: Sage.

Fairclough, N. 2003. *Analysing Discourse: Textual Analysis for Social Research*. London: Routledge.

Foucault, M. 2000a. Governmentality, in *The Essential Works of Foucault, 1954–1984: Power*. London: Penguin.

Foucault, M. 2000b. Omnes et Singulatum, in *The Essential Works of Foucault, 1954–1984: Power*. London: Penguin.

Foucault, M. 2000c. The Subject and Power, in *The Essential Works of Foucault, 1954–1984: Power*. London: Penguin.

Foucault, M. 2007. *Security, Territory, Population: Lectures at the College de France 1977–1978*. Basingstoke: Palgrave Macmillan.

Glasier, A., Gulmezoglu, A.M., Schmid, G.P., Moreno, C.G. and Van Look, P. 2006. Sexual and Reproductive Health: A Matter of Life and Death. *The Lancet*, 4 November 368 (9547), 1595–607.

Hindess, B. 1998. Knowledge and Political Reason. *Critical Review of International Social and Political Philosophy* 1(2): 63–84.

Houston, K. 2009. The Logic of Structured Dialogue between Religious Associations and the Institutions of the European Union. *Religion, State and Society* 37(1/2): 207–22.

Inglehart, R. and Norris, P. 2003. *Rising Tide: Gender Equality and Cultural Change Around the World*. Cambridge: Cambridge University Press.

IPS 1994a. [Inter Press Service] Islamic Opposition Grows to UN Population Conference, 21 August.

Jones, G.W. 2006. A Demographic Perspective on the Muslim World. *Journal of Population Research* 23(2): 243–65.

Kepel, G. 1995. *The Revenge of God: The Resurgence of Islam, Christianity and Judaism in the Modern World*. Pennsylvania: Pennsylvania University Press.

Kooiman, J. 2003. *Governing as Governance*. London: Sage.

Mayer, A.E. 2007. *Islam and Human Rights: Tradition and Politics*. Fourth Edition, Oxford: Westview Press.

MCB 2006. Joint Statement about the veil from Muslim groups, scholars and leaders. [Online: Muslim Council of Britain website]. Available at http://www.mcb.org.uk/uploads/Joint%20Statement.pdf [accessed 31 August 2011].

MCB 2007a. Towards Greater Understanding: Meeting the needs of Muslim pupils in state schools – Information and Guidance for Schools. [Online: Muslim Council of Britain website]. Available at http://www.mcb.org.uk/downloads/Schoolinfoguidancev2.pdf [accessed 31 August 2011].

MCB 2007b. MCB Statement on SORs. [Online: Muslim Council of Britain website]. Available at http://www.mcb.org.uk/media/presstext.php?ann_id=250 [accessed 31 August 2011].

MCB 2008. Statement: Muslim Marriage Certificate. [Online: Muslim Council of Britain website]. Available at http://www.mcb.org.uk/article_detail.php?article=announcement-734 [accessed 31 August 2011].

Merlingen, M. 2006. Foucault and World Politics: Promises and Challenges of Extending Governmentality Theory to the European and Beyond. *Millennium: Journal of International Studies* 35(1): 181–96.

Modood, T. and Ahmad, F. 2007. British Muslim Perspectives on Multiculturalism. *Theory, Culture and Society* 24(2): 187–213.

Muslim Institute 2008. Muslim Marriage Contract. [Online: Muslim Institute website]. Available at http://www.muslimparliament.org.uk/Documentation/Muslim%20Marriage%20Contract.pdf [accessed 31 August 2011].

Norris, P. and Inglehart, R. 2004. *Sacred and Secular: Religion and Politics Worldwide*. Cambridge: Cambridge University Press.

OIC 1990. [Organisation if the Islamic Conference] Cairo Declaration on Human Rights in Islam. [Online: UNHCR website]. Available at http://www.unhcr.org/refworld/publisher,ARAB,,3ae6b3822c,0.html [accessed 31 August 2011].

O'Malley, P., Weir, L. and Shearing, C. 1997. Governmentality, Criticism, Politics. *Economy and Society* 26(4): 501–17.

Patel, P. 2008. Faith in the State? Asian Women's Struggles for Human Rights in the UK. *Feminist Legal Studies* 16(9): 9–36.

Patel, P. 2011. Cohesion, Multi-faithism and the Erosion of Secular Spaces in the UK: Implications for the Human Rights of Minority Women. *IDS Bulletin* 42(1).

Ratzinger, J. 2006a. *Without Roots: The West, Relativism, Christianity and Islam*. New York: Basic Books.

Ratzinger, J. 2006b. *Christianity and the Crisis of Cultures*. San Francisco: Ignatius Press.

Rose, N. 1999. *Powers of Freedom: Reframing Political Thought*. Cambridge: Cambridge University Press.

Russian Orthodox Church 2009. The Russian Orthodox Church's Teaching on Human Dignity, Freedom and Rights – Freedom of Choice and Freedom from Evil. [Online: Russian Patriarch website]. Available at http://www.mospat.ru/index.php?mid=465 [accessed 31 August 2011].

SBS 2011. [Southall Black Sisters] *Cohesion, Faith and Gender: A Report on the Impact of the Cohesion and Faith-based Approach on Black and Minority Women in Ealing*. Southall Black Sisters Trust: Russell Press.

Sending, O.J. and Neumann, I.B. 2006. Governance to Governmentality: Analysing NGOs, States, and Power. *International Studies Quarterly* 50(1): 651–72.

Strenski, I. 2010. *Why Politics Can't be Freed from Religion*. London: Wiley-Blackwell.

UN Cairo Declaration 1994. Cairo Declaration on Population & Development. [Online UN website]. Available at http://www.un.org/popin/icpd/conference/bkg/egypt.html [accessed 31 August 2011].

UN-ICPD 1994a. Report of the International Conference on Population and Development, Cairo 5–13 September 1994. [Online: UN website as UN doc A/CONF.171/13]. Available at http://www.un.org/popin/icpd/conference/offeng/poa.html [accessed 31 August 2011].

UN-ICPD 1994b. Statement of Holy See, H E Archbishop Renato R Martino. [Online: UN website]. Available at http://www.un.org/popin/icpd/conference/gov/940908193315.html [accessed 31 August 2011].

UN-ICPD 1994c. Statement of World Council of Churches. [Online: UN website]. Available at http://www.un.org/popin/icpd/conference/ngo/940909231007.html [accessed 31 August 2011].

UN-ICPD 1995a. Report of the Fourth World Conference on Women, Beijing, 4-15 September 1995. [Online: UN website as UN doc A/CONF.177/20]. Available at http://www.un.org/documents/ga/conf177/aconf177-20en.htm [accessed 31 August 2011].

UN-ICPD 1995b. Holy See Statement of Prof. Mary Ann Glendon, Head of the Delegation of the Holy See to the Fourth world Conference on Women. [Online: UN website]. Available at http://www.un.org/esa/gopher-data/conf/fwcw/conf/gov/950905214652.txt [accessed 31 August 2011].

UN-ICPD 1995c. Statement of His Excellency Dr. Hamid Algabid OIC Secretary General at the World Conference on Women Beijing 4-15 September, 1995. [Online: UN website]. Available at http://www.un.org/esa/gopher-data/conf/fwcw/conf/una/950911155632.txt [accessed 31 August 2011].

UN-S/GA 1999. General Assembly: Twenty-First Special Session, 9th Meeting. [Online: UN website as UN Doc A/S-21/PV.9]. Available at http://www.un.org/ga/search/view_doc.asp?symbol=A/S-21/PV.9andLang=E [accessed 31 August 2011].

UN-S/GA 2001a. General Assembly: Twenty-Sixth Special Session, 1st Meeting. [Online: UN website as UN Doc A/S-26/PV.1]. Available at http://www.un.org/ga/search/view_doc.asp?symbol=A/S-26/PV.1andLang=E [accessed 31 August 2011].

UN-S/GA 2001b. General Assembly: Twenty-Sixth Special Session, 7th Meeting. [Online: UN website as UN Doc A/S-26/PV.7]. Available at http://www.un.org/ga/search/view_doc.asp?symbol=A/S-26/PV.7andLang=E [accessed 31 August 2011].

UN-S/GA 2001c. General Assembly: Twenty-Sixth Special Session, 8th Meeting. [Online: UN website as UN Doc A/S-26/PV.8]. Available at http://www.un.org/ga/search/view_doc.asp?symbol=A/S-26/PV.8andLang=E [accessed 31 August 2011].

UN-S/GA 2002. General Assembly: Twenty-Seventh Special Session, 6th Meeting. [Online: UN website as UN Doc A/S-27/PV.6]. Available at http://www. un.org/ga/search/view_doc.asp?symbol=A/S-27/PV.6andLang=E [accessed 31 August 2011].

UN Report 2010. Millennium Development Goals Report [Online: UN website]. Available at http://www.un.org/millenniumgoals/pdf/MDG%20Report%20 2010%20En%20r15%20-low%20res%2020100615%20-.pdf [accessed 31 August 2011].

Vatican 1994. Letter of his Holiness John Paul II to the Secretary General of the International Conference on Population and Development. [Online: Vatican website]. Available at http://www.vatican.va/holy_father/john_paul_ii/ letters/1994/documents/hf_jp-ii_let_19940318_cairo-population-sadik_ en.html [accessed 31 August 2011].

Vatican 1995. Letter of Pope John Paul II to Women. [Online: Vatican website]. Available at http://www.vatican.va/holy_father/john_paul_ii/letters/documents/ hf_jp-ii_let_29061995_women_en.html [accessed 31 August 2011].

Vatican 2003a. Ecclesia in Europa. [Online: Vatican website]. Available at http:// www.vatican.va/holy_father/john_paul_ii/apost_exhortations/documents/hf_ jp-ii_exh_20030628_ecclesia-in-europa_en.html [accessed 31 August 2011].

Vatican 2003b. Consideration Regarding Proposals to give Legal Recognition to Unions between Homosexual Persons. [Online: Vatican website]. Available at http://www.vatican.va/roman_curia/congregations/cfaith/documents/rc_con_ cfaith_doc_20030731_homosexual-unions_en.html [accessed 31 August 2011].

Vatican 2004b. Address of John Paul II to Hon. Mr Romano Prodi President of the European Commission. [Online: Vatican website]. Available at http://www. vatican.va/holy_father/john_paul_ii/speeches/2004/october/documents/hf_jp- ii_spe_20041028_romano-prodi_en.html [accessed 31 August 2011].

Vatican 2008. Address of His Holiness Benedict XVI to H.E. Mrs. Perols Ulla Birgitta Gudmundson New Ambassador of the Kingdom of Sweden to the Holy See. [Online: Vatican website]. Available at http://www.vatican.va/ holy_father/benedict_xvi/speeches/2008/december/documents/hf_ben-xvi_ spe_20081218_sweden_en.html [accessed 31 August 2011].

Vatican 2010. Address of His Holiness Pope Benedict XVI to the Members of the Diplomatic Corps For the Traditional Exchange of New Year Greetings. [Online: Vatican website]. Available at http://www.vatican.va/holy_father/ benedict_xvi/speeches/2010/january/documents/hf_ben-xvi_spe_20100111_ diplomatic-corps_en.html [accessed 31 August 2011].

Walters, W. and Haahr, J.H. 2005b. *Governing Europe: Discourse, Governmentality and European Integration*. London: Routledge.

Washington Post 1994. Catholics and Muslims Find Common Moral Ground: Disparate Faiths Agree That Portions of UN Population Document Are 'Unacceptable' 19 August.

Westerlund, D. (ed.) 1996. *Questioning the Secular State: The Worldwide Resurgence of Religion in Politics*. London: Hurst and Co.

Index

Tables are indexed in **bold** page numbers.